THREE ARTISTS: KURELEK, CHAMBERS & CURNOE

Also by Herman Goodden

BOOKS

The Goof
The Invisible Lone Ranger Suit
Counting Backwards from a Hundred
Towards a Forest City Mythology
Curtain Rising: The History of Theatre in London
In Good Faith
Not It
The River Project
No Continuing City

PLAYS

The Judgement of Slippery Jack
Suffering Fools
The Anniversary
Slippery or You Can't Get There from Here
The Dark Ages
Nature Abhors a Vacuum

THREE ARTISTS:
KURELEK, CHAMBERS & CURNOE

HERMAN GOODDEN

ELMWOOD

Excerpts from "Europe was the Place to be" appeared in the May 28, 2016 issue and "It can Happen Here" in the August 11, 2016 issue of *The London Yodeller*.

ISBN 978-0-9733583-3-9

Cataloguing data available from Library and Archives Canada

Cover Design & Layout: Kirtley Jarvis

ILLUSTRATIONS:

William Kurelek © The Estate of William Kurelek.
Courtesy of the Wynick/Tuck Gallery, Toronto

Jack Chambers © The Estate of Jack Chambers.
Courtesy of John & Diego Chambers

Greg Curnoe © The Estate of Greg Curnoe / SODRAC (2016).
Courtesy of Sheila Curnoe

Published by Elmwood Publications

Printed and bound in Canada by The Aylmer Express Ltd.

Dedicated to Ross Greig Woodman (1922–2014)
who helped all of us to see so much

Art is the transformation of the given.
— RGW

ACKNOWLEDGEMENTS

For generously sharing their time and insights with me in sometimes incidental conversations and sometimes very extensive interviews, I wish to thank Paula Adamick, Vince Cherniak, Sheila Curnoe, Christopher Dewdney, Chris Doty, Susan Downe, Bill Exley, Michael Gibson, Ted Goodden, Iain Hoadley, Av Isaacs, Iain MacGregor, Bill McGrath, Bob McKenzie, Michael D. O'Brien, Phil Prins, Nancy Poole, Carole Sabiston, and Ross and Marion Woodman.

Thanks also go to Maggie Lucchesi and Tom Taylor for proof-reading and to David Warren for his princely foreword. And most of all, thank you to The Catholic Art Guild for suggesting and funding a project so dear to my heart.

FOREWORD

Through a generation of "media," or two or three, Western, Christian man has lost his way entirely. (He had been losing it for a long time before.) This is often observed, and it should be, because it is the big fact of our epoch. By that word, "media," I intend an antithesis to poetry and literature, art and architecture, music and theatre and dance – "the arts" as we sometimes call them, for bureaucratic efficiency. We might also observe great mountains of skulls, still rising from the most violent of centuries, through the period I recognize as "post-modernity" – since technical progress blossomed in its ultimate accomplishment of planetary Total War, in August of 1914. Everything in this book comes after.

It is full of three artists who "valued what they had," in a time and country that seems to happen after everything good is over. Kurelek, Chambers, and Curnoe – each a little universe in himself – set out by ignoring the big fact and retrieving the small. Without patrons, without rules and inherited customs, without any sympathetic audience to begin with, each was "driven," or I think, "called."

I say this with confidence because in each case, a primal arrogance was beaten down. In true art there is only reverent humility.

Herman Goodden himself, as well as the Canadian artists evoked and discussed in this book, belongs to what I will call the Lost Tribe of the Found. What I mean by this paradox is, that in a time when media have generalized and homogenized human experience, each of the subjects of this book found a place, a location, a strand of continuity or orientation; which Goodden understands because he has lived it himself. And each came to it through circumstances over which he had, for all his wilfulness, little control.

Two of these painters "discovered" the Catholic Church, Curnoe remained a diehard "post-Protestant" to his sudden death. But I find all three God-haunted – and drawn along a passage through this earth very far from the generic. Each left a record of witness, whose attributes include beauty and truth, found in the most unlikely places; as well as a "rightness" that passes through the moral towards the mystical. Each was "made into an artist" by an agency outside of himself.

What "repression" in each of these lives, as Goodden adumbrates them!

What ripe territory for psychologizing! In fact we are dealing with the opposite of repression; with a kind of exaltation, instead. And you must read Goodden to comprehend this.

He tells the "back-stories," and why they are important. To understand them, we must submit to the conditions each artist imposed upon himself, along the pilgrim way. None, in his way, strayed far from "home" in the painting he attempted. Each lived "as if" post-modernity hadn't happened, in an almost shopkeeping homage to "location, location, location." This is quite different from "living in the past": the usual gesture of contempt we offer to those who step outside the confines of the insistent media present; who find a way towards a rich imagery, in a world full of beautiful particularities, seen as if for the first time.

Kurelek, Chambers, and Curnoe: all three are now "famous Canadians," but the national term is nearly meaningless, for different reasons in each case. It is only by adoption, or even appropriation, that they have become members of some Canadian Art pantheon. Yet not even Curnoe in his anti-American slurs showed allegiance to any political entity. His "patriotism" was to a room in the mansion of space and time, corresponding to London, Ontario. He made it his /Firenze/, and bicycled through its countryside with the fanatic loyalty of possession. Similarly, Kurelek and Chambers found all the universal themes they could handle, immediately at hand.

Note that Florence, Italy, through its artistic and cultural prime, had a population never larger than that of London, Ontario in the time of Curnoe and Chambers, Reaney, Dewdney, and others. It is a social world that Goodden describes from the inside, providing insights that might apply to many other places.

Goodden is himself an artist, a thinking reed in prose and stagecraft. He has painted for us these three portraits, better than any conventional biographies. Yet he has diligently done all the homework, and made himself an expert on each man, from out of an intimacy not of friendship, exactly, but of seer and subject. His portraits can be ruthless and surgical, in moments; but he is always presenting a whole character, never a placard or silhouette. Through the transformation of his very faults each of these much different characters is proceeding along a pilgrim's way: shedding the commonplace of sin in his passage, and entering into a /vita nuova/ unlike any life before.

He further turns these portraits inside out. For Goodden plays an artistic trick on us. We begin to see not only his subjects as spectacles in themselves, but ourselves and our world through their eyes. We begin to understand their art in a way that eludes the staleness of contemporary "art criticism." He does not omit the fine details. We begin to understand what the artist is witnessing. Or, we do if we are following with that attention which Goodden can enthral and reward.

The religious aspect of each painter's career is not quietly overlooked, as it is in the contemporary gallery scene. The book is no Catholic religious tract; it is no catechism; but it has the quality of a spiritual topography. Kurelek and Chambers were very unlikely Catholic converts, through whose dogged resistance, I think, Christ Himself found paths, to His Church which is no merely human institution. All three show pilgrim roads through the hills, presenting a succession of vistas.

Without reserve, I recommend this book to the reader, of any age, who wants to know what it is to be an artist – a real one, depicting what is real, in reverent humility; as opposed to a media poseur. Indeed, this book is a "classic" in that genre.

— *David Warren*

INTRODUCTION

Though they are all hinged together between the covers of one book, these essays on three 20th century Canadian artists, commissioned by the Catholic Art Guild, do not constitute a prose variation on a triptych. The longest (by a smidgen) of the three biographical 'panels' is the central one devoted to Jack Chambers. With William Kurelek on his right Chambers shared a passing personal acquaintance, a conversion to Catholicism, and a disciplinary devotion to the great past masters of European art. With Greg Curnoe on his left Chambers shared an intense and mutually inspiring friendship, a commitment to the idea of 'regionalism' (the artistic exploration and celebration of one's native ground) and an openness to new and non-traditional approaches to art making.

As all three artists, for a while at least, were represented by Toronto gallery owner Av Isaacs, it seems more than likely that Curnoe and Kurelek's paths must have crossed at some point but I have been unable to find any evidence that either ever had anything to say to or about the other. In terms of the subject matter to which they were drawn, it's hard to imagine two more disparate artistic temperaments than those of Kurelek and Curnoe. About the only thing they did unknowingly share was a fierce level of productivity; an ability (unlike the more fastidious and painstaking Chambers) to keep the wheels turning and readily move on from one project to another. Sadly, one other detail common to all three subjects, is that none of them made old bones.

So while there is a little interaction between Chambers and Kurelek, and a lot between Chambers and Curnoe, I am not lumping these men together. I am also attempting to present a more full-bodied understanding of each. Though all three artists were richly multi-faceted, for the sake of categorization Kurelek, Chambers and Curnoe became publicly identified as, respectively, a folk, a realist and a pop artist. These labels made it easier (particularly in the case of Kurelek but to an extent with all three) to dismiss them and deny them the serious appraisal they deserve. By digging into each of their lives and striving to see their legacies afresh, I hope to push back against this shortchanging. What you are about to read are three thematically discrete essays about three very different artists who each succeeded in creating that distinctive body of work which only he could have achieved.

— *Herman Goodden*

CHAPTERS

WILLIAM KURELEK

JACK CHAMBERS

GREG CURNOE

WILLIAM KURELEK

1

LIFE IN METRO'S HOUSE

My heart leaps up when I behold
A Rainbow in the sky:
So was it when my life began;
So is it now I am a Man;
So be it when I shall grow old;
Or let me die!
The Child is Father of the Man;
And I could wish my days to be
Bound each to each by natural piety.
                    – *William Wordsworth*

THERE IS A GREAT old quote with overtones both miraculous and menacing that is attributed to the Jesuit Order of teachers: "Give me a child
until he is seven and I will give you the man". The 'miraculous' connotation
chimes in a sort of unison with the Wordsworth poem quoted above; expressing that wonder we so often feel about how uncannily complete each human
personality already is, if not at birth (though perhaps even then if only we could
read the signs) then certainly in those first crucial years of infancy and childhood. Our traits, potentialities and predispositions all need to be schooled and
developed, of course, before we can become independent, functioning beings.
But it is a tenet of the Socratic school of education that no teacher or parent
can build onto something that wasn't already there in some definitely marked
form from the very beginning; that at least as much as the process of learning
is a taking on of something new from the outer world it is also an unveiling of
something within us, a further unwrapping of that very first and very greatest
birthday present that each of us received – our own unique and mysterious
selves.

The 'menacing' aspect of the Jesuit quote pertains to the capacity of a flawed
teacher or parent to warp a child's development in his earliest and most formative years so that he is cut off – perhaps for a time, perhaps permanently – from
his own innate potentialities. This was quite dramatically the case with William

Kurelek (1927-77), a born artist if ever there was one, who would spend virtually his entire life in reaction against his over-controlling and caustic father – a man whose tyranny over his son wouldn't begin to be mitigated by other forces until William was finally enrolled for school at the age of seven – the age by which the Jesuits believed the human template was irreversibly set.

It seems to me that William Kurelek's half century of life falls into three distinct acts, the first two roughly comprising 15 years each, the last one accounting for 20 years. The first 15 years of infancy and boyhood were all dominated by his father. Like any growing child he developed what skills he could but did so furtively and haltingly, within a paternally poisoned atmosphere of discouragement and uncertainty. There was no adequate foundation in place upon which to build anything very sturdy or dynamic. And when Kurelek started to move beyond his father's immediate range at the age of 15 – and for all that he managed to push himself through high school, university and art college and then go travelling first to Mexico and then to Britain and Europe – in many crucial ways he was only spinning his wheels. Certainly he saw things and he learned things but without some sort of existential traction he wasn't able to make any headway. There were fundamental problems to address and overcome, a radical reorientation to be effected, before he would be adequately equipped to make his way forward as an artist or a man. And then in his final and remarkably productive 20 years, driven by the almost desperate energy of one who has at last taken hold of a destiny that has been deferred for too long, Kurelek would waste little time on anything that did not directly contribute to his artistic legacy.

As both of William's parents – but particularly his father – played such a complex and troublesome part in his personal and artistic development, it is necessary for any sort of understanding that we sketch out at least some of the familial back story. William Kurelek was born on March 3, 1927 on a wheat farm outside of Whitford, Alberta, about 75 miles northeast of Edmonton. William was the first born son of Dmytro (often called Metro) and Mary Kurelek (nee Huculak). Both of William's parents hailed from farm families in the Ukrainian village of Borivtsi though Mary had been born in Canada and Metro came over at the age of 19.

Metro was the second born son in his family and as such he realized he would not be inheriting his father's land (nor much else for that matter) and the prospects for scrounging together some sort of livelihood on his own were even bleaker than usual in post-First World War Ukraine. The country had passed into Romanian control in the armistice agreements and the usual postwar plagues of poverty, crime and disease were all rattling away with unchecked vigour. In his frustration at trying to find some way to earn a living, Metro himself had resorted to crime as a young teenager, taking part in a smuggling ring operating between Poland and Ukraine ("to exchange items arbitrarily over-taxed in either country," William noted)[1] and was caught, roughed up and jailed for his efforts. On top of all this discouraging stagnation hemming him in at a time in life when a young person yearns to flex his abilities and strengths, Metro also faced the distinct possibility of being conscripted into the Romanian army where Ukrainians were assured of ill treatment.

Metro was more than ready to strike out on his own somewhere else where he might have a chance of some day farming his own land and when he caught wind of a settlement scheme promoted by the Cunard Shipping line whereby young Ukrainian men could pay off their passage to Canada by working for a full growing season on a western farm, he impulsively signed up, much to the dismay of his parents. Though his parents hated the idea, Metro was determined to go through with it and when his father saw that there was no way he could deter the young man he even abetted the scheme in a significant way by putting his son in touch with the man who would be his Canadian sponsor, Vasyl Hucalak, a fellow farmer from the Borivtsi region who had relocated to Alberta 24 years before and was doing well.

In spite of his father's help in making this overture and doing his bit to smooth his son's emigration, Metro bore some kind of resentment against his parents. William speculates that Metro's father had reneged on an earlier promise to sell off some property to raise a stake for his second son. Incredibly, after saying his goodbyes and sailing off to Canada early in 1923, Metro never communicated with his parents again.[2] Clearly, this was one very stubborn man who knew how to nurse a grudge, for decades if need be, even against those who'd given him life itself and – as we shall see – against those he gave life to.

In his autobiography William writes that Metro arrived in the new world with "nine dollars in his pocket . . . a small wooden suitcase . . . [and] a load of bitterness and suspicion from the troubled conditions of Middle Europe."[3] Metro met his wife-to-be when he turned up for his very first Canadian job as a hand on her family's farm. Mary was the eldest of Vasyl Hucalak's ten children which meant that some of her younger brothers and sisters, even though they were younger than her own first-born son, would nonetheless be William's aunts and uncles. The large Hucalak family was pretty well off by the prevailing standards of the then 56 year-old confederation but in many ways they had scarcely adapted their way of life or cultural references since leaving the Ukraine behind in 1899.

Ukrainian was the first language spoken at home and the Hucalaks attended a Russo-Ukrainian Orthodox church. So strong and nourishing were the ties that kept Canadian Ukrainian immigrants connected to the old country (William characterized the area where Metro and Mary lived and worked until he was seven years old as an "all Ukrainian district")[4] that Mary felt an immediate kinship with this just-arrived immigrant even though she'd been a nominal Canadian for all of her 16 years. The northern farmlands of Alberta were so sparsely populated and developed in the first decades of the 20th century, that to attend high school, Mary Hucalak would have had to board in Edmonton; a prospect that so intimidated the young girl that she elected to leave school before completing grade eight, thereby condemning herself to a life of near-pioneer toil like her mother before her. This reluctance to assert herself, to forge or stand up for her own ideas or convictions, would carry on throughout her life as both a wife and a mother. Mary was not the kind of mother who would ever challenge an overbearing father's treatment of her children but instead would fall in line with and even reinforce whatever sort of regimen he thought appropriate.

A little more than two years after Metro's arrival in Canada the young couple had an old world style wedding party in June of 1925 that lasted for three days with a special dancing platform set up beside the big Hucalak farmhouse. Mary was 18 and Metro was 21. Mary's father gave the newlyweds a cleared quarter section of his land complete with a rough shack that would be their first home until Metro himself could build something a little more substantial. But there would be no honeymoon. A wedding was perceived as a family event and a community event but there was no provision made for the more romantic concerns of the prime celebrants, no special time away from everybody just to be by themselves. After the big party wrapped up, Metro and Mary loaded up a wagon with their gifts and belongings and repaired to their shack at the other end of the property and were both out in the fields early the next morning to work.

To modern sensibilities, it all seems like a claustrophobically circumscribed existence. There can actually be a hidden blessing that falls to the second son who is not the heir apparent of his father's empire. With the lifting of the responsibilities of a preordained role comes a chance to consider other possibilities but Metro seems never to have had – and never to have desired to have – a single minute in which to entertain larger and more open-ended questions about his character and its potentialities. Having crossed the ocean in search of better farming prospects he sent down the deepest roots he could in the first patch of land he came to and then settled down with the daughter of his first employer and started up his new life on a corner of that very same farm that was part of his wife's dowry. Farming was what Metro knew. Ukrainian was the language and culture that he was raised in and formed by. This was precisely what he wanted. He never expected it to be easy and it wasn't.

Quite early on in their residency a barn would burn down. Then the family home would burn down. Later, when William was ten and the growing family had moved to Manitoba, the Kurelek farm was invaded by a plague of locusts.

All of these apocalyptic calamities, naturally, would eventually be recorded in paintings by William. In 1928 when William was a one year old toddler and Mary was pregnant with his brother John, Metro came down with an incapacitating and never-identified stomach ailment. On the advice of one doctor he travelled to Edmonton to have his appendix unnecessarily removed which only weakened him further as the pains continued and he was confined to his cot for almost the entire growing season of 1928. If it was some kind of an ulcerous condition, one can readily imagine its exacerbation as this notoriously driven and demanding man was forced onto the sidelines for such an extended period. William depicted this desperate scene in a 1964 painting called *Illness* which shows the young artist sitting on the dirt floor of their shack, distractedly tended by his bedridden father, while his mother can be seen through the open doorway handling the reins of a horse-drawn plough.

The very next year the stock market crashed and as markets dried up and grain prices plummeted, life became a lot harder yet for farmers everywhere, even those as apparently cushioned from austerity as Metro's father-in-law with his extensive land-lease deals with other area farmers and his brief proprietorship of the nearby Willingdon Hotel situated along the newly installed railway line. Ambitious as ever to get ahead and to secure a real foothold of his own, Metro had started to rent a second quarter section from Vasyl Hucalek and had also borrowed money from his father-in-law for farm machinery. The timing couldn't have been worse for such schemes of expansion and as Vasyl's own prosperity took a hit he was forced to repossess the second quarter and even placed a mortgage on the first – his dowry to his daughter – when Metro couldn't pay back all of the money he had borrowed.[5]

While Metro contended with a growing family and ominously shrinking prospects, William too was starting to feel displaced by his little brother John, nearly two years his junior, who was by William's own admission, more intelligent, more courageous and more adept at the kind of farm-related tasks that Metro valued in his sons. William couldn't help noticing that Metro seemed to favour, even prefer, the younger boy and whenever he and his brother got into trouble and some kind of punishment had to be administered, William felt that John got off lightly in comparison.

"We were to be constant companions all the way till our university days," William wrote in his autobiography. "But there was, I think, more than the usual jealous rivalry between us. I was early seen to be different – a dreamer. And I had to [see] my younger but naturally smarter brother stealing affection and praise from my parents when I thought I had first claim to them. Appropriately, I suppose, my very first memory of John is his hitting me over the head with a vanilla bottle."[6]

Well before the move to Manitoba which happened when William was almost seven years old, three enormously significant facts of his young life – all of them manifestations in one way or another of his already pronounced visual imagination – had declared themselves:

Even by the loosey-goosey standards of young boyhood, his grip on reality could be a little slack; he was powerfully drawn to art and visual imagery of all kinds; and he was hungry for God.

Let's take these in the order that they showed up.

William was distressed by hallucinations – waking nightmares – perhaps as early as the age of five. In his autobiography he describes these, introducing the subject as one more reason to envy his charmed younger brother who wasn't plagued with these disturbing visitations. "He slept with me in the same crib, yet he remained blithely immune to my suffering. This struck me as odd because even my sister saw the monsters."[7]

Having some experience of older brothers who prankishly persuaded me to see things that were not there, I have no doubt that his little sister Vasylyna (nicknamed Win), who might have been all of two years old at this time, only 'saw' these monsters at her oldest brother's urging. But that isn't quite what Kurelek says. Is the writer winking at us when he says that Win saw the visions as well? We just don't know. Here, as in many other of his autobiographical passages, Kurelek's writing is so carelessly calibrated or tuned that the reader can't be certain what he's getting at; in this case leaving the unsettling impression that writing as an adult he might still be recruiting his baby sister as some kind of validation regarding the veracity of visions that he knows weren't real. The logic isn't so much circular as a downward spiral.

He imagined a large cat like a lynx clawing at the underside of his crib. Most frightening of all was a huge turkey vulture that, Kurelek says, "wanted to get at me to peck at my face and eyes. But since I kept myself tightly covered all it could do was walk all over me. I distinctly felt the imprint of its feet as it stomped from one foot to the other. I held the blanket down so tightly that not even fresh air could get to me. This plus my terror made sweat pour off me many a night. One morning early, with sunlight already lighting up the bedroom, I woke and glancing out from under the cover saw John still sleeping. To my horror however I noticed that the vulture had dug its beak into my brother's scalp and was hanging there suspended like that. You can imagine how lightning fast I ducked back under my blanket! How I longed to sleep between my parents like my sister Winnie did! They only laughed when I told them of those monsters."

It was not long after these creepy sightings that their house burned down on a day when all the family was away and the Kureleks moved into a nearby and blessedly monster-free log shack for a few months while Metro rebuilt – indeed replicated – their home on its old charred stone foundation. When they moved back in to their new/old house, William noted with satisfaction and relief that his old monsters had apparently perished in the conflagration.

Growing up in a fairly remote Alberta farmhouse during the Depression the young William Kurelek wasn't exactly assailed by art wherever he looked but he managed to fasten onto whatever scraps he came across. He seems to have always been powerfully affected by the landscape around him even before he considered it as something that he might like to paint. And early in his autobiography he places this historical footnote in a description of his maternal grandmother's house:

"In the meat room, a cold room off the kitchen, hung a calendar with a reproduction of an old painting of a naval battle. I mention this because it was the very first inkling of my interest in paintings. I believe the very first sign of my interest in the actual production of art came at my grandmother's too. Or perhaps it was at our storekeeper's (great uncle's) place in Willingdon. One of the older children we were playing with had drawn a set of steps. I was fascinated by the technique of depicting steps by lines alone and observed that such a line drawing could either be looked at as from above or below the steps. Of course my observation was dismissed offhand by the others. But I treasured in my heart that fascinating discovery for a long time after – I must have, to be remembering it today."[8]

Just a few pages before that, describing the family's return to their rebuilt home, Kurelek notes, though this time not in a painterly way, the importance of imagery in providing some sense of ourselves and our place – both in this world and in the larger divine order:

"But a fire destroys more than things. It can destroy memories and affections. All those lovely old photos of mother, beautiful in her womanhood, which had adorned the living room, were gone. Gone too were those religious calendars on the walls from which I had acquired anthropomorphic concepts of God and Heaven. Mother and father, I gather, had believed and even prayed on their knees for a short time after their marriage. Now apparently the faith was gone for never again did I ever see a religious picture or icon grace their walls – not in Alberta, or Manitoba or Ontario."[9]

Patricia Morley makes an intriguing observation in her 1986 biography of Kurelek that despite the artist's insistence that he was indifferent or hostile to religion until his conversion in his mid '20s, the number of times that faith pops up in his writings about his childhood and in the subject matter of his early pre-conversion paintings suggests otherwise. She believes it was a storyteller's ruse employed for effect both in the writing of his autobiography and in how he chose to present himself to others in his personal life. "Bill had flair," Morley writes, "and one suspects that he found the conversion of an atheist a more striking and dramatic posture than the homecoming of a religious seeker."[10]

The novelist and painter, Michael D. O'Brien became friends with Kurelek toward the end of his life and has written what I regard as the single most insightful essay on the artist, *The Passion of William Kurelek*, first published in *Image*, Spring 1995 and subsequently incorporated into his illustrated book length study, *William Kurelek: Painter and Prophet*, published by Justin Press in 2013. His insights are so valuable because O'Brien writes not only as a friend and neighbour (in the Catholic community of Combermere in Northern Ontario where Kurelek summered and even did some desultory farming) but also as a fellow painter and fellow Catholic. O'Brien takes issue with many facets and contentions of Morley's biography (a book he regards as "ambivalent") and explained why in an interview I had with the artist in December of 2012.

"I knew Patricia Morley because she also collected my paintings. I think she purchased 20 over the years. She's now dead. In my conversations with Morley she was very hostile to [Kurelek's] position on moral issues. She was very pro-abortion, quite a feminist. On a whole host of sexual morality issues she was an ultra-liberal. Kind of an Anglican – went to church now and then – but an ultra-radical, modernist Anglican. She was deeply offended by Kurelek's positions which are our faith, certainly in terms of moral theology and the teachings of the Church. She tried to define these only in purely psychological terms. He was a repressed personality according to her; therefore he had to have a repressed moral theology. We had many discussions and arguments about this. She was both fascinated and repelled by certain aspects of him, especially his morality. But she was fascinated by him because she was extremely interested in the whole field of religion and art. She was very much a follower of Carl Jung. So it was kind of a stacked deck against a proper interpretation of Kurelek. She was a brilliant woman and a very good writer and a fastidious researcher but somewhat selective.

"I'm not sure exactly what Morley means [by trying to deny that he was ever an atheist]. She told me that Kurelek created his own myth of himself for public consumption. He created it as what he saw as part of his mission to save souls or to be an evangelist of some kind. She was emphatic that it was a myth, a self-created myth, and therefore was a distortion of reality. Now a crucial component of – quotation marks – "the myth" was that he had been an atheist who was shocked to find that God was real and present and the Saviour. I think she was projecting. If what Kurelek said about Christ, the Church, the cross, darkness and light, was something she herself had a fundamental problem with, she could not accept it, absolutely could not accept it as objective reality so it had to be something else. And steeped in Jungianism which is often seeing things in symbolic and mythological terms she would very naturally – or unnaturally – come to the conclusion that it had to be his own mental creation of himself, of his own image. But that's really ignoring a great many objective facts of his life."

Contra Morley, O'Brien takes Kurelek at his word and accepts that he was an atheist – "certainly on the intellectual level and the level of his convictions. Deep in the soul I don't believe anyone is an atheist. But remember, the human person is a composite of mind, body, emotion, spirit, soul. During that period of his life when he was a convinced atheist – I don't know how long or how deeply, a few years anyway – his suicide attempts would seem to indicate that he despaired of life and of God. At the same time, deep in his soul there would be a kind of knowledge of those moments when he'd experienced the divine presence. He may intellectually have rejected those moments as purely psychological events but during his unbelieving years he definitely did reject those experiences."

By early 1934 prospects in Alberta were so dire that Metro and his family – without even informing his in-laws – suddenly decamped to a 600 acre farm with an almost-palatial house (17 rooms) near Stonewall, Manitoba, 20 miles north of Winnipeg, which a fellow Ukrainian emigrant cousin had told Metro was available for a fire sale price of $12,000 and a down payment of only $500. It was a huge spread to take on and came with a large livestock barn, a pig sty and a chicken coop which meant that in a few years' time Metro would be diversifying into mixed farming instead of just growing wheat – something he would be very grateful for a few years later when a grasshopper plague wiped out all of that season's wheat crop except for a measly 13 bushels. Eight years into his Canadian adventure and now with a wife and three kids to look out for, Metro was starting all over again from scratch. Free of the meddlesome oversight of his in-laws (and the safety net they could grudgingly provide if worse came to worst) the new farm would either make or break Metro as a farmer.

2

HARD LESSONS

THE MOVE TO STONEWALL also heralded the beginning of William's formal education and that March he and John were both enrolled in grade one at the one-room Victoria Public School where they shared space with fellow pupils as old as 16 and 17. Over the course of the next nine years, William would be taught by a succession of five different teachers, all of them female. Some children, particularly those who are a little older as William was, actually look forward to starting school but he decidedly did not. A naturally bright and observant kid, over the course of his first seven years William had grown quite accustomed to learning in his own way and on his own schedule and he dreaded the change he sensed was coming. Even so, he was still surprised by how awful school actually was. His first faltering and terrified months at Victoria P.S. were soul-crushing agony.

Because the Kureleks predominantly spoke Ukrainian at home, both boys were at an immediate and enormous disadvantage in a learning environment where only English was to be spoken. Fellow students and sometimes even the teacher ostracized and humiliated the boys until they learned to fend for themselves in English; something which they were able to accomplish in about six months. Outside in the schoolyard and over the course of the mile-long walk between school and home, their treatment was even worse. Both the Kurelek boys were on the short and scrawny side, making them easy prey for older bullies of both sexes. Though William would eventually develop into an exemplary and hardworking pupil – a shy and conscientious student never prone to making trouble and even looked up to by his peers for his developing abilities as an artist – he later regarded those first few months of schooling as "the most traumatic experience of my pre-adult life."[11]

Most upsetting to him was not just the willingness of other children to be cruel but the obvious delight they took in it. "I discovered that there is a heartless mob streak in human nature that sees a fight, any fight, no matter how unequal, as an amusement."[12]

In his autobiography it is remarkable how much space is devoted to incredibly detailed accounts of fights and bullying campaigns that went down at this time, with miscreants and allies all named and strategies and outcomes all vividly recalled. It is the kind of material that most autobiographers don't bother delving into because, even if they remembered the particulars, what can all of it possibly mean to anyone 20 or 30 years later? Clearly it still rankled and when Kurelek was undergoing psychiatric care in England in the early 1950s, he was still poring over the indignities and injuries he'd sustained as a seven year old and made sure that his attending doctors took those schoolyard traumas into account when assessing his situation.

By the time he started school Kurelek had already developed that heightened sensitivity to injustice and cruelty that he would carry all the rest of his life as well as a shuddering aversion to discord of any kind. There can be little question that the young boy developed these sensitivities in reaction to the emotionally caustic atmosphere he experienced at home. And bouncing between that cold and uncomforting home and a school whose regimen he loathed, he acutely felt the lack of any sort of sanctuary in his world where he would be accepted and perhaps even cherished for who he was.

In the autobiography there's a heartbreaking scene (even though it recounts a collision between innocence and the way of the world that just about everybody experiences sooner or later) when William was supposed to head out for the second day at his dreaded new school without his brother John who had booked off sick:

"It was a very windy day. I got dressed for school, and had the school bag over my shoulder. But I lost courage before I even got past the other end of the farmyard. Dropping down at a big stone near the small chicken coop, I cried my heart out. Presently the shadow of Mother fell over me. 'How come you're not at school?'

"'Because it's too windy,' I sobbed, raising my tearful face up to her for sympathy.

"'Nonsense!' she shot back as she picked me up by the arm. I got such a warming-up on the backside I almost flew to school."[13]

Ordinarily it wasn't Mary who administered punishment; it was Metro. Considering the pressures he was under, it is small wonder that Metro had come to feel a little thwarted and stressed at the daunting prospects attending his livelihood. Unfortunately Metro did not have the kind of character that could gracefully accept these pressures as his lot and strive to overcome them while still extending comfort and security to his dependents. On the contrary, he was starting to take out his anger on those around him – most particularly on his dreamy, impractical, machinery-averse first-born son.

When Kurelek was a resident at the first of the English psychiatric hospitals where he went for help with debilitating depression and anxiety as well as a mysterious pain in his eyes that threatened his vocation as an artist, he tried to show his doctors exactly what his problems were by painting what they might see if they could only gain access to the inside of his skull. His 1953 painting, *The Maze*, is a starkly fanciful portrait of a skull that has been split down the middle with one half lifted away to reveal the other half entirely comprised of compartments, each of which contains a scene symbolizing a certain complex or issue that made his existence so disagreeable.

In his autobiography Kurelek explains why he chose "a wheat field eaten by grasshoppers under a blazing hot sun" as the backdrop for this allegorical painting of his cloven skull. That wasted field, he writes, "refers to my belief that my problems stemmed in a large part from my father taking out on me his raging impotence in the face of farming failures."[14]

William listed the kind of infractions and shortcomings that could make either parent (but usually his father) lash out. "Children were to be punished," he wrote, "not only for being bad – but also for making mistakes, for being afraid, for being ill, for being careless, for lacking vigilance."[15] Kurelek writes that as much as he dreaded corporeal punishment (which frankly wasn't administered all that often; perhaps half a dozen spankings and two or three well-placed boots up the backside) it was his father's "tongue-lashings" (a phrase Kurelek gave visual representation in at least two of his paintings) that did him the most damage. "'Stupid' was the most common adjective I got. 'Deaf,' 'dumb,''blind,' were close seconds." "Weak" and "useless" are two other standbys that he also cites.[16]

In that same passage Kurelek goes on in a remarkably obtuse way to speculate about the long term effects that this repressive parental discipline supposedly had on all of Mary and Metro's children. "But eventually the message got across; the Kureleks rarely bare their personal troubles or failures even to this day." That really is a little rich, appearing as it does in a published book which is anything but reticent in cataloguing the troubles and failures of not just the author but his entire family, and most particularly his father.

As William progressed as both a painter and a writer, he was absolutely shameless in his willingness to blame and demonise his father in the most public way. During his early manhood when he was most consumed by anger at Metro, he literally depicted him as a monster. In two different paintings – *I Spit on Life* (1953-54) and *Behold Man without God* (1955) – Metro is depicted with a reptilian forked tongue. In the first painting Mary is also poking out one of these slithery protuberances as the two parents sit at a table with William and two of his younger siblings and berate William alone. A framed sampler on the wall just above William's head reads, "Honor Thy Father and Mother" and "Home Sweet Home". In the latter painting, metal barbs knotted onto the ends of Metro's splintered tongue tear the flesh of young William's bowed back as he is depicted pulling his father along in a sort of rickshaw. It is fortunate that a streak of gallows humour appears in a number of William's darkest paintings as these eruptions of comic sanity help to mitigate against the impression that the artist suffers from a perfectly lethal dose of self pity. While they may humanize our perception of William, these humorous notes don't do as much for Metro who is now seen to be depicted as not just a monster but a buffoon as well.

William's flair for getting under Metro's skin (inadvertently and otherwise) was almost magical; eliciting the kind of wild over-reaction that usually can be unleashed only when a person sees some maddening aspect of himself that has been projected onto and is being reflected back from another. There was a horribly snarled constellation of expectations and disappointments that linked the stubborn father and his equally headstrong son in some apparently inextricable dance that neither partner could ever manage to shake themselves free of for very long.

Poking around in some of the evidence offered up by the Kurelek family back-story, one begins to construct possible psychological scenarios. I wonder for instance if it is possible that Metro might have harboured a deep and perhaps unconscious resentment of firstborn sons that could even extend to his own? After all it was nothing more than birth order that ensured his older brother an untroubled young manhood with everything laid out before him while Metro had to scramble and uproot himself to the other side of the world so as to get a shot at earning his own way forward.

Could Metro have been aiming some of the bitterness he felt toward his older brother at his own first-born son instead – this maddening boy who seemed to have no inclination to even appreciate, let alone capitalize on, the breaks that would ordinarily have come his way by dint of being first born? And in singling out John for praise and commendation and targeting William for the exact opposite, could Metro have been doing his bit to settle an old score and win a point or two for his perpetually overlooked team – the league of hard-done-by second-born sons who were never expected to add up to much?

And even though he had no interest in carrying on his father's way of life as a farmer, having been raised in such a conventional old-Eastern European atmosphere, it seems clear that young William nevertheless imbibed certain ideas and expectations about the privileges and status that should automatically accrue to the oldest son. William tips his own hand in this regard when he writes that he thought he had "first claim" to his parents' affection and praise. So it would seem that neither the father nor the first-born son felt that the other was fulfilling his half of the age-old compact that should have determined their roles.

Was Metro, as William repeatedly depicted him in paint and prose, a monster? None of his other children thought so. They knew he had a temper but they also knew how to handle it in a way that William never learned. It is a chronological fact of life observed in even the most serene and smooth-running of households that parents are significantly more strict and demanding with their first-borns than with later arrivals. As one child is born after another and another, material circumstances change – usually for the better – and parental anxiety ('Oh man, if I don't come down on this like a ton of bricks the child is going to turn out weird') is succeeded by an altogether calmer, almost laissez-faire confidence ('Yes, we know how to handle this and besides, they practically raise themselves').

Temperamentally at least, it is usually the pattern that younger children experience substantially more relaxed parents than their older siblings. Though none of William's younger siblings ever described Metro as an easygoing dad, not one of them (John, born 1928; Win, born 1930; Nancy, born 1936; Sandy, born 1944; Paul, born 1946; nor Iris, born 1948) would ever clash with Metro as spectacularly or incessantly as William.

William's youngest sister is quoted in Patricia Morley's biography, attesting that a couple of decades down the line, Metro – while still stubborn and demanding – had become a much more pliable father who on occasion could even be seen to take open delight in his children. "I was afraid of him too," Iris says. "When he was whistling, he was angry. His eyebrows bristled. You learned to look at his eyes. He was the kind of guy you had to read before you approached."

Iris then goes on to recall more relaxed and happier times; the like of which William never knew. "He'd play records and we'd dance. He enjoyed his later children more than his first."[17]

Kurelek admitted in his autobiography that his parental resentment was a hard habit to break, even after his religious conversion when he was persuaded that he should do so for the good of his own soul. "I quite frankly bore a grudge against both of them for what I considered unjust, disrespectful treatment. This was bad for me in that it poisoned me internally and caused such deep-grooved ruts of resentment that even today I find myself falling into them in dealings with other people. I memorized each wrong and stored it up to use as ammunition some day when I could make a comeback. One day, many years later, I was to discover that I was hurting only myself. Like the depersonalization [his name for the self-willed disengagement with life which he would cultivate to avoid pain and depression] that, too, was a kind of sleepwalk."[18]

Michael O'Brien identifies Kurelek's "primary wound" (and maintains the artist did as well) as "Fatherlessness" and says that it constituted, "a gash at the core of [Kurelek's] being, bleeding away vital energies."[19]

In a superficial sense O'Brien's diagnosis might seem crazy or at least counter-intuitive. Surely, some might surmise on the strength of the evidence here being examined, that poor 'bottom-kicked' and 'tongue-lashed' Kurelek was suffering from an oppressive surfeit of father. Get Metro to back off a little and offer up some fatherlessness for a change and prospects might actually improve for the kid. But it was on a far more profound level than this, O'Brien contends, that Kurelek lacked a father.

Yes, in the archetypal division of labour between parents, fathers are more demanding than mothers and their approval is administered in a more measured and qualified way. You could joke that dads are pleased as punch on the day you're born but once they've handed out the last of their congratulatory cigars, you've got to start earning your gold stars on a regular basis if you want to hold their attention.

But in the proper order of things this more discriminating bestowal of approval is always under laid with a largely unspoken but nonetheless sustaining atmosphere of helpfulness and encouragement. In any kind of pinch, the kid knows his Dad will be there for him. The Dad might not agree with him. He might not approve of what he did. But he will not turn away. He will not write him off. Though the kid may sometimes complain about the heavy demands laid upon him, he knows in his bones that his father has his best interests at heart and is always there to help him develop his best potentialities. And this necessary assurance was something Kurelek didn't have, as is made pitifully clear in the following story that hails from about his 12th year:

"Knowing my father's continual dissatisfaction with me, I found it impossible even to converse with him. I seemed always on the verge of breaking into sobs, but so as not to let such a humiliating display out I had to keep my mouth closed. This closed mouth habit drew as many scathing comments from mother as from him. Once, a seemingly small incident drew a more reasoned rebuke from her. Father had just stepped out of the barn and locked the door latch for it was winter, and I'd just arrived intending to enter. Because of my intense fear of him I couldn't even say, 'Please don't close it, I'm going in.' Dumbly, I just stood there till he'd moved off. Then I moved in. I guess he must have reported it to mother on reaching the house for she asked later that day, 'Why don't you talk to your father? You know he means well.' But I just couldn't believe her."

If the story stopped there, you might hope that this was one of those awful moments when father and son were equally paralyzed by some recent disappointment that held them back from doing right by each other; that this was a sort of emotional standoff that could have been overcome with a little mutual courage and frankness; that despite their defective delivery systems, both parties, in the parlance of Mary Kurelek, 'meant well'. But this passage concludes with another incident that bespeaks not just paternal defection on Metro's part but a devastating betrayal:

"In my case you might say words spoke louder than actions. When he was fencing we ran short of wire at the other end of the field and he sent me back for more. Just so he wouldn't scold me for bringing too short a piece, I avoided that by bringing the whole roll of wire. It was quite heavy. He smiled sardonically when I reached him, 'You know, William, I'm not sorry for you because you lugged that load all that way but because you're so stupid'."[20]

Just about every one of Metro's reported crimes committed against his first born son seems ultimately explicable, even forgivable, except this one. This one goes beyond being impatient or irritable, ignorant or stubborn, insensitive or thoughtless. This one, delivered not in the heat of some frazzled argument but coldly, calculatedly, after watching his son walk a considerable distance bearing a heavy weight in a pathetically uncertain attempt to please his father – this one seems truly hateful.

I find it hugely significant that Patricia Morley does not mention this incident, which stands out for me as so supremely damning, in her biography of Kurelek. In no way does she sugar-coat her portrait of Metro or, except for this one incident, shy away from recounting any of the significant clashes between father and son. She does however repeatedly throw doubt on the veracity, the trustworthiness, of some passages in William's autobiographical writings and to a considerable extent I sympathize with her on this score as well. William Kurelek can be a uniquely maddening writer, not only in terms of his ham-fisted style but also in what he chooses to focus on – sometimes ad nauseam – and what he glides right over in way too pat a treatment. But going by the man's frequently courageous sincerity and the fact that this particular incident was recounted in both versions of his autobiography – both written after his conversion and with five years between them which would have given him ample opportunity to remove any bits that struck him as untruthful or unjust – I think it would be a mistake to suggest that he made the story up.

Morley also repeatedly chides William for his lack of forgiveness towards Metro and here again I'm largely with her. Considering the suffering that this father/son mismatch inflicted on both of its principals and everyone they loved, and considering Kurelek's life-saving Christian conversion and that faith's commandment to honour his father which he wanted so devoutly to fulfill, who doesn't yearn to see William find some way to set down his horrible burden of resentment at his father's feet like a gargantuan roll of fencing wire and move on? But it seems to me that this particular putdown of his son likely represented the great insuperable hurdle in William's campaign to let go of his pain and anger.

In the second version of his autobiography (the version composed for public consumption; the first and longer version was specifically written as an aid to psychotherapy) Kurelek gives this story pride of place at the very end of the chapter entitled *Hard Times* in which he discusses his lifelong war with Metro. Mystifyingly, Morley quotes the first half of that final paragraph in her biography and then stops right where the fence wire story begins. Even weirder, she then inserts a snippet from her interview with John in which – at first glance at least – William's younger brother might seem to be denying that this particular incident ever took place:

"Bill's siblings hold a view of their father which is different and the same," Morley writes. "The shifting perspective is fascinating, given the fact that so much of Bill's life hung on his tragic relationship with his father. The Kurelek children emphasize that their father's efforts were admirable. 'We were better off than our neighbours. Some of them didn't have shoes. There was no way that Will could have had it much better by what Dad could do. I was fortunate in that it suited me'. John admitted to hating his father at times, and finding him most unreasonable. 'Dad was intelligent enough to know that you shouldn't deride your children.' He observed that their father's behaviour came out of a Slavic tradition where the father is always right, and that in that context his harshness was not extraordinary, nor, John implied, were his brother's difficulties: 'But perhaps he felt it more'."

But look at that key line again. "Dad was intelligent enough to know that you shouldn't deride your children." Yes, just about every father who ever drew breath would be intelligent enough to know that. But John doesn't say Metro didn't do it.[21]

I asked Michael O'Brien what he made of this omission in Morley's biography.

"[William Kurelek] had a pretty public life – his autobiography, a lot of the paintings – the whole story was splayed out there for the public. I think it would be pretty natural that the family might try to downplay the darker side of the family history and try to present their father in a better light . . . Bill never really received from his father at any point in his lifetime – not even in old age – unqualified approval. The last time I visited them at their farm in Combermere Bill and I took a walk and there was a drought that summer and the corn crop that Bill had planted died. And he said, "My father is coming to see me soon." I don't remember him ever saying, 'Dad'; always 'my father'. And he said it with a kind of tension: 'I wonder what he'll say when he sees this?'

"And even to the end of Bill's life his father maintained that Bill should have been a doctor instead of an artist. It's a very Slavic thing, you know – a peasant Slavic thing – to use emotional and sometimes physical violence on your children to train them for a dangerous world, to protect them. People like that don't see it as abuse. They see it as protecting their children. And I think Morley was trying to show that there were other sides to Dymtro Kurelek than just what was presented in the autobiography. And that was true. But the fact remains that he was a pretty brutal man – emotionally especially – and that left its mark on Bill for all of his life. However, the point being – and Bill is very emphatic about this after his conversion – that it was a way Christ used to help him learn what forgiveness is, what love is, to carry some of the sufferings of Christ. He made a trip to the Ukraine to try to understand his father better. He was always working towards that healing right up until the end of his life. But I think he was realist enough to know that it would not be complete until Paradise."

Indeed, the final act Kurelek carried out in this life was a long-desired visit of three weeks to the Ukrainian town of Borivitsi where Metro had been born and raised. He had been once before but Communist authorities would only let him stay for three hours. He campaigned relentlessly to be given a second opportunity and when permission was finally given, he set off at once in September of 1977 even though he already knew he wasn't well, returning late in the month barely able to stand with the 100 drawings and five paintings he'd worked on in his last functioning weeks. He entered St. Michael's Hospital almost as soon as he got back to Toronto and after receiving the last rites of the Church died there on November 3.

I asked O'Brien if he felt that Kurelek ever did forgive his father.

"Oh yes, I feel so. But the important thing to remember – and he was wise enough to understand it too – forgiveness is not necessarily sweet, sentimental feelings about a person. It's a choice to love and to let go of resentment. And he worked at that all his life. . . He was adamantly committed to the truth no matter how hard it was and how poorly it reflected on himself. My guess is that Morley was not trying to suggest that he was a liar but he was psychologically, emotionally damaged to such a degree that the whole truth was not being brought out. We talked a lot about Kurelek after his death and I never heard her accuse him of lying. I heard her endlessly categorize him as a severely wounded human being whose magnificent art came out of his psychological/emotional pathology. In that way I think she herself, blind to her own pathology, was basically trying to justify her rejection of his moral position."

We are told in our age of divorce and single motherhood when so many fathers either flee or are driven out of the home or don't even show up for a token year or two of duty once they've planted their seed, that developing any sort of faith in God as a divine father can be difficult for people who have such a limited or malign experience of their earthly fathers. For Kurelek, this process was more or less reversed. Kurelek's first experience of the blessings that a father can provide came from God. Until he was convinced of the redeeming love that God had for him, it was as if there was no ground beneath his feet, no continuity of purpose on which to build and develop anything. Until that simultaneously stabilizing and liberating base was secured, Kurelek suffered with a near-fatal unpreparedness to deal with either his life or his art. And once he'd found a God to worship, the daunting challenge that then faced him was how to obey the Fifth Commandment which told him he must honour his father and mother.

The first months of school had been a trauma for Kurelek but once he started to settle in, there were significant compensations that Victoria Public School provided for him. Never terribly athletic or physically adventurous (unlike his brother John who was noted for wearing out shoes and pants twice as quickly as William) Kurelek still had a tremendous capacity for work and in gradually starting to apply himself to his studies he was able to win some much-needed praise and distinction as a student who routinely earned top marks. If home was a place where he felt that he just couldn't win – and to a young child who didn't set foot in a school until he was seven years old, home was pretty much his entire world – what a relief it must have been to start spending seven hours a day in a place where he could.

Throughout his nine years at Victoria P.S. Kurelek consistently rang up a grade average of ninety per cent. How important this became to his fragile sense of self-worth is made clear when he writes about the one occasion when a Mennonite fellow student named John Giesbrecht displaced him at the top of the class in the middle of a term: "I am tongue-tied with disbelief. That night I swear an oath on the private altar of scholastic superiority: 'Never, never again this humiliation!'" And sure enough, just a few months later he had pulled himself back into first place and stayed there for the rest of his public school career.[22]

Another and perhaps more important service that Victoria P.S. provided its pupils, was free art supplies. Starting in grade one with a box of crayons and a Reeves Student Watercolour set, art supplies far superior to anything Kurelek had been able to rustle up at home were regularly handed out. This was another area where he could prove himself and establish that he wasn't the waste of space that his father derided him as, and he threw himself into visual art with typical Kurelekian vigour, quickly winning recognition from his peers and teachers.

Kurelek described the sort of attention he was receiving as an artist from his schoolmates by about grade four or five. "I was by then a steady 'sketcher'. It just came naturally. I also got plenty of attention from doting pupils. Sometimes they crowded so closely that a few would have to stand on the nearby desks to look down at me at work. The yearly holidays always brought fresh opportunities to show off my talent. I competed with myself in drawing and colouring. I was able to see if I could do a better Santa, a better shamrock or Valentine or Witch than the previous year. Very few of these were saved, however – only some cowboy, pirate, planes and war drawings which I found in a portfolio up in my parents' attic by chance very recently."[23]

He also had at least one teacher who was secretly on his side as well: "My desk had a mass of drawings in it at all times for, besides recess, I sometimes used to draw on the sly in the desk during class. Imagine my surprise a few years ago to get a letter from our longest-of-all school teacher, Mrs. Houghton. She said she'd read the magazine publicity of my work and wanted to tell me, among other things, that she had wished very much to help me develop my talent when I was her pupil, but the best she could do at that time was to pretend she didn't notice that 'stolen time' drawing."[24]

Other than cranking out seasonal emblems and other school-related art, Kurelek was drawing and painting for his own pleasure as well, creating images inspired by popular culture and his own imagination. When he came upon that stash of images in the attic as an adult, even the artist himself was taken aback by the violence of the imagery. "They're so frightfully violent," he wrote. "People's heads being ripped off by a cannon ball. An airship blasting a gun emplacement. An arrow coming through a knight's shield and stabbing him in the eye. My wife analyzes this as repressed violent feelings towards my tormentors."[25]

Many of these disturbing images were plastered on his bedroom walls at home where they elicited Metro's disapproval and concern. Patricia Morley writes, "His father considered art a waste of time at best, and at worst a perversity. Dmytro was upset to discover his son covering the walls with garish designs of priests and angels, nurses, snakes, tigers. The images that could frighten a grown man came from many sources: radio melodrama, comics, Westerns, Jehovah's Witnesses literature, even illness."[26]

Michael O'Brien makes the astute observation that in reacting so strongly against his son's "devil pictures" (an interesting choice of words from this generally unreligious man) the ever-morose Metro may have "feared his own pessimism being handed down through his son."[27] In his 1981 interview with Patricia Morley, the usually stalwart Metro confessed that these powerfully disturbing images made him frightened to go upstairs to the boy's room. "So I was afraid to go there." Metro demanded the pictures be taken down, though that didn't mean his son stopped producing more of their kind. "I said, don't do that, you're wasting your time, you'll fail school. He was quiet, and trying always to do what I wanted. So he tried to hide it from me. Half a year later, I found he was still doing it."[28]

Frankly it's not unusual for growing boys in the upper grades of elementary school to feel a sudden fascination for images of physical violence and horror and it was probably pointless of Metro (though not terribly surprising) to have tried to plug up his son's primary channel of self-expression in that way instead of letting him work it through. Kurelek was just then entering into the churning hormonal cauldron of adolescence which awakens all kinds of hitherto unsuspected appetites in its unwitting subjects. Some of those appetites are rude and disruptive, others are sweet and soothing and some of them are neither wholly one nor the other but tantalizingly hint that these previously disparate aspects might even be combined in intriguing ways.

"And then something happened," Kurelek wrote of another interior storm he underwent at this time when he came upon a stack of Sunday School magazines piled up on a desk at the back of the school room. "I'd seen this picture before of Christ standing on the bow of a boat stilling the waves. Although it was just an illustration, suddenly it had a totally strange and unexpected impact. An indescribable feeling of elation flooded over me. I just wasn't prepared to cope with it so I didn't know what to do. Anyway, I got to my front seat alright, and sat down looking ahead, hoping no one had seen the change come over me.

"This religious experience (if indeed it was that) brought with it a spontaneous desire to worship. In Spring I went into our bush behind the implement shed and cut myself a thick willow branch – which incidentally had a fragrance similar to incense – and from this I whittled a crucifix. During the day I would occasionally steal into my room to pray before it. Sometimes at night, I would get out of bed hoping against hope that my brother, with whom I always slept, would not awaken, and see what I was doing. I don't recall if I also tried to be a better person – that is whether I also was Christian in practice. Nor do I remember how long this devotional period lasted. It was probably not longer than the summer. It has never returned, not even to this day."[29]

Kurelek's touchingly evocative painting from 1961, *Winter Windows and Praying Boy*, commemorates this brief and awkward period of grace which couldn't be sustained. Michael O'Brien explains its inevitable evaporation: "But the burst of spirituality was raw and undirected. There was no one with whom he could discuss the questions which inevitably arose. There were disappointments about 'unanswered prayers'. And shortly after, puberty began in full force. He stopped praying and the years of unbelief began."[30]

What Kurelek has described here is not only a strong religious predisposition but even a mystical capacity for something like rapture. Sadly (or do I perhaps mean heroically?) the last line ("It has never returned, not even to this day") speaks to the degree to which faith for Kurelek as an adult would be an act of logos and will, almost entirely lacking those great revivifying infusions of spiritual helium that can suddenly lift us out of the everydayness of our lives, evoking that same "indescribable feeling of elation" that overtook him as a young teenager. I raise the possibility of heroism because I'm reminded here of St. Teresa of Calcutta's decades of feeling cut off from God and nonetheless doggedly carrying on with her devotions and her extraordinary, gruelling work serving the poorest of the poor.

Kurelek didn't trust emotion as a theological engine as it could so readily lead to a shifting chaos of subjectivism, which, of course, posed a particular threat to someone with his depressive disposition. Writing about the aftermath of his adult conversion, Kurelek strikes that same cheerless note of strictly unemotional commitment: "There was one very important thing I'd learned about emotion. It is a fleeting, fickle thing. It's good to have in so far as it helps with devotion, but never, never count on it . . . No, there had to be another kind of conversion – one of the WILL. It's like discovering that two and two make four. You know it's true. Period. And it will continue to be true no matter what you feel like. You, for your part, must make the best possible effort to live by it. Sometimes it will be easy, sometimes difficult. Sometimes you'll feel uplifted, sometimes dry as dust, or even in that state which religious people know as 'the dark night of the soul'."[31]

There's a 50 page section in the home stretch of the first version of *Someone with Me* (which was wisely cut way back in the second) where Kurelek pretty well sets aside the story of his life altogether and engages in some utterly leaden proselytising, laying out what he considers an irrefutable argument for the existence of God. Even readers who are on his side may find themselves muttering, "Oh, please, just stop this," as they wearily flip over another page to see a not very accomplished sketch of a tea cup, some sugar cubes and a teaspoon with a nail in its cradle that St. William Aquinas has placed here to illustrate his pedantic musings on the difference between materiality and non-materiality. It's just awful.

It's quite scary to consider his wife's claim in her introduction to the second edition of *Someone With Me* that in his last couple of years Kurelek was seriously considering whether he shouldn't give up painting and write full time. All of his life William Kurelek had an immense respect for the written word. He frequently lifted titles, lines and phrases from life-shaping books and poems as titles for his paintings. Routinely Kurelek would compose extensive forewords for his gallery exhibitions which contained large captions (or short essays, if you prefer) explaining what the individual paintings were about. This double-barrelled approach of visually showing and verbally elucidating, he hoped, would ensure that this painter, who saw himself primarily as a 'messenger,' always got his message across. If you take him at his own word, it would appear that Kurelek believed painting was a poor second cousin to writing.

In the concluding section of his autobiography, Kurelek says as much. Writing about the "moral decline of our ever more materialistic society" which he believes will almost certainly lead to "total nuclear war and political tyranny" in which "most of our art may well be destroyed", Kurelek ponders what is the point of painting at all. 'What's the use of painting beauty only, if this beauty will soon be destroyed?' I ask myself. The logical thing for me would be to turn to preaching the gospel of 'repent and be saved,' but if God had meant me to do strictly that, then He'd not have given me the talent to paint and draw. So all angles considered, it ends up that I'm doing exactly what I am supposed to be doing. Paintings may not have nearly the power to convert people that the printed or spoken word has, but each man has his part to play in the human and divine drama – some persons just a few lines, others whole pages."[32]

The man could proselytise beautifully and powerfully – but in images that effortlessly convey strong emotions – not in his dry-as-dust words. While some of his more in-your-face didactic paintings depicting the sin and depravity of Toronto's Yonge Street or bloody fetus-strewn streams behind public hospitals may repel more viewers than they attract, no such qualms are raised when he cranks back the outrage factor and instead seeks to convey quiet sanctity. I particularly love the paintings he developed for his sublimely effective 1976 picture book, *A Northern Nativity* in which he depicts the Holy Family in 20 different Canadian locales from an igloo to a boxcar, from a Newfoundland outpost to a Saskatchewan grain silo, riding in a horse-drawn Mennonite cart in Ontario or a packhorse through the Rockies or standing in the crowd at Niagara where Mary has to hold Jesus up high so he can see beyond the assembled crowd staring at the frozen falls. In paintings such as these Kurelek wields, if not the "power to convert people," then the power at least to open their hearts, in a way that he never does in his plodding, apologetic writing.

3

OUT INTO THE WORLD

BY THE TIME THAT William and John concluded their nine-year stay at Victoria P.S. to attend high school commencing with grade ten (they had taken grade nine studies by correspondence, overseen by their Victoria teacher) material circumstances at home had markedly (and temporarily, it would turn out) improved. Metro's great gamble in leaving the Alberta Huculak family compound to run his own farm in Manitoba was paying handsome dividends. While the war had dried up the supply of young men to hire as hands, Metro could now turn more reliably to his ever more able-bodied sons to help with farm work – particularly John. And the war had also brought a miraculous increase in produce prices so the family now could afford a car. His 16th summer saw William's first-ever visit to "a large body of water," when the family visited Winnipeg Beach.

Though William still felt picked on and disrespected by Metro, some significant changes in the dynamics between them were slowly becoming evident during the war years. Before we get into those we should also acknowledge that there were things about his father that William always had admired, indeed (to use his own phraseology) "worshipped". Even during their worst periods of discord, William always gave his father full points as a first rate storyteller. "I recall, as a boy sitting in the kitchen corner after work was over, listening to my father tell stories to his hired man of the brutality and even comic confusion of war. Father was a natural born storyteller, and hired men came and went, so I heard those stories over and over."[33]

Kurelek himself also had this storytelling gift though in his case, that gift would be rendered by far most effectively in his paintings. The narrative hook is one of the qualities that make his paintings so compellingly popular with not particularly art-savvy people. Virtually anyone who looks at his scenes, so elaborately set up and usually peopled with human characters who intrigue us or touch us, will instinctively wonder, "What's going on here?" and immediately start piecing together a story or a situation.

"There's something extraordinary operating there," Michael O'Brien says about Kurelek's knack for narrative painting. "Some of it is illustration, it's not art. But a good deal of it is illustration that starts to move beyond simply telling a visual story into the realm of high art. And I think you could look to Peter Breugel and Hieronymus Bosch whose work he saw in Vienna. They were basically illustrators who were also great artists. He didn't see any strong demarcation line between telling a visual story and great art. The lines were not hard and fast for him."

While Metro drove all of his children to work very hard at their farm and household chores (which could extend from before dawn until after sunset during the peak summertime growing season) and also drove them to excel at their schoolwork, he was never any less demanding of himself. Certainly there can be no doubt from which parent William inherited his formidable work ethic. Speaking about his father's drive to succeed in the wake of the grasshopper plague, Kurelek wrote, "Here was the long awaited chance to make good as well as to snatch the homestead out of the jaws of disaster, and father drove himself and us mercilessly. There were times he seemed to be heroic, as in a play which made a deep impression on me when we read it in high school. The name of it, appropriately, was *Dark Harvest*."[34]

Kurelek follows that commendation with a few of his usual sniping notes about Metro's heavy-handedness. As William moves into his teenaged years in his various autobiographical accounts and keeps picking away at these paternal injustices, one might be tempted to feel exasperation but the more apt response is pity at the degree to which the relationship with his father had been ruined beyond all earthly repair. Without some kind of supernatural aid, William was constitutionally incapable of picking up on the new cues that Metro was starting to send his way.

Around the time that William and John moved into high school, a definite sea change was underway in Metro's heart. It is incredibly difficult, even at the best of times, for children and parents to suddenly draw a fresh bead on one another and come to a new understanding about what the other party is up to. Such soul work can only be achieved over an extended period of time if both parties are open-minded and well-intentioned; two conditions that were woefully lacking here.

The strongest evidence that Metro was maturing as a father and starting to consider what – by his own lights, mind you – would be best for his children was his decision not just to send William and John to a proper high school for grades ten through twelve (something neither he nor his wife had been able to benefit from) but to send them to a high school in Winnipeg where the standards would be among the highest in the province. This meant paying their food and lodging at a series of rooming houses for their first year and, when that didn't work out to everyone's satisfaction (too many bad smells and argumentative landlords), buying a bungalow near Isaac Newton High School in their second year when William and John's sister Winnie joined them as a student and gave some rather desperately needed assistance in cooking. Also resident in the house in a sort of overseeing role were the Melnyks, an older couple of Ukrainian descent, but as they're scarcely mentioned in Kurelek's account of this period, it seems their interaction with he and his siblings was pretty minimal.

There is one section in the first version of his autobiography where Kurelek comes close to thanking Metro for what he did for him at this time. Unfortunately he chose to throw this passage out of the second version, which is the one that was widely published a couple years after William died and while Metro was still alive:

"I suppose my father had dreamed and planned on making something special of us through higher education for years. But to us it came like a thunderclap out of the blue at the end of grade nine. We weren't going to Stonewall, but to the big city, Winnipeg itself, for high school! I sometimes wonder what I'd have done if father had not wanted to take on the expense of higher education. Would we have dropped out into the workaday world like children of less ambitious parents? . . . It was obvious John and I had the intelligence to go in for [higher education]. But the drive to do so – well, as I said, father provided that simply by announcing, 'You're going to high school in Winnipeg'."[35]

Kurelek's description of their first day at Isaac Newton is one of the most delightfully written sections in both versions of the autobiography. Even though he is describing a social humiliation of the very first order, he brings a lightness of touch to the telling and sees the incident for what it is and no more and doesn't try to play it up into some life-wrenching trauma:

"We didn't even know until we got to Isaac Newton that morning, that we were one week late starting school. I gathered some time later that father had needed our help as long as possible on the farm with the threshing. And an agreement had been reached between him and the principal, Mr. Floyd, that our first week could be skipped . . . As it was, we not only hadn't time to knock the hayseeds out of our hair; we were dumped into a system already in operation."[36]

In terms of the rapid cultural adaptation required of these rural, one-room school grads suddenly pitched into a much larger, urban high school, it scarcely mattered that Isaac Newton was the smallest of all the Winnipeg high schools. Neither they nor Metro had any idea what they were in for. After stopping by the office to get them enrolled, Metro accompanied his sons to Room 12 which they assumed would be their full time classroom and then took his leave. The boys were late on their very first day and had to enter into a packed classroom of students (most of whom already knew each other, not just from the previous week but from the previous grade nine school year) who stared wordlessly at the newcomers.

Utterly unprepared for the different setups and routines that pertain in high school, the intimidated brothers had stumbled into what would turn out to only be their home room class, carrying all of the textbooks they would need that term in unwieldy and disintegrating paper parcels. No one had thought to explain to them about lockers. They had no sooner settled into desks at the back of their home room, hoping to lie low for a while and figure out the lay of the land, when everybody suddenly stood up and headed off to their first class of the day. They tried to follow some of the boys they'd noticed in their home room, until they lost track of them in the milling crush of students all heading this way and that at top and purposeful speed. Then another bell rang, all the classroom doors up and down the hall were suddenly pulled shut, and William and John, once again, were the only people in the whole school who didn't know where they were supposed to be. They peered through the windows in classroom doors looking for anybody they recognized, finally barging into a history class where they started to appreciate how far behind in their studies they were. That class eventually broke up and they were unsure where to go for their second class, again wandering the echoing hallways of both floors with John on the brink of tears. They spotted a vaguely familiar face in the typing class and barged in there, late again, no sooner taking their seats then they realized they were supposed to be in German class.

Within a few days the boys had found their high school legs, knew exactly where to turn up when, and were soon able to redirect all that nervous energy expended in their initiatory week into more productive channels and apply themselves to their work. Isaac Newton being a high school of some academic rigour and distinction, William was no longer routinely racking up grades of 90% or more but (except for a bit of a breakdown in the Easter term of Grade 11 when he failed) he pushed himself as hard as ever and always placed in the top quadrant of his classes.

There was no ostracism or bullying as the boys had first experienced at Victoria P.S. and the more easygoing John soon made a wide circle of friends (to the point where he would start to fall behind academically and even fail his grade 11 year) while William did not. Beyond the orbit of their home community with its mix of young relatives and people he knew well because they were always around whether he actually liked them or not, William found it hard to make new friends. The pattern which would play out over and over again throughout his teenaged years and on through to his late 20s, was that whenever he did latch onto someone with friendship potential, utterly starved for companionship, he would come on way too hard and usually repel them in pretty short order.

All of the friendships he tried to make during this period tended to be one-sided affairs that burned out quickly, often leaving him feeling foolish and lonelier than ever. Alternately naive and suspicious, Kurelek wasn't good at reading people and his neediness was so pronounced that he was an easy mark for emotional or financial mooches looking to fatten their egos or wallets without giving anything much in return. Later on in university and art college he would start to make what he hoped would blossom into solid friendships with budding Communists who were only looking to make ideological converts or homosexuals hoping to score and Kurelek would bail out as soon as he discerned their real motivations.

If one-on-one friendships were elusive, he wasn't any better at hanging out with groups of guys who always wanted to brag about their various feats involving booze and girls. Kurelek sensed early on that his was a potentially addictive personality and shunned alcohol as both a personal danger and a waste of scarce money. Nor could he bear to be around young men when they talked about girls in a predatory way. Kurelek wanted a wife some day and understood in principle that before you could make someone your wife, you'd have to go out on dates and court her. But no girl had yet appealed to him strongly enough that he could summon the courage to face what he felt certain would be an awkward and discouraging ordeal.

Considering their markedly different natures, it perhaps wasn't so surprising that the sensitive and studious older brother and his more rough and tumble younger brother started to get on each other's nerves, occasionally erupting into wrestling matches and food fights. William describes one of their more desultory set-tos where they faced off across the kitchen table in their Winnipeg bungalow flicking cold spoonfuls of soup at one another. When Winnie showed up as a housemate in their second year at Isaac Newton, some of the tension between the brothers dissipated as they more and more were able to go their separate ways.

Friendless and increasingly cut off even from his brother, Kurelek threw himself into his school work to such an extent that his body and brain started to rebel. Eating cheaply and meagrely to minimize his dependence on Metro and virtually chaining himself to his desk for marathon study sessions (goaded on by the Churchillian slogan pinned to his wall, "Nothing matters now but victory!") Kurelek started to suffer spells of anemia and light-headedness and once passed out altogether when rising from a protracted study session.

Most worrying of all his eyes started playing tricks. His vision dimmed, images blurred. When eye strain started to flare up, he developed an unhelpful strategy of alternately covering one eye and reading with the other and this, combined with his anxieties about what on Earth was happening, only exacerbated the problem and the pain until he feared that he might go blind. His eye problems would persist until he booked himself into a psychiatric hospital in England. In retrospect he understood these to be psychosomatic. Michael

O'Brien believes his ocular difficulties were reflective of his over-reliance on sight as the only sense he could trust: "Seeing was of great importance to the boy . . . touch was not a sense used to express love. Hearing was the channel through which he received mockery. Sight, therefore, would become a prized possession . . . The theme of vision was central in Kurelek's life."[37]

With his own eyes focussed on material success and respectability, Metro wanted his oldest son to become a doctor which would never have been a very good fit for someone as physically abstemious as William. Because he still found it difficult to openly stand up to Metro, William hummed and hawed through a couple of one-sided encounters and then appeared to submit to his father's grand plan for his future profession, even enrolling and handsomely passing a summer cram course in Winnipeg where he imbibed three years' worth of Latin language training in six weeks. That working knowledge of Latin came in very handy a decade later when he converted to Roman Catholicism.

Though he never bought into Metro's dream of doctoring, William played along with it to avoid a knockdown, drag-out fight and because he didn't want to pass up the opportunity to get out from under his father's influence for whole weeks at a stretch. The boys were required to return home to Stonewall every second weekend to help out around the farm; a small enough price to pay for the 12 consecutive days of unsupervised liberty that preceded and followed those working visits. Privately Kurelek knew that a career in medicine was not to be: "But doctoring? No, a hundred times no!" he writes in his autobiography. "The thought of associating intimately, aggressively with people as a doctor had to do, to touch their bodies, to cut them open . . . well, I just couldn't face the idea of it."[38]

By his grade 12 year, Kurelek had persuaded Metro to let him aim himself in the direction of a teaching degree which might not carry the same sort of earning potential as medicine but was certainly more respectable than trying to be an artist. Kurelek later admitted that this too was a "front" that he had little intention of following through on, though if push came to shove, he probably could have taught whereas he never would have made it as a doctor. Best of all, this phony vocational realignment meant that he now could immerse himself in the full range of options (something short of a smorgasbord) that Isaac Newton High had to offer for the aspiring visual artist – one class a week.

It is interesting to note that just as soon as Kurelek was out from under the full time oppression of living under Metro's roof, he and John had enrolled at the local Ukrainian Greek Orthodox Cathedral, St. Mary The Protectress, where they not only attended Mass regularly (though in William's case without personal conviction) but took night classes in Ukrainian language and history and participated in a full range of cultural and social activities like concerts, plays and dances. While the first approach to the Cathedral had been made at

Metro's behest, Kurelek surprised himself by how quickly and even passionately he took to the place. There were girls there (and one in particular) that he adored from afar, never daring to declare his interests and risk rejection but who unwittingly served as idols of aspiration – idealized goddesses whom he would improve himself in order to be worthy of.

While he held himself aloof religiously, paying only lip service during Mass, he was converted to the cause of Ukrainian nationalism and also 'worshipped' in a manner of speaking and only for a while, the priest at St. Mary's, Father Mayevsky. "I went completely overboard in admiration for this substitute father . . . As he told us the history of the Ukraine, described her natural riches, her cultural beauty, I realized his zeal was passing from him to me. Now I was on fire too. I was really moved by the tragedies of Pid Kova, Mozeppa, Shevchenki and the Free Ukrainian Republic. Father Mayevsky was also a noted Ukrainian choir conductor and in listening to the concerts he put on, I began to hear again the haunting beauty of the Ukrainian folk songs my father used to sing in the years before the Great Depression."[39]

Unquestionably these Church-related activities took some of the edge off Kurelek's loneliness in the big, cold city of Winnipeg but I suspect they also helped to assuage the pangs of something that can only be called homesickness. Even though the harsh atmosphere of his own childhood home was not something he longed to return to, he knew there was some sort of emotional, existential nourishment that he had never received and which was crucial and which a healthily functioning home ordinarily provided. If his own true father couldn't be trusted, he would instead worship this substitute father as a hero and would even risk the haunting torture of hearing again songs which conjured up images of Metro. Cut off from his real family, he would immerse himself in the larger story of his family's cultural background and take whatever strength could be extracted from that.

In a very real sense the teenaged William Kurelek was a displaced person who fled his toxic childhood home for the sake of his own survival but recognized that he was fundamentally unequipped to make his own way forward without some kind of extra-familial help. The disorienting experience of immigration wasn't just a factor in his family's background. It was also his own personal reality, cut off as he was from any of the consolations and supports that family and a home community can provide.

Even though he was a born Canadian, he identified with newcomers to our land in their lonely and precarious struggle to find a way to live here. How fitting it is that so many of the paintings for which he would become best known and which won him his first popularity, chronicle the struggles of vulnerable European and Slavic immigrants trying to make a go of it in the strange and dauntingly large and empty landscape of Canada. And how well Kurelek's outsider's outlook on the world as a place where he didn't belong would eventually jibe with his conversion to Roman Catholicism and its conviction that all of us are strangers in a strange land who do not have an abiding home this side of Eternity. But until he won that consolation through membership in the Roman Catholic Church, he remained a nervous and uncertain young man who was painfully conscious of not fitting in anywhere.

As the summer of Kurelek's grade 12 year approached, Metro again surprised his sons by suggesting that one of them should try to find work in Winnipeg as he could get by on the farm that season with just one helper. John who would eventually become an engineer made the rounds of every electrical firm in town and struck out. William hit pay dirt with his very first application to a sign painting firm. Though he had to cycle 18 miles out to Stonewall and back most weekends to help out there, Kurelek was thrilled at last to be not only earning his own keep but socking away nearly all of the money he would need to pay for his tuition at the University of Manitoba.

In fact he would never work a long stretch on Metro's farm again. Once free of his father's corrosive influence, he never returned home for more than holidays, short visits or working weekends. Over the summer holidays between university terms, he stood up against Metro's assumptions and wishes that he would help out at the Stonewall farm and took on summer jobs in remote Northern Ontario lumber camps instead. Scrawny and slight of stature as he may have been, he was a hard worker who not only earned his foreman's respect but his own as well. On his first visit to the Stonewall farm after his first summer in the bush, he defiantly wore his lumberjack boots at all times even though there were constant complaints lodged about the noise and dirt they kicked up. Those great galumphing boots were his way of signalling to his parents with every plodding footfall: "See? I can stand on my own two feet."

Kurelek was proud that he could stick it out and even excel at a dangerous and demanding job that a lot of other young men couldn't abide for more than a few days. And the mid to late '40s were the last pre-mechanized days of real lumber-jacking; a vanishing way of life he would celebrate in paintings and one of his best picture books called simply, *Lumberjack*. In other holidays he picked up construction jobs (once helping to build an extension to a terminal grain elevator in Port Arthur) and a few notches below that in occupational prestige, worked at a car wash, sorted out piles of clothing for a dry cleaner and did a stint as a waiter in a restaurant. The work was menial and demanding but it was a huge boon to his sense of adequacy to prove that he could earn his own keep and be his own man.

While life under Metro's roof had never been luxurious, as Kurelek started to earn his own money, he pared things back even further, developing penny-pinching habits that would stick with him for the rest of his life. Particularly during his last 20 years of success, he could be incredibly generous in his charitable giving of both money and time but where he and his family were concerned he strove to maintain an almost penitential frugality which became a bone of contention with his wife. Late in the first version of his autobiography (he wisely edited it out of the second) he drops in a petulant note aimed at his wife where he sounds more than a little like Metro trying to toughen up his offspring by withholding inessential comforts that might make them go soft. "Actually about the only unhappiness I have today is not having my wife's respect. She cannot, or will not, see the future as I do. And I will not force her to especially since I'm so alone in my vision. So I have to stand aside and see my children raised according to her protective philosophy, and all the while knowing it would be kinder to them to let them learn endurance now."[40]

Perhaps the most extreme manifestation of this tendency was the less than ideal space he allotted for himself as a studio. Even as one of the most successful artists in Canada, Kurelek worked in a cramped, windowless, airless room in the basement of his Toronto house, an eight by four foot coal cellar that Kurelek had originally adapted as a bomb shelter before taking it over as his studio. Not just uncomfortable, it was frankly an unsafe environment that almost certainly shortened his life.

"Yeah. I was down in there once," Michael O'Brien told me. "It was awful. It was horrible. Just a tiny, tiny subterranean cubicle. I don't know how anyone could work in there."

I mentioned that some people contend that working in that room killed him.

"I think so too," O'Brien concurred. "I think it was probably a major factor. A lot of those spray paints [he used] were extremely toxic and it was not a well-ventilated painting place. On the rare occasions that I've done similar work with such paint, I got violent headaches and felt nauseous. So I've stopped using it, thinking about what happened to Bill. He got cancer of the liver and pancreas and that's where these things hit."

Ascetic economy is a skill which most developing artists have to inculcate but even in the most cash-strapped stretches of their youth, a ship of good fortune makes it into harbour now and again and the 'beans-and-day-old bread' regime is occasionally and gratefully punctuated by riotous splurges of bohemian extravagance. It is notable that Kurelek never seems to have indulged himself in that way. Even before his Christian conversion, such indulgence was a break he did not want to give to himself, that he did not think he deserved.

There are a few sections in the autobiographical writings where he boasts about how little he was able to get by on, such as this bit hailing from his art college years where he writes about modelling himself on the examples of James Joyce's young artistic hero, Stephen Dedalus, and that poster boy for starving artists everywhere, Vincent Van Gogh:

"I rebelled as I understood a proper artist was compelled to do – if he was worth his salt – against conventionality, and I would face the contempt and poverty that being such a social outcast entails . . . It seemed that I had to live as full, intense, and varied a life as my literary artist heroes apparently had to in order to acquire a background of experience from which to draw their subject matter. I really tried to fashion my life on theirs . . . I was proud of my poverty, of not having proper food, or enough of it, of wearing shabby clothes and not bathing or shaving . . . proud I chummed with communists and eccentrics, even that I suffered from periods of depression because I believed that out of all this I was destined to produce great art."[41]

While he eventually came to regard his emulation of Dedalus and Van Gogh as just another "costume" he had donned in his search for a personal identity, Kurelek couldn't just shake off his penny-pinching habits at will, even when not doing so made him look stingy and mean-spirited. There's an account in his autobiography where he takes part in a guided tour in Ireland and surprises himself by having a really wonderful time – indeed, an experience of (to use his own words) "Wordsworthian . . . ecstasy" – the impact of which he then defuses in that passage's conclusion by writing, "Only having to give the guide a good fat tip like the other tourists did, marred a memorable day."[42]

This is the sort of thing I mean (as well as that jab at his wife, above, for being too soft on their kids) when I describe Kurelek's writing as 'ham-fisted'. A more sophisticated writer, mindful of the primary impression they want to leave with the reader, wouldn't drop that kind of clanger at the end which does so much to spoil everything that's gone before. Not so much with the texts in his picture books which were overseen by editors (with whom he'd regularly get into tussles, usually over what he construed as moral points) but certainly in the autobiographical writings, there are times when you just want to shake the poor man for undercutting his work in this way.

I suppose that what one feels the lack of in so much of his writing is charm, a more sophisticated understanding of how impressions are made and how allowances must be granted or consideration shown for different temperaments and points of view. As a writer he doesn't expend any time or effort in trying to win you over. He just plops down whatever comes into his mind. I suppose you could argue that it's an honest approach but it's not a winning one.

Of course one also can examine Kurelek's paintings and similarly find no trace of such refinements and niceties but there such absences don't matter because at his not infrequent best, he is in such absolute control as an artist. If art works at all, it works quickly and irrefutably ('Seeing is believing,' goes the old saw) whereas writing works persuasively and takes more time. Art is what it is. Even if you can't explain it, you almost instantly get the artist's conception or you don't and there's really not much point in arguing with it. But that's not the way writing works. Prose and even a lot of poetry don't present you with a vision which you will largely accept or reject right away so much as they develop an argument or describe a situation which you will incrementally learn to trust depending on how fairly or artfully the material is being presented.

In writing or painting, William Kurelek worked quickly without a whole lot of agonizing or tweaking. With his visual art this wasn't a problem — indeed the unmediated directness, even the innocence of the conception and the execution are real strengths — but such an approach didn't serve his writing well. In his autobiographies there are numerous sections where you wish he'd gone back over the material and worked it up a little better just to make it more readily comprehensible, let alone more evocative.

Even though he recognized in moments of frank self-appraisal that he didn't have pronounced literary gifts, he could be remarkably stubborn and protective about his writing and resistant to suggestions about how to improve it. In addition to the hypersensitivity to criticism that many unseasoned writers evince, Kurelek was also wary that people wanted him to water down his Christian message. He consulted with a number of fixers before publishing the second edition of his autobiography; the shorter version aimed at a broader public which McClelland & Stewart published three years after his death. One of the prose doctors called in to help out was author and editor, Barry Callaghan, and he told Patricia Morley, "He wanted that book to read well, to be published, be persuasive. I could feel it almost like a lust in him. He wanted his story 'out there'. But he didn't want to yield to any judgement of his prose. I had to operate with great care, almost apologetically . . . He really wanted a blessing, not criticism . . . He couldn't write to save his soul."[43]

His art almost never suffered by his preferred modus operandi of 'damn the torpedoes and full speed ahead'. I put that one mild qualifier in there remembering a painting like *Terry Ryan's Lunch* from his *Kurelek's Canada* book. It's one of the Ontario paintings, based on a story he heard from a friend, of workers installing hydro lines in the north and playing a crude joke on one of the newbies on their crew by furtively raiding his lunch pail and smearing a cow pat over his sandwich. I'm sure it made a great joke at the time but as the central subject for a full page painting . . ? Well, let's just hope that was one of the days when he produced three or four canvases and the others were a lot more substantive.

Except for a couple of dry periods in his 20s when depression seized up his gears, the fast turnover of work seemed to be a necessary constant with Kurelek. Never a fan of down time, he was always painting and sketching, even on plane trips and while waiting around for appointments. Unbroken momentum kept him primed as an artist. In his introductory essay to *The Messenger* catalogue,

Kurelek's dealer Avrom Isaacs tellingly notes that "Most artists produce one exhibition every two years. Bill easily came up with two exhibitions a year . . . Bill's genius was the gift he had of an endless supply/memory of stored literal images. When he approached a painting there was no hesitation, no problem to resolve. He had a warehouse of images that were crystal clear in his mind. This allowed him to work rapidly and contributed directly to his being so prolific. When he approached his canvas (usually a gesso-covered masonite board) he didn't have to work out his vision. He already had a fully realized picture in mind."[44]

That first pre-university summer away from Stonewall, Kurelek attempted to get to the bottom of what was ailing him physically. He booked an appointment with a dentist and had one rotten tooth extracted and also saw an eye doctor whose pricey prescriptions for ointments and glasses did absolutely nothing to ease the bouts of ocular fatigue and pain that were brought on by intense study. A little later on in his university career, Kurelek approached a general practitioner about his anemia and occasional light-headedness and was prescribed pills to goose up his basal metabolic rate as the doctor suspected his thyroid gland was underperforming. Kurelek dubbed these his "B.M.R. pills" and believed he became addicted to them for a few years. They seemed to fix his listless spells but they also erratically affected his moods, bringing on alternating bursts of euphoria and despair. The troughs were no fun at all but the peaks – in which he was full of self-confidence and hatched great schemes of the art he would make – made them worthwhile.

"Perhaps it wasn't strictly drug addiction I got from the B.M.R. tablets but it sure resembled it. Somehow, I don't know how, I got a perpetually renewable prescription. Once the B.M.R. was up to normal I was supposed to lay off those pills. But I kept taking them as an antidote for depression. This went on for three years, off and on. I'll copy my diary observations . . . 'In about two weeks I began to feel its effects. The fire of life in me that before had flickered anemically now began to blaze forth in violent bursts. I now feel I am developing, potentially capable of great accomplishments – but the sleeplessness remains – the fluctuations of exuberance and despair, before slight, now travel in mighty sweeps. Particularly in the hot peak of the cycle, do strange and powerfully romantic and optimistic planning and theorizing seize me. My only regret is that these moments soon burn themselves out and I lose faith in myself.' Back up on another peak I wrote on: 'I want to drop everything and plunge headlong to my life goals. I want to travel and learn and feel and live and prepare fully for a great destiny.'"[45]

At first still playing along with the bluff for Metro's sake that he would become a teacher, Kurelek majored at university in history, English literature and Latin and also took courses in art history and psychology. From this last course

he picked up the idea that a lot of his ailments – his listlessness, his eye problems, his recurring depressions and funks – might be psychological in origin
and he resolved to one day see if some form of psychiatric treatment might help.
He did well enough in his studies to earn a couple of minor scholarships and
graduate with his Bachelor of Arts degree but except for his reading of James
Joyce's *Portrait of the Artist as a Young Man*, and Irving Stone's novelized biography of Vincent Van Gogh, *Lust for Life*, nothing much from his three years at
the University of Winnipeg seems to have made a lasting impression on him.

Indeed it appears that he learned a lot more about himself and the world
and gained more confidence while working to earn his tuition and living ex-
penses than he did in any university classroom or lecture hall. He criticized virtually all of his professors for their lazy and unengaged presentations of curric-
ula and was equally judgemental of the shallowness of his fellow students with
whom he had his usual difficulties making friends. By the end of his third year
he cared so little for the academic world that he neglected to attend his graduation: "Strange how nothing else stands out academically in that University year
other than the impact of Joyce's book. All I have is a picture of myself walking
toward the bus, past the Administration Building, thinking how wonderful it
was to be on fire with ideas. I must have been on one of my B.M.R. peaks . . .
Perhaps I really didn't care towards the end, because I know I refused to attend
graduation. I refused to be drafted into a cap and gown, or even get a photo of
me taken in one. I was going to be a Stephen Daedalus. I would wear my own
phoney costume, not the establishment's phoney costume!"[46]

In the spring of 1949 as Kurelek wrapped up his studies at the University
of Manitoba, Metro moved the whole growing family one more province to
the east to a much smaller 50 acre farm in Vinemont, Ontario, just outside of
Hamilton. Kurelek, of course, had worked a couple of stints as a lumberjack
in the north but the southern portion of Ontario was a revelation to him. The
rest of the family had gone ahead to Vinemont by car and Kurelek and his sister
Winnie followed by train from Winnipeg at the end of the school year: "I'll
never forget the astounding impression Southern Ontario made on me when I
first saw it. I must have been at an intense burn peak in my B.M.R. cycle. I was
almost rushing from window to window in the coach. To me who'd grown up
on the monotone flat prairies it was like eating a banana split after plain bread.
It was so beautiful, so warm, so quaint, so lush, so picturesque, so civilized, so
interesting, so mature. I could have strung adjectives on and on."[47]

What brought on this latest and final domiciliary move isn't clear. Patricia
Morley who did an excellent job of explaining all of Metro's earlier moves in
her biography of Kurelek, draws a comparative blank on this one: "The reason
for the sale of the Stonewall farm remains mysterious. Neither Bill's writings
nor the surviving Kureleks clarify the matter. Like his famous son, Dmytro was

secretive by nature or habit. Perhaps wartime prices for agricultural products had made it possible for him to opt for a pleasanter climate and a much smaller farm. As with the earlier move in 1934, he chose an area where many Ukranians had already settled, as post-war immigration continued to alter population patterns."[48]

Morley seems to suggest that prices were sufficiently bounteous that Metro decided he could ease up on his scale of operations but such an attitude is completely at odds with everything we know about the ambitious and workaholic Metro. And we also know that finances tightened up significantly with this latest move. None of William, John and Winnie's younger siblings would have higher education laid on at Metro's expense. "I will not be able to afford it and they will have to work in factories," Metro wrote in a letter to his eldest child a couple of years later.[49]

Kurelek himself presents a thoroughly bleak picture of Metro's state of mind in Vinemount in this description of the new homestead. "I used to go home to the farm by bus on the weekends sometimes. But there was no longer much to help with. There was so little land and father walked or sat around moping a lot for his lost kingdom in Manitoba. He'd had his ambition kicked out from under him."

Later in that same passage he describes Metro blowing up at two of his younger siblings for making too much noise – kids Kurelek scarcely knew since he'd left home for high school and university six years earlier, describing them as almost like another generation. Metro "leapt up, yanked Paul out of his chair and delivered the two of them roughly out of the room. It seemed so unreasonable. Paul, the poor little fellow, was quite shaken. The wave of pity for him that engulfed me as I heard him crying in the next room was so deep that I can still feel it just by recalling the hurt expression on his face. It was like seeing myself from outside in."[50]

In one of his very finest paintings, 1964's *In the Autumn of Life* [Plate 1], Kurelek depicts the Vinemount farm in a large canvas that successfully brought many of the different streams of his art together within one frame. At first glance one seems only to be looking down on an autumnal rural landscape – harvested fields in the background, a pond and laneway with three parked cars to the right, barns and outbuildings to the left – and in the centre a huddled family group of grandparents, children and their spouses, and miscellaneous kiddies (all of them faithful likenesses of the Kurelek clan) – are posed together in front of a modest farmhouse as their picture is snapped.

But then one notices the dead and stunted tree in the left foreground, cruciform in shape with its upper limbs and foliage all hacked away, and then you make out the head of Christ crowned with thorns and his right leg just visible as he hangs suspended on the far side of the tree with a pack of four wolves licking the blood at the base of the trunk. I personally would prefer it if the painting stopped there but Kurelek being Kurlek, toward the top of the painting on the horizon line he painted a small and even discreet (by Kurelekian standards) white cloud indicating that the city of Hamilton has just been hit by an atomic bomb. One is reminded of all of those dreadful, pretentious art films of the '60s where auteur directors would slip in a stock clip of bomb detonations when they needed some profound gravitas. (My good friend Chris Aikenhead's brilliant send-up of crappy student films, *Ivory Founts*, concluded with three of them tacked on one after another.)

But with or without the nuclear cloud, Kurelek's message is the same: 'See here, O man, even with all of your striving and your industry and your worldly success, your life is in vain if, like my father, you ignore God and his salvific love for you.' The painting was originally exhibited in 1964 as the concluding panel of 20 paintings that were designed to honour Metro, recounting his trip from the Ukraine to Canada and presenting scenes from his three farms in Alberta, Manitoba and Ontario. Working on the series, Kurelek went to great lengths to re-imagine his father's odyssey from the inside but here again we see that in forgiving his father and creating this body of work in honour of his father, he was prepared to let go of past bitterness but not to sugar coat his story.

In a note he placed next to the painting when it was exhibited two years later in Winnipeg, Kurelek wrote: "What I'm trying to say is that my father's life, hard as it may have been, is not a happy ending story, even though it may appear to be on the surface, judging by the large healthy family he has raised and the extent of his possessions. He will still have to meet "the day of judgement". And Christ, whom he has ignored all his life, and maybe even helped crucify with his sins, is like a 'skeleton' in his closet. It's an unpleasant scene, that he may try to keep off his property, but it's still there nevertheless."[51]

In 1967 the National Film Board made a ten minute documentary called *Kurelek* based on the exhibition and their treatment – indeed their bowdlerization – of the back story to the paintings contributed to the simplification of Kurelek as a happy/chappy painter of rural scenes which made it so easy for cultural mandarins to disregard him. On the National Film Board website, the promo for *Kurelek* reads: "A documentary about the self-taught painter William Kurelek, told through his paintings. There are scenes of village life in the Ukraine and the early days of struggle on a prairie homestead and the growing comforts of family life. In Ontario, Kurelek paints the present life of Canada with the same pleasure he painted the old."

Of course, the one Ontario painting, the concluding image of the film, is *In the Autumn of Life*, and the filmmakers crop it in such a way that Christ nailed to the tree is never seen at all and the mushroom cloud (utterly uncommented on) is only partially seen and just seems to be a fluffy white cumulus of the non-nuclear variety that pleasantly hovers above a jolly family scene.

With his ever increasing independence from Metro came an increased courage to follow his own star. Kurelek announced that the next rung in his education would not be teacher's college but art college – the Ontario College of Art in nearby Toronto where he'd be renting his own place to live – though he tried to soften his father's disapproval by lying that he would be focussing primarily on commercial art.

Though Kurelek had a few good things to say about some of what he imbibed at OCA – in particular the lectures in art history at the Royal Ontario Museum, working for the first time with nude models in life drawing, some classes in lettering, the examples of certain professors and some of the more promising students as productive or at least promising makers of art – there is an unmistakable note of aloofness in his recollections about his time at OCA. One definite factor was his advanced age. Most of his fellow students had gone straight into art college from high school and he found them juvenile and hard to relate to.

Once again lacking anything that could be described as real friendships, he was set upon by young and ardent pinko cranks and spends almost as much time in his autobiography recalling his not-terribly engrossing arguments with Commies-in-training as he does talking about the courses he took. Given his own family's background it's hard to imagine that he was ever for a second actually attracted by Communism or considered it to be a good thing. I suspect that his propensity for putting up with their hooey was more the result of his own loneliness (if he had to listen to this blather in order to have some interaction with other young human beings, then so be it) and it also was perhaps a fairly passive (if pointless) way to rebel against Metro. Even though I doubt that their political philosophy had any serious appeal for him, there would've been something in these callow proselytisers that perhaps carried echoes of the loner, Stephen Dedalus-type rebels that he so admired.

Perhaps if he too had gone into art college three years earlier, the curriculum at OCA might have taken hold of him in a more involving way but there is an unmistakable sense in his autobiography that arriving there as he did at the age of 22, it was all a case of too little too late; that as much as there were a few techniques and approaches presented that he found useful, he had already developed beyond this perfunctory level. In his second term he stopped attending the full roster of classes and only took those he was interested in. Though he'd been longing for years to receive a full and proper art education, now that he was finally in a place that supposedly could provide that and just that, it wasn't enough. Kurelek became antsy to move on and decided to bail out early in the third term of his first year. "I decided OCA didn't have the creative ferment or atmosphere or whatever it's called for a dedicated fine artist and that's what I thought I was . . . 'I am setting out,' I announced to myself, 'on a long journey – in search of myself as an artist.' The first place would be Mexico."[52]

In art books at the college Kurelek had seen and admired some work by social realist (ie: Communist or, at least, virulently anti-bourgeois) Mexican muralists like Jose Orozco, Diego Rivera and David Siqueiros and learned of an English-language school at San Miguel de Allende where Siqueiros taught and which some other OCA students had attended and found worthwhile. In what sounds like one of his B.M.R. frenzies, he hatched a very loose plan. "Once I got there they might grant me a scholarship. But since I didn't have any money to get there I'd have to earn it first. 'Perhaps,' I calculated, 'I can combine that money earning with a search for myself – for example, going back over the old ground to see what made me and where the roots of my artistic creations may lie. Yes, that's it!' I felt excitement rising, 'I'll go back to Manitoba and Alberta. I'll work in Edmonton to make my stake for Mexico!'"[53]

It took him six months to raise his stake. He hitch-hiked part of the way out west to familiarize himself with the mode of transport he intended to use for getting himself down to Mexico and stayed for a considerable stretch of that time with a maternal uncle in Alberta while working a series of short term jobs in construction, another one cleaning out tanks at an oil refinery and other more menial fare such as scooping hot loaves of bread off an assembly line at a huge bakery. In every spare moment he was sketching and painting and was excited by the progress he was making. On the weekends he made side trips to see various people and haunts associated with his childhood, including a particularly meaningful visit to the farm near Whitford where he'd been born.

He set out for Mexico in the late fall, just ahead of the snow and soon realized he should have left earlier if he'd wanted to avoid some distressingly cold evenings when, if the hitch-hiking wasn't going well, he'd duck into all night cafes and nurse cups of coffee until dawn or flag down buses and fork over a few bucks to buy himself some mobile warmth and the chance to move himself along a little closer to his destination while catching a few winks.

He stopped off in San Francisco to visit the big art gallery there and spent a few days in Los Angeles getting reacquainted with Father Mayevsky, the Ukrainian Orthodox priest he'd admired so much (for non-religious reasons) back in his first years of high school in Winnipeg. The priest was a generous and gracious host but Kurelek found their re-encounter disillusioning as this once heroic substitute father had put on weight, was inclined to bicker with his wife over petty matters and seemed to be succumbing to materialism.

In his rejection of materialism and his peripatetic way of life Kurelek almost seems to prefigure the hippies who wouldn't fully emerge on the scene for another couple of decades yet. And in recounting his moral disapproval of the once-revered man who put him up and fed him and ferried him around town for three or four days, one unmistakably detects that fatuous Aquarian note of disdain for those who provide comforts that are simultaneously consumed and abjured. Indeed, one wonders if the bickering which Kurelek found so objectionable may not have arisen from Mrs. Mayevsky's reluctance to keep feeding this glum freeloader who wouldn't shove off.

From L.A. and Father Mayevsky, Kurelek made his way inland to Las Vegas and the Boulder Dam and then aimed himself directly south to Texas and Mexico via the main highway that passed through the Arizona Desert. It was out there after 36 sleepless hours that he found himself alone, exhausted and buffeted by a strong, cold wind that made him shiver. He was having miserable luck with the hitchhiking and once the sun went down he knew the odds of landing a ride had decreased yet further but still he walked on through the better part of the night for about 20 more miles, turning around to wave his thumb at an occasional oblivious car and turning back to walk some more and stumbling into roadside thorn bushes until his last stores of energy and will utterly collapsed and he knew he could go no further. With no cafe or even a telephone booth to slip into for warmth, he decided to crawl into a culvert and call it a day, perhaps even call it a life.

"Finally 'freeze or no freeze' I decided to chance lying down. I crawled under one of those useless looking road bridges which are only for flash floods and pushing aside thorns, lay on the bare ground. This time there weren't any cardboards or newspapers for covers. Whether I fell fully asleep I don't know, but next thing I was aware of was that there was someone with me. He appeared to be a person in a long, white robe. And he was urging me to rise. 'Get up,' he said. 'We must look after the sheep, or you will freeze to death!' I did get up and set off at a near-run down the road, shaking violently from the chill. Presently I noticed the sheep around me had become nothing but those ragged pieces of mist floating across the road, and the 'other person' just seemed to blend into myself."[54]

"I'll never forget that night till the day I die," Kurelek wrote, and he took the title for both versions of his autobiography – *Someone With Me* – from his account of this incident. (Perhaps at the urging of one of his manuscript doctors the unbelievably klutzy phrase, 'ragged pieces of mist' was changed in the rewrite to the marginally better, 'ragged fluffs of mist'.) Though this visitation came to him at a time when his atheist convictions were at their most impregnable and caused no immediate reappraisal of his position, later, after his conversion, he understood and treasured the experience for what it was – an act of divine mercy extended to him at one of his lowest ebbs. His only other reference to it is found in the very conclusion of both versions of the autobiography where he explains why it is that he no longer falls prey to pessimism or despair no matter how discouraging things might seem:

"We see only the underside as yet of the tapestry God weaves and so we can't make out the whole pattern of the human predicament. What I am sure of, however, is that I am not really alone anymore in the rest of my journey through this tragic, puzzling, yet wonderful world. There is someone with me and always has been. And He has asked me to get up because there is work to be done."[55]

The whole pattern of his present predicament became all too wretchedly clear a few days later when he finally rolled into San Miguel de Allende to find that the English language art school he traversed the continent to attend had just been disbanded and the artist he most wanted to study with, David Siqui-eros, had moved on to Mexico City. An offshoot school was being cobbled to-gether called the Instituto Allende with five other less renowned teachers and a scarcely more populous student body mostly comprised, Kurelek said, of "tour-ists, retired ladies who painted more for the pleasure than for a serious career. In fact, it was this tourist aspect of the whole school that set me most against it. And though I did stay for five months, I never quite made peace with it."[56]

Kurelek travelled to Mexico City to try to make connections with the big name muralists that drew him to Mexico in the first place but lacking any sort of introductions to them and being shy and socially awkward, this all came to nought. What he really wanted was a master/apprentice sort of relationship with someone whose work he unreservedly admired but there was no way to make that happen. And so he queued up with the lady tourists and signed on for courses at the Instituto in life drawing, lithography, anatomy and a special course in framing taught by a local craftsman that might actually have planted a few ideas in his head that came in handy later.

Again, it's hard to know what good the place did him because, as with his accounts of his time at university and art college in Canada, far more attention is lavished on his extracurricular discoveries and experiences than anything that transpired in the classroom. There are, of course, the usual stories about hoped for friendships that turn boring or rancid when the candidates turn out to be hectoring Communists or needy homosexuals who have no interest in William Kurelek the person.

But on a wider, cultural scale, and on a deeper and as yet disregarded spir-itual level, there was lots to take in. Exposure to a whole new kind of landscape and architecture was never wasted on Kurelek. He quickly picked up the Span-ish language to the point where he could competently converse. And Mexico was his first acquaintance with widespread poverty and a society that wasn't so completely hooked up to the capitalist creed.

And again and again – though it roused his suspicion and even a measure of pity for the poor saps who believed in it – he bumped into devout Catholics whose expressions of faith inexplicably moved him. Two young women, "a Chinese from Hawaii" and the other "a rich rancher's daughter from Texas," acted as guides on a number of tours he took and they could never pass by a Catholic church without dropping in to say a prayer. They invited him to participate as well but he was having none of that.

Nonetheless he watched. "They'd put mantillas (which they carried in their handbags) on their heads, and crossing themselves with holy water, they would kneel down, their faces all seriousness. 'It's superstition,' I told myself, 'but beautiful superstition'."[57]

I asked Michael O'Brien if he felt that Kurelek got any benefit from his stints at university and two different art colleges. He took a good long pause before giving an answer: "He certainly developed through the art college training in a number of skills. But I believe really he was quite a natural genius. His greatness as a creative artist would have developed regardless but the art college and various other forms of training helped the process, sped the process, gave him technical skills. But his vision of what it is to be an artist was essentially that of a vocation, a spiritual charism for a Christian artist. And as for his academic training, I think all it gave him was a picture of how lost the modern age is intellectually and spiritually."

Kurelek hitch-hiked and bussed his way back up to Canada and then had a short and decidedly tense visit at the family farm in Vinemount. Kurelek had sent Metro a barnburner of a letter from Mexico in which he'd laid out his shortcomings as a father and asserted his determination to make his way as an artist, with or without his father's approval. Metro claimed that he hadn't even read the letter yet and wasn't prepared to go picking through any minefield of hurt feelings and disappointments with an eye to improving his relationship with his first-born son. So Kurelek cleared out, determined to earn another stake that would get him over to Britain and Europe. After flailing about in Montreal, he found another job with a lumber-jacking crew in northern Quebec and then moved over to Northern Ontario for another round of the same, finally socking $1800 away for his efforts.

He spent most of December back in Vinemount working on an enormous stylized painting that he conceived as a gift for Metro to prove his mettle as an artist. It was a gift that was loaded with bitter and defiant meaning and was received, Kurelek tell us, "reluctantly". *Zaporozhian Cossacks,* which Kurelek worked on for four full weeks, exudes an almost cartoonish energy, expressing fierce masculine power at its most pitiless, and depicts a scene from Nikolai Gogol's *Taras Bulba* in which the title character kills his son for defecting, for the sake of love, to the enemy's side.

From Vinemount he went on to Montreal in January of 1952 to arrange his passage to Europe. Ever on the lookout for ways to economise, Kurelek discovered a deal that was available with Cunard Steamships (the same line that had brought Metro to the new world 29 years before) that would get him over to Swansea, Wales for the rock bottom price of $112. Part of that deal was that he would have to hang around for 14 weeks, waiting for the spring break-up in the St. Lawrence. He used this time supremely well, signing on for some lessons in conversational French, thinking that he might like to study art in Paris for a stretch but that never happened, largely because he discovered *The Natural Way to Draw* by Kimon Nicolaides, a book which revolutionized his approach to picture making and which Kurelek felt not only supplanted the need for any further art education but called into question the validity of everything he'd already learned.

First published in 1941 (three years after Nicolaides' death) the approach put forth in this enduringly popular book is to get the developing artist to shed all of the habits and predispositions they've relied on so far and focus anew on the two key elements of gesture and contour.

"First the essence of a pose or stance is done with a quick scribble called gesture, and secondly the slow, painstaking contour drawing is made by feeling the outside of a thing," Kurelek wrote. "As you become fluent the two approaches meet and marry, and you find yourself doing the right thing without having to worry if you are or not. In the beginning however, it is essential that you scrap all you've learned about drawing and painting, most of which is bad, and start all over again. By his method you get the inner feeling of things; their weight, their physical realness. And Nicolaides was right! I did make the vital breakthrough."[58]

Nicolaides suggests that his course should take an aspiring artist about a year to work through. Typically Kurelek crammed it all into his three months in Montreal. The contour work he did in his rented room, stripping down and working in front of a mirror. The gesture work was carried out in the city at large, visiting cafes and construction sites and bus and train stations. Though he did not fully realize it yet himself, Kurelek's formal education was now completed. From here on in he would learn how to paint by painting and by visiting art galleries and studying firsthand what other artists had done.

Just before Kurelek sailed to Europe that spring, he finally received a response from Metro to his own great intemperate tome of a letter from Mexico. We don't have William's original letter to Metro to help us adjudicate this dispute which would probably be a fool's errand anyway. What is blazingly clear from Metro's response (translated from Ukrainian into English by William and thereby applying one more layer of obfuscating filter onto our understanding) is the depth to which Metro had been wounded by his son's words:

"I see that I have been mistaken according to your way of thinking," Metro wrote, finally signalling that he was ready to go digging through the smoking debris of their relationship and suggesting that William come back to Vinemount for one last visit before setting sail. "I must admit to you that I finished reading that letter of yours from Mexico just two weeks ago. I intended several times to read it but I could not swallow more than two or three pages because something choked me in the throat and my eyes became wet and I could not see further. But I have finished it now. And since you write that I did not educate you for your good but so that I could have the glory and that I tortured you so you'd become a doctor and not some kind of artist, then certainly you won't want me to extol myself with your paintings. I do admit I wanted you to be a doctor or anything else as long as you'd not end up cleaning stables."[59]

If Metro wasn't willing to talk about it before, William wasn't willing to talk about it now. He might be able to tough his way through entire seasons in the bush but he knew he wasn't strong enough to withstand another annihilating bout of Metro's recriminations and self-justification. It was time to put an ocean between himself and the land of his birth and formation. And once he was immersed in that other and much older culture, he would undertake a Nicolaides-type experiment on his own very being, first taking himself apart and then rebuilding himself on sounder principles and according to a better plan. He knew that his vocation was to be an artist and that his problems with chronic depression and inexplicable eye pains were holding him back from fully realizing that call. He was now determined to deal once and for all with these obstacles.

4

THE BREAKDOWN

KURELEK HAD READ about the Maudsley Hospital in central London (and its sister psychiatric facility southeast of the city, Netherne Hospital), and noted that these were training hospitals where much attention was paid to the psychotherapeutic potential of encouraging patients to paint. Kurelek had written to Maudsley from Montreal a few months earlier, asking if he could receive treatment there and Dr. D.L. Davies, a senior physician, told Patricia Morley, "I told him no, he wasn't eligible unless he became ill while in Britain." [60]

Well, as of June 1st, 1952 Kurelek was in Britain and on the 4th he made his way to Maudsley Hospital in central London, told them he was ill and asked for help. He was given an out patient's appointment for two weeks hence and was found to be "severely ill" and five days after that he was admitted to the hospital (on Dr. Davies' ward) for one month's worth of observation and treatment on June 23rd. It was all so simple and straightforward and gracious. And compared to his botched Mexican trek where he made his way down there only to find his school had vanished, this time his equally reckless scheme had come off like clockwork. To the end of his days, Kurelek maintained warm feelings for the British for so readily taking him in.

Very early on in this first stay, reassured that his eye strain wasn't some harbinger of a developing blindness but was likely brought on by groundless worrying, Kurelek was quickly able to put it out of mind so that it almost magically went away. Unfortunately, his difficulties with depression and lethargy and depersonalization could not be so readily uprooted but, initially at least, he was content that these too would soon prove treatable.

Though his incarceration and treatment at a psychiatric hospital wasn't something he'd be likely to mention to just anybody, Kurelek was blessedly free of any sort of shame or stigma regarding his need for such services. He included accounts of his treatment in both versions of his autobiography and opened the second version – the one prepared for wide public consumption – with a forthright discussion of his time at the English hospitals. "I had freely chosen to admit myself as an inmate. I am obliged to point this out because even in our enlightened age there is a tendency to think that anyone who has been in a psychiatric hospital must be 'mental.' Depressed, unhappy, emotionally disturbed, yes; mental, no."

His reason for coming clean on this delicate matter is explained in the opening page of chapter one: "Knowing what people would think, I kept my hospitalization a secret for many years upon my return to Canada. It was only later, when I realized that I could help a lot of unhappy people, that I decided I would tell my story as it really was."[61]

Kurelek was released from his first hospital stay in August with an understanding that he would continue to paint (as this was so obviously his best avenue of recovery) and meet once a week with Dr. Bruno Cormier, a Quebecer on staff at Maudsley. Kurelek rented a flat near Maudsley and landed a job as a labourer with the London Transport Board, (LTC), sticking it out for two months even though he was squeamishly appalled by the vulgarity and laziness of his fellow members on the road crew whose job it was to lift the rails off central London streets and repair the roadbed below. Just before commencing that job Kurelek crossed the channel and mooched his way through the great galleries and museums of Europe for a few weeks, encountering Van Eycks and Vermeers in Paris and Flanders, Boschs and Rembrandts in Belgium and Holland and spending three full days feasting his eyes on the collection of Bruegels at Vienna.

Coming face to face with such masterpieces both inspired Kurelek and depressed him. Back in England he confessed to Dr. Cormier that his European trek had been a big mistake, that he had learned nothing from his art gallery tour except how inadequate his own skills were. Patricia Morley, I think, rightly suggests that this "conviction [only] reflected his depressed state at that time." [62] Certainly, going by the evidence of *Tramlines*, the large, sweeping painting he produced at this time of transport workers engaged in his job of lifting old rails out of the road in Brixton, Kurelek was wielding some decidedly Bruegel-esque skills in a bold new way in his creation of this crowded street scene. *Tramlines* was the first painting Kurelek ever sold – to the LTC for 32 pounds – determining its price by tabulating the hours he put into its creation at the same rate of pay he'd been earning as their labourer. While not quite so stylized as *Zaporozhian Cossacks* (the painting he'd given to Metro before leaving Canada) and even carrying suggestive influences of Diego Rivera, *Tramlines* similarly succeeds in its energetic depiction of an exclusively male world and also conveys the respect he always extended to work, no matter how menial.

And hitting a different note altogether were the small 'trompe-l'oeil' paintings depicting banknotes, coins, stamps, a key on a string, a burnt matchstick, a newspaper clipping, which he quickly whipped off to bring in rent money. These uncannily real-life minimalist still-lifes suggest, had he so chosen, that Kurelek could have earned high distinction as a photo-realist painter. But accomplished as these very different works were, Kurelek still felt stalled and inadequate.

Ticked off at what he perceived as the niggling ineffectiveness of his once-a-week counselling sessions, Kurelek penned the following screed to Dr. Cormier "in bold hand on a very large sheet of paper," he notes. (The sight of such an emphatic script must have elicited a sigh from the overworked doctor who doubtless had dozens of needy patients to tend to.) At great length Kurelek outlined a common complaint of those undergoing the perfunctory ministrations of a professional therapist when their heart's deepest desire is to be radically – and if possible, immediately – transformed.

"You and Dr. Charatan have accused me of irrationally asking for a snap cure. That's not true. But I want right now to begin the cure. I want something to work on day by day so that I can see I'm making progress; I want you to tell me what to do. It must be a deep emotional experience or a series of experiences compared to which these talks are trivial. It's not enough just to know what my problem is – SOMETHING HAS TO BE DONE. The interviews are too few, too short. You say you have too many patients and can't spare more time than three-quarters of an hour a week, so I'm selfish to expect more. You're right but I'm no less frustrated for knowing that. Either give me a stimulant – drugs, hypnotism, or whatever you have – or else interviews that are three to five hours long. You are too vague in your guidance – in fact you don't guide at all. Any solid advice, if there is any, is buried under words. Tell me what to do during the week; give me some hard work to do. Then I'd have a distinct challenge and be compelled to face it. If you were to tell me to stand on my head or burn a hundred dollar bill, or any crazy thing towards a cure, I'd do it. Perhaps you as a psychiatrist are not allowed by the rules to actually get personally involved in a patient's problem. But I do expect you to be idealistically attached to a high standard of work and dedicated to serving mankind. If you were, you'd grasp eagerly at every scrap of information you could get about me so that these interviews wouldn't be wasted on mere 'getting acquainted' sessions. You're not even coming half way to meet me. You're not even reading my autobiography I gave you."[63]

The letter didn't effect any noticeable changes in the frequency, duration or nature of Dr. Cormier's attentions. There was no magic elixir to be imbibed that would suddenly make Kurelek's brain start functioning in new and healthy ways. Nor could the doctor take out his eraser and rub his way through his appointment calendar so as to clear the deck for five-hour sessions of heart-to-heart talks with nobody but Kurelek. Such lavishings of attention just aren't possible in the therapeutic world.

But Kurelek hadn't slaved in a lumber camp to raise his passage and then hauled his estranged and suffering carcass across the Atlantic Ocean just so he could partake in a measured way of a few helpful tips for thinking happier thoughts. He couldn't go on this way any longer. And he wouldn't. Life as he'd known it for the first quarter century (for what would turn out to be half of his allotted time in total) was, quite simply, no way to live. If this was as good as human existence could get, then, as he titled one of his bitterest paintings created in this darkest of times, "I Spit on Life." He was desperate for nothing less than total reorientation of mind and soul and he would risk anything to win that. With alarming coolness he decided to sharply up the ante in this un-engaging game with medical professionals who were not being sufficiently forthcoming.

"Dr. Cormier refused to budge out of his professional serenity and aloofness. If he wasn't going to, then I'd have to 'do something,' to break the stalemate. Just as the protest marchers of today despair of attracting attention by peaceful means, and sometimes set themselves alight with gasoline or do physical damage to property, I decided violence against myself was the only recourse I now had. Planning it all carefully beforehand, the day before an interview I exposed my arm and made a series of cuts from the wrist up, with a razor blade . . . I now had something concrete to show Dr. Cormier and I did. He blanched but didn't otherwise panic, inquiring instead into the circumstances. A day or so later I was invited by the hospital to re-enter as an in-patient. Dr. Cormier had had enough. Dr. Carstairs took over."[64]

Kurelek was readmitted to Maudsley in April of 1953. Unquestionably Dr. Carstairs was a better fit. "I took an immediate liking to him. Somehow I had the feeling that there was more than the average doctor's wisdom and understanding in him . . . I was given a private room, which also doubled as a studio, and there he would come and give me something more like psychoanalysis. I'd lay on my bed, with him sitting behind my head out of sight."[65]

Kurelek admits that during his stays at both Maudsley and Netherne Hospitals he enjoyed the best set-ups he'd ever known for producing art. Free of all financial worries such as rent and food he was able to put in ten and twelve hour days painting and other patients and doctors (some of whom knew a thing or two about art) would regularly drop by to admire his progress and give him the sort of feedback he always hungered for. Some doctors even took his work to show to other prominent artists for evaluation. An overture was made to Stanley Spencer, an artist Kurelek much admired, and while Spencer initially agreed to meet with Kurelek, nothing came of it, perhaps because of Spencer's failing health.[66] Mindful of that disappointment as well as his failure to connect with the big name muralists he'd travelled to Mexico to study with, throughout his career Kurlek always made time for students and developing artists who requested meetings and consultations.

In truth there are only three great validating forces in this world that can heal our deepest wounds and radically reorient a lost and struggling soul such as

Kurelek was at this time. And all three of these forces are forms of love. They are a loving relationship with another person, a loving relationship with God and a love for one's work. With his pronounced work ethic already in place, his innate talent and a yearning hunger for a sense of vocation or calling, Kurelek was already magnificently equipped for this third form of love. And by giving him his own space within Maudsley Hospital in which to live and hone his skills as a painter, Dr. Carstairs was validating the artistic path to wholeness and inviting Kurelek to make art "for specifically psychological purposes".

This he proceeded to do with typically Kurelekian forthrightness by painting *The Maze* which he called a "deliberate self-analytical painting using visual symbols . . . depicting all my psychic problems tied together in a neat package." One can imagine a more sophisticated artist shuddering at the very idea of working in so deliberate, so automatic or calculating a way but thankfully that sort of precious standoffishness which, out of vanity or some kind of self-regard, might insist on a more obscure or mysterious approach, was never an impediment for Kurelek.

He liked nothing better than a viewer who would look at his work and if anything puzzled him, would come right out and ask, "What does this mean? What is this supposed to be? Can you explain this bit?" Kurelek wanted to be understood as completely as possible and would routinely post little and some not-so-little essays beside the paintings or in his exhibition catalogues explaining in the most perfunctory way exactly what was going on in each of the art works.

The first two forms of love suddenly came to him in the form of Margaret Smith, the occupational therapist at Maudsley who not only provided Kurelek with paints and canvases and supplies but would visit with him for an hour or two at the end of each day and get him to talk about whatever was on his mind. Her approach was so gentle and natural and generous that her visits quickly became the highlight of each day. He responded to her with total confidence and trust, which surprised him. After all, she worked for the hospital and whereas he'd "felt nothing but a cold clinical gap" between himself and the doctors as they asked their probing questions, he opened up to this woman in a way he never could with them. Early on in their meetings he was discussing something he found quite painful and suddenly burst into tears. "I distinctly remember being amazed even as it happened, for I'd never had such an experience before. I can't remember now whether she actually put her hand on my shoulder or whether it was just the expression of sympathy on her face, but I experienced a deep sense of relief."[67]

Following a discussion in which they discovered a shared enthusiasm for poetry, Smith loaned Kurelek an anthology of poetry to read and to protect the book jacket, she wrapped the volume in a sheet of newspaper – a Catholic newspaper, Kurelek couldn't help noticing. Still a staunch atheist at this time, Kurelek incredulously asked if she was Catholic and Smith, without defensiveness of any kind, replied that she was. If he hadn't liked and admired her so much, Kurelek might have gone on the attack as he recently had with a fellow patient who was Jewish. Instead he was intrigued. Could the serenity and strength and decency of this woman have something to do with the faith she so quietly and confidently professed?

Smith never lectured or proselytized which only made Kurelek more curious: "I began to ask a question here, a question there, gingerly working around the edges of a subject which I still had no use for. Sometimes she couldn't answer these questions to her satisfaction so she'd bring along a pamphlet or a booklet. Dipping into these I found out about the Catholic practice of praying for others. Finally I asked her if by any chance she were praying for me. Once again came the simple answer – nothing more, nothing less: 'Yes, I am'."[68]

Late in 1953 Kurelek was moved over to Netherne Hospital on the Brighton Road just south of London where he was put under the care of Dr. Sybil Yates; a woman he deemed well-intentioned but ineffective. Netherne was a long term care facility which allayed (or at least delayed) his concerns about how he would support himself but Kurelek dreaded the move. Mostly this was because his meetings with Margaret Smith became much less frequent; she could only make the trek down to Netherne on her own time about once every two weeks. Shortly after this move he inexplicably snapped awake one night shortly after midnight, sat up in his bed and surveyed the world around him:

"The moon was shining brightly on the cabbage field outside our villa and on the pine woods beyond. The other patients in the dormitory were all asleep, making no more noise than my workmates in the bush camp used to after a hard day's work. It was a peaceful scene and yet I became aware of a sense of complete and utter abandonment, the like of which I had experienced only a few times back in childhood. Oddly, the presence of the other sleeping patients didn't seem to comfort me in the least. I was a consciousness lost in the universe. I wanted to wake one of the patients or call the night nurse and say, 'Could you help me please – I feel abandoned.' But that would have made me seem childish and I decided not to. I don't know how long I sat, completely at a loss as to what to do, when it occurred to me to try what Margaret might suggest. For the first time since I was a boy of eleven in Manitoba, I tried praying from the heart to God. But even as I made the attempt I realized I didn't know how or what to say. I decided to ask the Catholic chaplain at the hospital about prayer. Somehow this decision alone did the trick, for it gave me enough peace to lose myself in sleep for the rest of the night."[69]

Kurelek painted this scene which marked the beginning of his final turn toward Christ in mixed media on masonite in 1970. It is one of the largest single panel works he ever created (122 X 122 centimetres) and one of his most haunting. He took its title, *All Things Betray Thee Who Betrayest Me,* from the English Catholic poet, Francis Thompson's most famous poem, *The Hound of Heaven*; a poem which serves as an answer to the Blessed John Henry Newman's questions regarding the divine derivation of conscience in *A Grammar of Assent*: "'The wicked flees, when no one pursueth,' then, why does he flee? Whence his terror? Who is it that sees in solitude, in darkness, in the hidden chambers of his heart?" Though he substitutes a feline for a canine, C.S. Lewis alluded to the same sort of celestial pursuit when he scoffed at pompous seekers talking about their 'search' for some maddeningly elusive God: "As well speak about the mouse's search for the cat!"

All of the paintings in Kurelek's 1970 exhibition – and the name of the exhibition itself: *Nature, Poor Stepdame* – took their titles from phrases to be found in Thompson's 1890 ode on religious conversion including *Thunder Driven, The Young Skyey Blossoms, I Triumphed and I Saddened with All Weather,* and *Glimmering Tapers 'Round the Day's Dead Sanctities.*

In *All Things Betray Thee Who Betrayest Me*, a young man sits up on a metal-framed hospital bed hugging himself in dreadful fear. To his right an enormous picture window (nightmarishly larger than anything you'd find in a hospital; it extends so far that it tapers in the distance) frames a coldly luminous scene of a full moon casting its muted blue light over a field of bulbous cabbages arrayed in perfect rows. There is a fringe of dark forest at the very back of the landscape and just beyond the cabbage field, far enough away that we can scarcely make him out, a dog sits and waits – the relentless Hound of Heaven.

Kurelek's meeting with the Catholic chaplain took place two days later by which time he was almost embarrassed by the urgency he'd felt on that desolate night. For his part – perhaps picking up on Kurelek's coolness – the chaplain wasn't particularly helpful either. Kurelek felt any interest the chaplain might have had in him fell away when he said that he wasn't Catholic but just had a few general questions about prayer. The chaplain offered a few platitudes, a couple of suggestions . . . none of it penetrated Kurelek's shell of depersonalization.

It might appear that he had reverted to his atheistic state, rejecting all notions of seeking help from God but this wouldn't quite be an accurate assessment. A lot of his reading at this time was Christian literature. More and more religious concepts and references were appearing in his artwork. He was mindful of it, attracted to it, intrigued by it intellectually, but emotionally – at the level of trust and conviction – he simply couldn't bring himself to pray.

Feeling abandoned at Netherne, over the course of the next few months Kurelek descended to new depths of despair and hopelessness. The Freudian-style 'regression therapy' he was desultorily going through with Dr. Yates wasn't helping at all. In a letter to Dr. Carstairs at Maudsley that Patricia Morley quotes, he mockingly wrote about how his newest doctor was getting him to construct small dolls that were supposed to represent his infant self:

"I am seeing Dr. Yates only an hour a week now having what I think is psychotherapy – the two of us sit in chairs by her fireplace and chat 'seriously'. She has traced my main trouble right back to early babyhood from some free style drawings I did for her (so she says) and today I made a little baby about four inches long out of plasticene which I am to carry in my pocket and 'nurse'. Till I see her with it on Wednesday I've made it safe by putting it in a wrapping within a wrapping within a wrapping within a wrapping within a big egg within a steel drum within a box."[70]

"The latter sentence is perhaps the strangest Bill ever wrote," Morley uncomprehendingly comments in her biography. I beg to differ. I think it's one of the truest, funniest and darkest. It is the perfect narrative complement to the confessional paintings he was working on at this time, such as *Pre-Maze* [Plate 2] and *Where Am I? Who Am I? Why Am I?*, in which isolated straw puppet men with gloves on their hands and buttons for eyes pointlessly grope about in sterile and desolate landscapes where they can't make contact with anything or anybody.

This was a period of intense searching and analyzing when Kurelek wasn't rattling off as many as three canvases a day as he sometimes did in the early '70s when demand for his work was at its peak. In these sometimes brutally personal paintings, he wasn't preoccupied with cultivating or keeping an audience; he was painting in as direct and compelling a way as he could in a desperate fight to salvage his sanity and his soul. There was no moderating filter in place and nobody's feelings were spared in these confessional and nightmarish paintings. In such large scale canvases as *The Tower of Babel* (1954), *I Spit on Life* (1953-54) and *Behold Man Without God* (1955), Kurelek presents complex panoramas of troubling vignettes (many drawn from his own life and depicting the brutality of his father, other children and various human institutions) that are arranged in either the free-flowing manner of a movie poster with one scene spilling into another, or are each contained in separate compartments in the manner of a Thomas Hart Benton mural.

While the Bruegel-esque nature of the human figures in so many of Kurelek's farm scenes has been widely noted, with these grim and sprawling canvases that picture scenes of degradation, humiliation and torture, the more apt comparison is with the apocalyptic paintings of Hieronymus Bosch. And just as Bosch's *Garden of Earthly Delights* turned up on album covers by such doomy and pretentious rock bands as Pearls Before Swine and Deep Purple, so a few images from Kurelek's *The Maze* (1953) were featured on Van Halen's *Fair Warning* (1981); the album where that band sought to shake off their reputation as house party rockers so as to don more substantial airs.

There's an incredible amount of dark and depressing information to be absorbed in those paintings whereas in three other of these self-referential paintings from the same period – *Pre-Maze* (1953), *Where Am I? Who Am I? Why Am I?* (1953-54) and *Lord That I May See* (1955) – Kurelek strips back the operatic profusion of those panoramic canvases to present just one stark and grimly fanciful image of a groping, stumbling man, always eyeless, struggling to discern his place in a bewildering world. Yet there is a chronological progress charted in these three paintings, reflective of his own journey from the bewildering and dispiriting depths of atheism and depression to Christian belief and the affixing of a workable handle to his world.

In *Pre-Maze* the figure depicted wears a bag over his head, buttons for eyes, tape slapped over his mouth, thick gloves on his hands as he hopelessly plods his way around the perimeter of a barren silo, decorated only with one utilitarian chair and a large institutional clock such as you'd find in a classroom or a hospital ward. The floor is marked with hundreds of footprints, telling us that he has fruitlessly been working this circuit for a long time and getting no further ahead. This was an image Kurelek devised to express what he called his "depersonalization" – his utter disengagement with human life, his mere existence as "a sawdust-filled puppet". In his autobiography Kurelek explains that he cultivated "depersonalization" as "a concentration camp type of 'out'." In that state, "a person need not feel hurt, or nearly as hurt, because he is not a person."[71] In the second painting the figure is out of doors. He still has no eyes but at least he can feel the wind on his face and his bare hands, held out in front, are free to explore and apprehend. It is a night time scene, the sky almost as brown as the earth on which he walks, with one single dead tree dimly silhouetted on the horizon.

The third painting, larger than the other two, is drenched in glorious daylight and bright colour. The still eyeless figure is this time depicted on his knees, perhaps as the result of a stumble but more likely (considering the title) in an attitude of prayer. He is facing the viewer and behind him a stony path ascends a hill with a green and leafy tree (perhaps a representation of the cross as the tree of life) at its apex, a large bird wheeling in the sky overhead and two other human figures in silhouette racing upward to the tree. Our blind man may be facing the wrong way but the rocky path on which he kneels is the right one. He has asked the Lord for sight and it does not seem that this request will be unfulfilled for much longer.

The comparative serenity and hope depicted in that third painting from 1955 were still out of reach in the early afternoon of August 11, 1954. Again he lacerated his arms with a razor blade but this time he also hacked up his face and then swallowed eight days' worth of sleeping pills which he had deliberately stashed away for the purpose of killing himself. Thoroughly bloodied and groggy, he hid himself in a linen cupboard where he wasn't discovered until the supper hour and was rushed by ambulance to the main hospital building where his stomach was pumped and bandages were applied to his self-inflicted wounds.

The very next day he was offered Electro-Convulsive Therapy (ECT), popularly (or unpopularly) known as shock treatment, and readily, indeed joyfully, consented. How many times had Kurelek complained to his doctors that they weren't doing anything for him? He was fed up with talking and nursing plasticene dolls. He wanted something real and dramatic and ECT promised to be that. He'd seen the radical change of demeanour – from listlessness to a sort of "dazed buoyancy" – that transpired in other patients who'd undergone shock therapy and wanted some of that for himself.

Kurelek didn't expect the treatments to be pleasant and they weren't. His first treatment was so violent that he sprained his back and as Kurelek came to in the incurable ward where he'd been sent to recover, he noticed an immediate change in himself because of the way he was regarding others – his crippled and senile ward mates: "This was my first acquaintance with incurables – the lowest of the low in illness. My being there seemed to be fated, as if I personally had to realize at last the essential weakness and fragility of mankind. Here were men who to outward appearance seemed nothing more than suffering vegetables, and for the first time in my life I was touched with pity, real pity for someone else besides myself."[72]

Something was finally breaking through the shell of his depersonalization – something divine – and it was shock therapy that had made the opening. Kurelek was given fourteen convulsion treatments in all, and the process didn't get any easier as it went along. He wrote that it was like being executed fourteen times over. "There is an instinctive dread in a person of being annihilated. And so instead of one getting more and more 'used' to it, it is dreaded all the more each time. I noticed that some of the patients lined up opposite me were moving their lips almost imperceptibly. They were praying. It is said that sorrow remarries us to God and how true that is. Here was an experience horrendous enough to knock the self-sufficiency out of any man. One prays best when one is really and helplessly up against it. That is when I, too, resumed prayer. I've been praying ever since."[73]

There is a fascinating note, perhaps deliberately autobiographical or unconsciously so, that is struck in the 105th panel of Kurelek's *Passion* series, entitled, *And so they reached a place called Golgotha, that is, the place named after a skull*. [Plate 3] The scene laid out below us in a broad vista depicts the final approach of Christ and the two condemned thieves to the crucifixion site. In a procession led and followed by red-robed centurions, the thieves carry crossbars which will be attached to two poles already planted in the ground. Simon the Cyrene, walking just behind Christ, hauls the Lord's entire cross which will be set in the hole between those two poles.

Golgotha is a rounded outcropping of rock, so named because of its re-semblance to the bald crown of a human skull. But Kurelek's Golgotha, while somewhat elevated from the rest of the landscape, most resembles a skull not in its likeness to a rounded dome of bone but in the outline of the crucifixion site itself which is delineated by a low encircling wall of piled stones. As I say, intentionally or not, this outline of piled rock very closely resembles the boney outline of the cloven skull in Kurelek's *The Maze*. Considering that he likened each dose of shock treatment to an execution, I don't think it is being too fanci-ful to suggest that Kurelek is telling us here that his own Golgotha, the place of his greatest suffering which he freely accepted fourteen times over, was within the outline of his skull and that it was the agony he underwent there that turned him to Christ and brought him to salvation.

Shortly after Christmas of 1954, with Margaret Smith's encouragement and promise of ongoing moral support, Kurelek left Netherne Hospital and set up on his own in a small rented room. He would not set foot in any kind of hospital again until his death from cancer more than 23 years later. Through a connection from Netherne, Kurelek found work with London's most distin-guished framing shop, F.A. Pollak Limited, situated at 20 Blue Ball Yard near St. James's Palace. This firm also restored antique frames and furniture and many of the skills he developed there – gilding, spattering, smudging, sealing, "gessoing the ground" were applicable to his work as a painter as well.

"Another task I was given, especially when business was slow, was frame stripping. I was given half a dozen assorted dentist's tools and told to strip a gold frame which might be several hundred years old, inch by inch, right down to the original coat of gold. It might take weeks to do just one frame and if only two inches were done in a day that was good progress."[74]

On the side Kurelek also produced the small still lifes, the trompe-l'oeils, which readily fetched him an additional four pounds a week from local galleries which would then turn around and sell them for three to four times as much money. He knew he was being ripped off but didn't mind. The paintings he produced and his work at Pollak's weren't garnering him a name or a reputa-tion but he was developing his skills and could taste his progress. For now he was content to work quietly and obscurely. This almost hidden atmosphere was well-suited to this fragile period of transition as he carefully, thoughtfully and prayerfully reassembled his life.

He marked the first anniversary of his release from hospital by travelling to the Marian shrine at Lourdes where he prayed for the gift of complete faith. His religious attitude at this time was an entirely new experience for one who was ordinarily so anxious to see a thing resolved one way or the other right now. Though not yet a Catholic, he was serenely confident that before too much longer he would be. He was acting in good faith regarding the faith, regularly attending Mass even though he could not receive the Eucharist, steadily reading and reasoning his way toward a certain goal and accumulating strength and resolve in the process itself. There could be no surer sign of his new sturdiness and resolve than his decision to return to Canada for the summer.

He set out with four definite goals in mind. He was ready to face his family again and devoutly wanted to improve his relationship with Metro in accordance with the Church's teaching on the fealty owed to one's parents. He wanted some time away from England to sort out what his true feelings were for Margaret Smith. He knew he loved her as a very dear friend but did that mean he also wanted to marry her and be her husband? The incredibly fine detailed work he'd been carrying out on trompe-l'oeils had brought on some ocular strain and he wanted to give his eyes a rest. And he planned to find work in Canada to raise another stake of money to fund a trip to conduct research in the Holy Land which would help him flesh out the series of paintings he was starting to plan out, illustrating St. Matthew's account of the Passion of Christ.

5

ARTIST ON A MISSION

BACK AT THE FAMILY farm in Vinemount there were tensions and some off-limits subjects that couldn't be gone into with his parents but overall the situation there was enormously improved from its raw and ragged state five years earlier. The first sign that a new era had dawned took place as Kurelek stepped out onto the platform at the Hamilton railway station and Metro rushed forward to greet him with a teary hug and a kiss – his "first ever" Kurelek noted. While these two would never share a loving and fully supportive father/son relationship, the years of sniping and dumping on one another were thankfully over. Both of his parents had been profoundly shaken to learn of his near-suicide in 1954 and that disaster, so narrowly averted, obviously influenced their more ginger approach with him now. This was particularly evident regarding Kurelek's intense interest in Catholicism.

"It was obviously not liked. John said so openly. Mother and father were more guarded. To use their words, "It's something to hold onto, even if not true." I myself avoided preaching even when I defended the faith. It didn't seem right to urge others to accept something I wasn't one hundred per cent convinced of myself. The only really sticky occasions that developed were when I'd refuse to eat meat on Friday or attended Mass. That last really looked crazy to my parents because when the car wasn't available, I'd walk or cycle to church. It was only about three miles distant but there was a mountain in between. Going down to church was easy but the return climb really worked up a sweat."[75]

Kurelek was struck by how much Metro had aged and by how little work he had to do on the Vinemount farm. He conceived the idea of soon returning to Canada for good, settling in Toronto, and starting up some sort of framing business where he could employ Metro to make the frames which he would design and finish. He knew it would be unwise to try living with Metro or even work alongside him but he wanted to do something to help his father out financially and give his days a little more purpose. Though this plan never worked out (among other reasons, Kurelek didn't have sufficient capital to start up a small business) it shows how fundamentally his attitude toward his father had changed and how determined he was to make what amends he could and do right by his father.

Kurelek worked that summer for Grimsby Brick and Tile, first loading hot tiles onto a truck and when that made his back pains from his shock therapy sessions flare up again, he quickly earned his chauffeur's licence and drove the company truck instead. At the end of the season, Kurelek had $600 saved up on top of his boat fare and returned to England and his work at Pollak's. "Tentatively," he says, he proposed marriage (or the idea of marriage) to Margaret Smith and was forthrightly turned down. One can imagine a time when being spurned in this way would've quickly and utterly crushed him but his grip on life was much steadier now and he accepted the rejection remarkably well and even with a measure of relief.

"She gave me a firm 'No' and went on to explain I no longer needed her as a crutch. In the days that followed I slowly came to some realizations about her and me. One of them was that I had been afraid all along that I was seeking the faith only to please her. Her rejection of my proposal revealed my fear to be unfounded. I had really been after the faith for myself."[76]

His first order of business now was to enter the Catholic Church. Margaret Smith happily agreed to stand as one of his sponsors and Kurelek immediately started taking instruction and counselling from two English priests, Father Thomas Lynch and Father Edward Holloway. On February 11th, 1957 he was formally accepted into the Church – a date he was delighted to discover happened to be the feast day of Our Lady of Lourdes. His prayer at Lourdes the year before for the gift of complete faith had indeed been answered.

Kurelek now immersed himself in Catholic social circles and clubs as well as the Guild of Catholic Artists and Craftsmen. With the faith as their common drawing card, he found that all the usual stresses that attended his social interactions in the past were no longer in play. He enjoyed an ease of repartee and a sense of communion and trust with other people such as he had never known before.

Kurelek made his long-anticipated trip to the Holy Land in the spring of 1959, studying the geography and terrain, the architecture and layout of the streets, and returned with all his notes and drawings and photographs to England for seven final weeks to wrap up his affairs before returning to Canada for good that summer. During that final interim, *The Sunday Observer* newspaper ran an un-credited reproduction of Kurelek's *The Maze* as the visual complement to a feature article entitled, *Labyrinth of the Sick Mind*. Reproducing artists' work without payment or credit was not an issue at that time. Kurelek dispatched a letter to the editor, not to complain about any such oversights but to assure readers, "that there was a happy ending to the story. Although I left hospital after various treatments not fully well, I had while there made an English friend who through good example introduced me to the Roman Catholic

Church. Later, after much study, I received the Faith and it has helped me to bear with the remainder of my trouble and to begin a normal life."

And then, ever the grateful guest, Kurelek signed off with this: "I am returning to Canada next month, so I would like also to take this opportunity to say 'thank you' for all the social security, kindness and respect which I came needing and have been treated to during my six years stay in this country."[77] Back in Canada for keeps, Kurelek took a room in Toronto near the Ontario College of Education where he hoped to earn his teacher's certificate to raise the capital for his framing business. He was accepted there for a grand total of four days and then, perhaps having learned about his recent hospitalization, the authorities turfed him out of the program, explaining that he was "obviously the sensitive type of person who couldn't take the nervous strain of controlling a class. High school children are cruel. They'll take advantage of you and kill you."[78]

Unquestionably the rejection was a blow but Kurelek now had two allies in his corner, backing him up and offering support. One of course, was the Church, his faith. The other, amazingly enough, was his family. The cash-strapped Metro had even offered to co-sign for a loan to see him through teacher's college. "I was now left to help myself, of course, but it was a weight off my mind to know that those close to me were behind me instead of against me."[79]

Kurelek immediately set to work on his deliberately filmic *Passion of Christ* series, completing the 160 paintings over the next several years which would eventually be bought en masse by Olha and Mykola Kolankiwsky and permanently installed in the Niagara Falls Art Gallery they specifically built to house this series. What makes this series 'filmic' is not the sort of high realism that he executed in his trompe l'oeils. On the contrary, here the style is almost cartoony and becomes looser as the series goes along and he had less time to devote to it. The individual paintings (each with a beautifully lettered caption underneath taken from St. Matthew's account of Christ's Passion) are set in sequence like the panels on a filmmaker's storyboard, cutting at will from an establishing shot, to a group shot, zooming in on this figure or that, switching around the point of view during scenes of confrontation or conflict, featuring certain angles of perspective or pumping up the light or the shadows to heighten atmosphere and mood.

As he had during his last couple of years in England, Kurelek immersed himself in the life of the local Church and became deeply involved in the social and cultural events operating out of the Catholic Information Centre at the corner of Bloor and Bathurst. It was at this group's annual picnic the next summer that he would meet Jean Andrews, the woman he would marry just a few months later in the fall of 1960.

Though Jean and their four children turn up from time to time in Kurelek's paintings, and though he wrote a couple of paragraphs about each of them in the later edition of his autobiography, any student of Kurelek can't help but be struck by the enormous disparity, in both extent and candour, regarding his treatment in paint and words of his family of origin and the family he and Jean created. All indications are that it was an old world marriage with an old world understanding of the division of labour and the roles appropriate to husband and wife. Kurelek always said he was happiest when creating art and if artistic productivity is the yardstick, then the boggling quantity of work he produced in the final 17 years of his life as a husband and father – with at least one exhibition every year and ten very popular picture books being produced – would seem to indicate supreme contentment on the domestic front.

I asked Michael O'Brien if he thought Kurelek was a happy man in his final twenty or so years and he took a longer than usual pause to formulate his thoughts.

"Good question," he said at last. "I think he had a lot of interior suffering right to the end but I think he had moments of joy and he had a profound spiritual peace. I mean, what is happiness? Concepts of that kind are pretty subjective. I would say yes, he was ultimately happy in Christ but he was not a jolly kind of fellow you might find sharing jokes around a barbecue in the backyard. His identity really was very much integrated with his sense of mission as an artist and an evangelist. That's where he found himself and was most completely himself. And I think happiness comes from being who we truly are in Christ. That doesn't mean we're not going to suffer interiorly."

The year he got married is also the year when Kurelek's career as an artist started to take off. That March he'd held his first solo exhibition in Toronto and simultaneously made perhaps the most important and one of the most unlikely friendships of his life with an art dealer most famous for showcasing avant garde and abstract artists. Seeking work as a framer to fund his great project of the Passion paintings, Kurelek approached Toronto art dealer Avrom Isaacs in the fall of 1959. Isaac's four year old Greenwich Art Gallery would change its name to The Isaacs Gallery just a couple of months before Kurelek's first of many shows there.

For most of his career, first in England and now in Toronto, Kurelek supplemented his earnings as an artist by his exquisite work as a framer and gilder, winning such distinction in this field that he and one of his colleagues at the Isaacs Gallery were invited to take part in creating the frame for Rex Wood's recreation of Robert Harris' *Fathers of Confederation* – the original of which was destroyed in the 1916 fire at the old Parliament Building. Conceived as a centennial project by the aptly named insurance firm, Confederation Life, the newly framed recreation of Harris' most famous painting was unveiled in the House of Commons Centre Block in 1969.

Because of this training Kurelek was able to not only frame all of his own work himself but frequently used those frames in ingenious and sometimes outrageous ways as an extension, an amplification, a counterpoint, and even an integral element of his paintings. In a canvas as seemingly straightforward as 1974's *Cold Dawn in Saskatchewan*, a narrow horizon line of orange-fading-outward-to-yellow bleeds light into a deep blue sky atop an utterly flat and almost equally deep blue field of snow that is regularly dotted with cruciform telephone poles. And that deepest hue of orange at the very centre of the horizon is featured in an even narrower line in the grey barn board frame that sublimely encases the scene.

In a lot of his 'ethnic' paintings chronicling the experiences of immigrants leaving their lands of origin and settling in Canada, Kurelek would take some decorative motif from that culture and work it into the framing or matting. In 1968's *Cross-Section of Vinnitsia in the Ukraine*, 1939 (the top half depicting the scene of a concert in a park; the bottom half showing two pits stuffed with corpses six feet beneath that turf) the frame constitutes the outer rim of a prison window whose bars are laid over top of the painting. In his mind-blowing *Reminiscences of Youth* which also hails from 1968 the canvas acts as a memory window looking out onto a brilliant winter scene of children playing on a snow-covered haystack. And on the large surrounding frame, Kurelek depicts a darker scene, an interior, of a young man stretched out on his cot beneath the window in nostalgic reverie on a warm summer evening, a single light bulb burning in the socket overhead and some classical music playing on the record player at the head of his bed.

"I was the first one to give him a show," Av Isaacs told me with obvious pride. "He was pretty well penniless at the time so I gave him a job making frames in my picture framing shop as well. Almost from the very beginning his work was selling as fast as he was making it and sold very well. When he first approached me to apply for a framing job, he showed me some samples of his work. I took one look at them and I gave him a show.

"There was a striking uniqueness and a physical accomplishment to his work. Even though he'd gone to the Ontario College of Art and to university – in both cases for a short period of time – he really taught himself to paint and he painted beautifully. He was a perfectionist. He was so intent about getting things right. He had this imagery in his head so when it came time to put it on canvas, he already had the image he wanted. So he didn't hesitate long. Therefore he could do paintings in a very short period of time. He approached the canvas with a complete image of what he wanted to say and he said it quickly. He could take suggestions but I assure you most of the time, he was working out his own direction. So the idea was that I would give him a show pretty much from the beginning."

It might seem uncanny how quickly everything took off for Kurelek. But when you look at the incredible range of work he was able to draw on for that first show – he pulled in some trompe-l'oeils, both of his self portraits, the stunning *Farm Children's Games in Western Canada* (perhaps his finest tip of the hat to the genius of Breugel) and two of his most arresting didactic pieces, *The Modern Tower of Babel* and *Behold Man Without God* – you can start to imagine the jaw-dropping impact his sudden arrival on the Canadian art scene must have had. His first show drew the biggest crowds that The Isaacs Gallery had ever known.

Word of Kurelek's arrival spread fast across the country and the very next year, Alfred Barr, the director of collections at New York's Museum of Modern Art, brought him to international attention. Barr was invited by the Women's Committee of the Art Gallery of Ontario to choose any Canadian painting as their gift to the MOMA. Individual dealers had brought what they considered the likeliest candidates to win Barr's approval and whichever painting he chose (and everybody assumed it would be abstract) the AGO would immediately buy as their gift and hand over. Most of the dealers and artists were in attendance at the show except for Kurelek. He didn't even know Isaacs had entered his *Hailstorm in Alberta* in the competition. The assembled crowd watched Barr go back and forth over the contenders and keep returning to the Kurelek piece. Once he definitively made his decision, a call was put through to Kurelek to hurry on down to the AGO. He said he'd be right there; he'd get a streetcar and be there in no time. 'Get a taxi,' they demanded, and for perhaps the first time in his life, he went for the pricier option.

In the final pages of his autobiography, Kurelek revisits an artist's talk he once gave in which he comes close to laying out his artistic credo. It was Christian humility he contends that "gave forth the greatest flowering of art, that of the later Middle Ages. I feel it was superior even to the Renaissance. In both these periods the subject matter was religious. And yet the big difference is that in the former period Art was used to serve religion. In the second, the tables were turned, so to speak, and religion was used to serve Art. In other words, in the Renaissance, art had already turned somewhat hypocritical. It really glorified man himself and this is the trend that has continued to this day. One of the amazing things about the Middle Ages, for example, is that sculptors and painters were often anonymous. The perfect example of man giving glory to God really and truly can be seen in the sculptures that adorn the roofs of Gothic Cathedrals. No one can possibly see the loving details of it way up there. Today, however, artists sign their paintings big and bold as if to say, "I did it – – – all my own work – – – aren't I the greatest!"

A little further on, he writes, "There is another wholesome and humble aspect of the medieval artist, I gather. It's that he wasn't so awfully conscious of art or of being an artist. In fact he merely thought of himself as a craftsman – in the case of a painter, for example, as a *picture maker*. Another craftsman would be a stonemason or a goldsmith or a tapestry weaver. So what it really meant was that a customer, usually the Church but sometimes a wealthy townsman or noble, would ask for a *picture*. Usually it was of a particular subject, and the craftsman executed it for him to the best of his ability. It was just as simple as that. He had a shop like any other craftsman, employed assistants or apprentices or even his own family assisted him in the making of a picture. We hear of certain portions of certain masterpieces way back then being perhaps the work of such and such an apprentice. Later that apprentice became a master painter in his own right. Can one imagine that of today's artists? Sacrilege!"[80]

Taking this medieval example completely to heart in the first years following his conversion, Kurelek didn't sign his paintings at all unless specifically requested by a customer to do so, in which case he would hide his signature so completely within the body of the work that sometimes even the artist himself couldn't find it later. Characteristic of the man as this gesture was, and commendable as it might seem from a Christian perspective, artistic anonymity was an intolerable affront to smooth commercial operations in the world of modern art and when Av Isaacs had words with him about the impossibility of continuing in this way, Kurelek came up with a compromise, signing his works with a small monogram that featured a cross set above and between the initials 'WK'.

6

WHAT REMAINS

REPEATEDLY KURELEK maintained that as hard a slog as his formative years were, he was grateful that he hadn't won commercial success earlier in his life as its distractions might have thrown him off his true path. One wonders if critical approval might have posed the same threat to his integrity but perhaps luckily, he never had to contend with much of that at all.

My brother Ted is a stained glass artist and when he learned I was working on a study of William Kurelek, he sent along some of his thoughts about the artist and his standing in the arts community: "The world of art is, as you observe, fickle, but the dismissal of K.'s work as "folk art" is not the whole story, at least as I understand it. The height of his popularity was also the low point of his reputation in what I might call 'the Fine Art world' (there are worlds within worlds here). I was taking an evening drawing class at McGill in the early seventies and there was a quote posted over the door (I remember it as being ascribed to Piet Mondrian [1872-1940, Dutch non-representational painter who developed the art form called Neo-Plasticism], though I may be wrong) that read: "ART IS A WAY OF THINKING – NOT AN ILLUSTRATION OF THOUGHT". K's *A Prairie Boy's Winter* was in bookstores at that time, selling briskly, and I bought one for Terry.

"It was beneath regard as far as my art instructor was concerned, because Kurelek was an illustrator, not an artist. K.'s penchant for offering written commentary on his paintings, as he does in *Prairie Boy* and elsewhere, reinforced this perception. I do think that K usually had a clear thought in his head before he went to work, and in this regard he went a step beyond mere documentation or exploration, into the realms of commentary, often with unambiguous value judgements built in to the work itself. Along with the horizon line – one of the ways I identify a Kurelek painting at a glance has to do with his consistently surprising use of the horizon line – this is a characteristic of his work. The paintings were personal, partisan, and committed to his values.

"In terms of this fickle world we're talking about, I sense that Kurelek's stock is rising now; a shift has taken place since his death that allows him to be celebrated as a folk artist rather than an illustrator (some selection is necessary here – there are themes in his oeuvre that will only appeal to those who share those specific values and judgements). And of course, there is an intense interest in his life, the tragic misfit side of things, which conforms in broad outline to the template of Van Gogh – we can't get enough of the severed ear."

Ted is certainly right about Kurelek's rising stock. In the fall of 2012, right about the time he wrote me that letter, Heffel, the Canadian fine art auction house sold Kurelek's *King of the Mountain*, a large canvas depicting boys playing a game of dominance on a snow covered haystack, for more than $380,000. Once he got his life sorted out by about the age of thirty, commercial popularity was never the problem. Right from that very first show at the Isaacs Gallery in 1960, Kurelek's work flew off the walls as quickly as he could make it. It was serious commentary and feedback that he was starved for.

His shyness and his religious preoccupations cut him off from most of his colleagues in the art world. "I don't think he had much to do with other artists," Avrom Isaacs told me. "He just went along his own way. One thing that comes to mind is there was a show of Gordon Rayner's one night and Bill and his wife Jean showed up to my amazement because Bill never came to openings. So I said to Bill, 'Nice to see you. What are you doing here?' And he said, 'Well, my wife wanted to see what artists look like.' Other than his own openings, of course, that was about the only time he appeared."

Kurelek took a livelier interest in painters who shared his Christian convictions. He admired Jack Chambers' work and even did a canvas of his own, *Don Valley on a Grey Day* (1972) in homage to Chambers' *401 Towards London No. 1* (1968-69). Michael O'Brien made contact with Kurelek in his mid 20s when he was looking to commit his whole life to Christian art. "I was a successful artist but not painting overtly Christian work even though I was a strong believer. I was visiting Madonna House and telling them about my dream of being a full time Christian artist and they suggested that I write to William Kurelek in Toronto who was a friend of the community and had a farm up here.

"So I wrote to him and he wrote back a very warm letter and invited me to visit him in Toronto. This would have been the spring of 1977. I had a wonderful day with him there. He took me out to lunch and encouraged me not to give up, to keep going. And he said, 'I want to help you so let's keep in contact and tell me how you're doing in terms of the creative work and inspiration.'

"So in the summer I visited him and his family at their farm in Combermere and we made arrangements. I had my first full exhibit of my Christian work in Ottawa scheduled for that November. He was very happy about that. He was leaving for Ukraine – his father's old homeland. By the time he got back, the doctors told him he had cancer. I wrote to him a few weeks before my exhibit was to open and his wife wrote me back, and said, 'Bill is in hospital. He has only days to live. We're really sorry we can't come to your exhibit in Ottawa.' My exhibit opened the week he died. There was a review of my exhibit deep in *The Ottawa Citizen* and the announcement of his death was on the front page the same day. It was a real grief for me."

In his 2013 book, *William Kurelek: Painter & Prophet*, Michael O'Brien relates how in 1961 Father Émile-Marie Brière, a priest at Madonna House, was amazed on a visit to Toronto to come upon one of Kurelek's paintings of a "monstrance surrounded by multitudes of people worshipping Christ," on display in the front window of a secular art gallery – the Isaacs Gallery. He filed away the artist's name and recognized it a couple of winters later when Kurelek paid his first visit to the community of Catholic lay people and priests in the Madawaska Valley which had been founded by exiled Russian Baroness Catherine de Hueck Doherty (1896-1985). The place became his spiritual home and did much to channel and inform his faith.

O'Brien writes: "Father Brière . . . offered to give him a tour of the Madonna House property. When Kurelek entered the bare room of the poustinia, he saw on the wall an art print of the flagellated Christ. He was drawn to the image, looked at it closely, then collapsed on his knees and erupted in heartbroken sobs. Father Brière was astonished but did not try to console the man. The priest stood beside him but perceived this 'as an amazing experience of God, of sorrow, of grace.' When the tears subsided, Kurelek remained on his knees for some time, gazing at the image with attention, very still, inwardly calm. The two did not discuss the incident afterwards."[81]

I asked O'Brien what Madonna House provided for Kurelek.

"There he found a community of people who were truly living the whole Gospel as a living reality, who were loving our Lord Jesus as a Redeemer – living, alive and present. He found people who had given their whole lives, day by day, in obedience to the will of God and to do it with love. He found a community full of love. They recognized the Spirit at work in him – not just that he was a great Christian artist but he was a man carrying a cross, he had some swords in his heart, but he was continuously turning them over to Christ. He was a man of prayer. He was a man of the sacraments. He was a person who bore for decades the criticism of the dominant secular media which marvelled over his technical skill but lamented his antiquated worldview. He took a lot of flak, a lot of contempt – from the family contempt of his childhood and youth to the world's contempt as a mature man. All his wounds, his sins were laid out in public. He was hiding nothing. And he was pointing to the fact that he needed a saviour and mankind needed a saviour and the good news is the saviour is with us. It cost. It cost a lot."

For most of his career William Kurelek was considered 'beyond the pale' critically. He was predominantly a creature of the commercial and not the public gallery system and except for one travel grant awarded by the Canada Council in 1969 to study poverty in Hong Kong, South Africa and India (for a series of paintings and sketches that would illustrate a poem, *Pacem in Terris,* by Father Murray Abraham, a Canadian missionary in North India) Kurelek seems never to have partaken of public arts grants – that lifeline without which many of his best known colleagues would not have been able to keep their careers afloat.

With his penchant for rural landscapes peopled by farmers and peasants and his insistence on delivering a censorious and none-too-subtle Christian message in many of his canvases, Kurelek came off as a bit of a square and a throwback. When best-selling books and prints and calendars featuring his work started to appear in the 70s (and sell like the proverbial hotcakes), it seemed he might even start to incur resentment and a bit of a backlash à la Norman Rockwell, but I expect his singular lack of slickness saved him here.

Kurelek was so manifestly operating out of his own deepest impulses unsullied by commercial or trendy considerations that you simply couldn't go after him as a phoney or a hack. You might personally find his work cloddish or embarrassing but you knew he meant every stroke of it. And then with the least bit of research into his life and career (referring either to his autobiography or the documentary film about him, *The Maze*, in both of which no secret is made of his horrific struggles with depression) you came up against the fact that this was a man who had suffered terribly to win his position as an artist. It would require a pretty monstrous arrogance to deny that Kurelek had earned a credibility that could not be assailed.

It was easier to just ignore him. In the first edition of his *Concise History of Canadian Painting* (Oxford University Press, 1973), published just four years before his death when Kurelek had already imprinted himself on the Canadian consciousness in a way that no other living Canadian artist had, Ottawa-based art historian, curator and critic Dennis Reid did not so much as mention him. When the book was revised and expanded for a second edition in 1988, three paragraphs were worked into a new concluding chapter which included the line, "When he died [Kurelek] had the broadest public following of any contemporary artist in Canada."

If Reid's book had been entitled, *Canadian Artists I Happen to Like,* the original oversight would have been excusable but for a supposed history of Canadian painting (however 'concise') to not even acknowledge the existence of the most popular and one of the most prolific artists of his time is . . . well . . . emblematic of my contention that most of the Canadian art cognoscenti would rather pretend that William Kurelek never existed.

It would be hard to overstate the importance of the 2011/2012 touring show, *William Kurelek: The Messenger,* in fleshing out a more complete understanding of the artist. Prior to this show Kurelek was – simultaneously – one of the most popular and least comprehended of 20th century Canadian artists. Organized by Andrew Kear, Tobi Bruce and Mary Jo Hughes and exhibited at the three major Canadian galleries where they served as curators (respectively, the Winnipeg Art Gallery, the Art Gallery of Hamilton and the Art Gallery of Greater Victoria), *The Messenger* was not only the largest Kurelek retrospective ever mounted but it brought together for the first time all of the different streams in Kurelek's art.

Dubbed the 'People's Painter' largely because of his commitment to figurative painting and because of the phenomenal appeal of his rural and country scenes peopled by immigrant farmers and children that were gathered into calendars and best-selling picture books (like *A Prairie Boy's Summer, A Prairie Boy's Winter* and *Kurelek's Canada*) there was an immediacy of appeal, a common recognisability to Kurelek's work that made it approachable by a far wider swath of the Canadian populace than most artists can ever hope to reach.

But as his popularity increased to a greater and yet greater extent (and as often happens when that kind of mass appeal has been achieved) this remarkably multifaceted artist largely became known for only one (and that the least troubling and least challenging) aspect of his work – what most art critics would classify as 'folk art' even though it was far more accomplished than the work of most other artists so designated such as Grandma Moses or Maude Lewis. In addition to showing us the full range of his work, one of the gifts bequeathed to viewers of *The Messenger* in all of its boggling entirety is that we now bring new eyes to even what previously might have seemed the most unassuming of Kurelek's pastoral paintings and can divine deeper and more ambivalent messages than we were previously equipped to see.

By gathering together 85 paintings from every period of his career and presenting an unprecedentedly broad and complex monument of this artist's accomplishments, *The Messenger* handily exploded the trite conception of William Kurelek as a simple folksy painter of prairie scenes. During his almost 20 years as an exhibiting artist, Kurelek knew that his prairie-scapes and farm scenes were the paintings with the broadest appeal and called them his "potboilers." Though he felt a greater sense of urgency when working on his "didactic" paintings which imparted some kind of Christian lesson or warning, he was cannily persuaded by his Catholic confidant and friend Helen Cannon to keep both streams going. Not only did Cannon believe that Kurelek's landscapes and farm scenes were imbued with more meaning because he believed in a Creator; she wanted to see him amass as many viewers and patrons as possible. "'Do both kinds of paintings,' she urged me," Kurelek writes in his autobiography. "'The others are just as important if you want a wide audience.'"[82]

And Kurelek made no bones about it, he wanted and he won as wide an audience as possible, both because it would validate his worth in his own eyes and his father's and, most importantly, because he saw it as his special mission as a Christian to impart a moral lesson or message in his work. There was no standoffishness or feigned embarrassment on Kurelek's part regarding his success; no nagging fear that he must be doing something wrong if his work spoke so powerfully to so many people; no nagging suspicion that his work might be more significant if its appeal was less obvious, its message more obscure.

With a total lifetime output of well over 2,000 paintings, this driven and almost frighteningly prolific artist also produced two self-portraits in 1950 and 1957 which act as bookends to his crucible-like years of geographic travel, psychiatric travail and religious questing and attainment. Both were included in *The Messenger*. The first, entitled *Portrait of the Artist as a Young Man*, was executed just before he headed down to Mexico, and pays self-conscious homage to James Joyce's novel about the need for the budding artist to jettison limiting cultural and theological trappings so as to finally encounter "the reality of experience and to forge in the smithy of my soul the uncreated conscience of my race." Kurelek originally entitled it, *The Romantic*, he said, "because I represented myself as a dreamer: the Joycean artist about to burst into beautiful bloom, but not quite there yet."[83]

This decidedly bohemian self-portrait – long tow-coloured hair draping across his brow, wearing a faded work shirt, open at the throat, and sleeves rolled up to the elbows – is set against a background of what he called an "imaginary temple" in which various painted devices (fancifully ornate columns, a window and a doorway, two wooden moulding strips bent together in the onion-shaped outline of an ogee arch) act as frames surrounding scenes of an orchestra playing, a man emerging from an egg, a young naked boy dancing in the moonlight. It is the portrait of an aspiring artist setting out on a quest of self-formation.

In the second self-portrait, simply entitled, *Self Portrait* [Plate 4], a more confident but therefore more impervious Kurelek faces the viewer square on. His darker hair is combed off his brow. He wears a dark dress shirt buttoned to the neck and graced with an ochre-coloured tie, and is standing in front of a bulletin board entirely covered with souvenirs of his development such as family photographs and pictures of some of his earlier paintings but with the most prominent placement reserved for holy cards, a photograph of the English priest who helped him in his conversion to the Catholic faith and postcards of the Basilica at Lourdes and the imprint of Christ's face on the Shroud of Turin.

This is the portrait of an artist who has crossed continents and oceans and scrambled out to the crumbling outer rim of sanity and miraculously made it back again. He has encountered the 'reality of experience' and forged his own conscience in that harrowing process. This is a man who knows what he stands for and will not be shy about sharing what he has learned and what he believes with others. From this point on, one senses, all vanity burned away, he will not be susceptible to the siren call of false prophets. His head will not be turned. His heart will not be swayed. He has seen the light and found his path. The once-questing artist has indeed become the messenger.

Even in the wake of that definitive exhibition, many critics still fail to recognize Kurelek's accomplishments and achievement. Robert Enright (founding editor of the arts quarterly *Border Crossings* and a regular reviewer for both CBC Radio and *The Globe & Mail*) confessed when reviewing *The Messenger* in the fall of 2011 that he had hitherto missed the point about William Kurelek. Enright admitted that when he'd seen the previous major Kurelek retrospective in 1982 (*Kurelek's Vision of Canada*, curated by Joan Murray for Oshawa's Robert McLaughlin Gallery and comprising 48 paintings that were exhibited at 15 galleries across the country), he "judged him to be a minor folk painter concentrating on religious subjects, a kind of naive, flatland Bruegel."

This latest exhibition, Enright declared, "has fundamentally changed my mind about his achievement" so that he now sees him "as an artist of intense commitment and dedicated skill," as well as one of "the most bizarre painters this country has produced . . . . His work reads quite differently today than it did in the sixties, when he seemed a lone and curious figurative artist in an art world dominated by abstract painting. The open-ended plurality of current art making, and a postmodern tolerance for aesthetic and personal eccentricity make Kurelek more contemporary now than when he was alive. . . . In 2011, he seems like a Prairie Hieronymus Bosch, his naiveté replaced by a single-minded apocalyptic vision."

So, from a 'naive flatland Bruegel' to a 'bizarre . . . Prairie Hieronymus Bosch'– I guess that qualifies as a significant critical upgrade in some circles. In spite of Enright's professed change of heart, it's still hard not to sense some underlying animosity and condescension in play here. But then even Joan Murray (who curated the 1982 retrospective Enright cited above) wrote in the penultimate paragraph of her introduction to that exhibition's catalogue: "By the time Kurelek died, at fifty, he had just barely improved as a painter. The table-top composition remained, but by 1975 he could achieve small miracles of colour and mood (as in *Stooking*). A big show of his landscape paintings teaches you to hate the finicky detail and ever-present green grass. In his work, in fact, there's much to hate – an unformed sense of picture making, for instance."[84]

I asked Michael O'Brien if he could fathom this curator's problem with 'tabletop painting'. (And by the way, wouldn't working on a flat surface rather than an upright one almost certainly contribute to his unique placement of the horizon line?)

O'Brien told me, "What they don't understand is that most of the art of Christendom until the advent of the Renaissance was tempera paints used in very thin layers and very liquid layers so it has to dry flat and it dries slowly. I paint the same way. I paint on a tabletop. I never use an evil . . . an easel. Whoa, that's a Freudian slip. I find there's so much projection onto his life and it just reveals the lack of understanding on his critics' part. It's pathetic really."

Then, citing the impact of *The Messenger* as it criss-crossed the country, drawing record breaking crowds, O'Brien added, "There's a whole new genera-tion that really doesn't know much about him. And people are staggered by this resurgence of interest in a phenomenal Canadian artist – a world artist – who lived among us. I think his reputation will just grow and grow from now on. He's not going to go away."

I visited *The Messenger* at the Art Gallery of Hamilton on Good Friday of 2012, three weeks before the show was set to move on to Victoria and almost 35 years after the artist's death. Any hopes I secretly harboured that the buzz may have died down and the crowds might have thinned out a little were ut-terly dashed by the fact that, quite unknown to me, the gallery had waived the admission fee for this holiday and holiest of days that held such supreme impor-tance for Kurelek. The viewing rooms were packed with dozens upon dozens of enthusiastic viewers of all ages, many of them by dint of their attire and their noisy interaction with the paintings, giving off a decidedly non-cognoscenti aura.

This press of humanity meant that for some of the more popular works, I had to wait for five or so minutes, bobbing my head this way or that as I worked my way to the front of the crowd to finally win a clear and unobstructed view which I in turn would soon have to relinquish out of courtesy for those who had now assembled behind me. But it also meant that I got to witness first hand Kurelek's knack, undimmed by death, for reaching people of all sorts and con-ditions. And I was perfectly situated to hear a spontaneous two-word art review that I think would've thrilled the artist to the soles of his paint-spattered shoes.

A lot of the overtly religious works were displayed in one of the first rooms that visitors came to. I was originally scared off by the crowd in there and worked my way back to it a few hours later. While I was gazing upon Kurelek's painting of the Last Supper, entitled *When Evening Came* (one of the works from *The Passion of Christ* series) my personal space was invaded by a man with Down's syndrome, perhaps in his 30s, who was leading an older couple I presumed to be his parents to feast their eyeballs on it as well. I demurred as the woman apologised for the younger man's exuberance and then I started to tear up as he tugged on her arm to draw her attention away from me and back to this wonderful painting of Christ and all of the Apostles meeting for the last time. "That's today," he announced to his parents, grinning with excitement and pride for having made this connection between life and art. "That's today."

PLATE 1 William Kurelek: In The Autumn of Life, oil on tempered hardboard, 59 ʺ x 120.3 cm. 1964. Art Gallery of Ontario, gift from the McLean Foundation, 1964, 64/9

PLATE 2   William Kurelek: Pre-Maze, watercolour and graphite on paper, 25.3 x 37.7 cm, c.1953. Art Gallery of Ontario, gift from the collection of Bruno M. and Ruby Cormier, 1983, 83/300

AND SO THEY REACHED A PLACE CALLED
GOLGOTHA, THAT IS, THE PLACE NAMED AFTER
A SKULL.

PLATE 3 William Kurelek: The Passion of Christ (And So They Reached A Place Called Golgotha),
gouache on paper, 52.2 x 48.1 cm, 1960-1963. Niagara Falls Art Gallery

PLATE 4 William Kurelek: Self Portrait, watercolour, gouache and ink on paper, 47.5 x 38 cm, 1957. The Thomson Collection © Art Gallery of Ontario, 103679

WILLIAM KURELEK

Works cited in this essay:

KB	Morley, Patricia. *Kurelek: A Biography.* Toronto: MacMillan of Canada, 1986.
KPP	O'Brien, Michael D. *William Kurelek: Painter & Prophet.* Ottawa: Justin Press, 2013.
KVC	Murray, Joan. *Kurelek's Vision of Canada.* Edmonton: Hurtig, 1983.
PWK	O'Brien, Michael D. "The Passion of William Kurelek." Denville, NJ: *Image* (Spring issue 1995): pp. 75-93.
SWM 1	Kurelek, William. *Someone With Me,* 1st edition. Ithaca: Cornell University Press, 1973.
SWM 2	Kurelek, William. *Someone With Me,* 2nd edition. Toronto: McClelland and Stewart, 1980.
WKM	Bruce, Tobi; Hughes, Mary Jo; Kear, Andrew (curators); Dedora, Brian; Isaacs, Avrom; Smylski, Brian (essays). *William Kurelek: The Messenger.* Catalogue of a travelling exhibition first held at the Winnipeg Art Gallery from Sept. 29 to Dec. 31, 2011 and then travelling to the Art Gallery of Hamilton from Jan. 28 to Apr. 29, 2012 and the Art Gallery of Greater Victoria from May 25 to Sept. 3, 2012.

CHAPTER 1: LIFE IN METRO'S HOUSE
1. *SWM 1*, p. 4
2. *KB*, p. 14
3. *SWM 1*, p. 6
4. *SWM 1*, p. 8
5. *PM*, p. 20
6. *SWM 1*, p. 15
7. *SWM 1*, p. 17
8. *SWM 1*, p. 26
9. *SWM 1*, p. 20
10. *KB*, p. 54

CHAPTER 2: HARD LESSONS
11. *SWM 2*, p. 48
12. *SWM 2*, p. 51
13. *SWM 1*, p. 38
14. *SWM 1*, p. 307
15. *SWM 1*, p. 18
16. *SWM 1*, p. 134

17. *KB*, p. 43
18. *SWM 1*, p. 135
19. *PWK*
20. *SWM 1*, p. 134
21. *KB*, p. 42
22. *SWM 2*, p. 54
23. *SWM 1*, p. 82
24. *SWM 1*, p. 83
25. *SWM 1*, p. 82
26. *KB*, p. 35
27. *PWK*
28. *KB*, p. 306
29. *SWM 1*, p. 61
30. *PWK*
31. *SWM 2*, p. 157
32. *SWM 1*, p. 508

CHAPTER 3: OUT INTO THE WORLD
33. *SWM 1*, p. 3
34. *SWM 1*, p. 122
35. *SWM 1*, p. 138
36. *SWM 1*, p.140
37. *PWK*
38. *SWM 2*, p. 83
39. *SWM 2*, p. 84
40. *SWM 1*, p. 517
41. *SWM 1*, p. 220
42. *SWM 1*, p. 448
43. *KB*, p. 280
44. WKM, p. 20
45. *SWM 1*, p. 203
46. *SWM 1*, p. 206
47. *SWM 1*, p. 206
48. *KB*, p. 62
49. *SWM 1*, p. 285
50. *SWM 1*, p. 214
51. *KB*, p. 210
52. *SWM 1*, p. 217
53. *SWM 1*, p. 225
54. *SWM 1*, p. 254
55. *SWM 2*, p. 176
56. *SWM 1*, p. 257

57. *SWM 1*, p. 268
58. *SWM 1*, p. 284
59. *SWM 1*, p. 285

CHAPTER 4: THE BREAKDOWN
60. *KB*, p. 76
61. *SWM 2*, p. 7
62. *KB*, p. 80
63. *SWM 1*, p. 304
64. *SWM 1*, p. 305
65. *SWM 1*, p. 306
66. *KB*, p. 80
67. *SWM 2*, p. 328
68. *SWM 2*, p. 330
69. *SWM 2*, p. 27
70. *KB*, p. 98
71. *SWM 1*, p. 129
72. *SWM 2*, p. 30
73. *SWM 2*, p. 32
74. *SWM 2*, p. 159

CHAPTER 5: ARTIST ON A MISSION
75. *SWM 2*, p. 147
76. *SWM 2*, p. 149
77. *KB*, p. 144
78. *SWM 1*, p. 486
79. *SWM 1*, p. 487
80. *SWM 1*, p. 503

CHAPTER 6: WHAT REMAINS
81. *KPP,* p. 114
82. *SWM 1*, p. 499
83. *SWM 2*, p. 116
84. *KVC* intro

JACK CHAMBERS

7

A TRIP TO THE BEACH

IN THE FINAL YEAR OF HIS too-short life, ravaged by the last stage of the acute myeloblastic leukemia he'd battled for nine long years (and which he was told at the time of his diagnosis might well finish him off in less than one) Jack Chambers (1931–78) wrote his memoirs at the behest of his agent, Nancy Poole. It was originally planned that art critic and writer Paul Duvall should write Chambers' life story but when Duvall confessed that he couldn't produce the book fast enough to meet the proposed deadline, Chambers took on the job himself less than six months before his death, using his own extensive stash of notebooks and journals to both map out and flesh out the text. The resultant book clocked in at about 20,000 words concerning his life and an additional 7,000 words of 'Technical Explanations' and journal excerpts giving an insider's look at how he made many of his paintings and other works.

The entire limited print run of 300 numbered and signed copies of *Jack Chambers* was pre-sold and distributed to its subscribers within a month of Chambers' death in May of 1978 at the age of 47. The 177-page book is chock full of colour and black and white reproductions of his work as well as an assortment of small family photographs, and came in a slipcase with a separately bound folder containing a fine art print of his muted 1964-65 painting of daffodils in a vase called *Daffs*. Originally priced at $350, today a single copy at London's Attic Books will cost you $750.

"I insisted on it because I felt that he was going to be so important and there had not been the proper attention paid to him," Nancy Poole explained to me. "So I thought he has to do this. I think that we both recognized that he wasn't going to have that much more time. He would understand that in my request. We didn't discuss that aspect but we both recognized that this was not something to be put off, that it needed to be done. I wanted his story from his point of view and his choice of what to put down, what was important to him. But what I wanted most was the technical stuff so that conservators would know what they were dealing with — when he was using boards that he should never have used, when he was not doing proper priming, when he was doing mixtures of paints that would drive them crazy 50 years from now."

There wasn't enough time nor did Chambers any longer have the strength to leave us with an exhaustive or even complete exposition of his life, even if he had wanted to do so. Indeed, he was checking out page proofs on his hospital death bed. The prose is quite unmarked by any sense of urgency even though he knew this would be his last chance to verbally express any important truths that needed to be said before shuffling off into another dimension. There's a too self-conscious artfulness to some of the writing, as if he was so determined to avoid conventionality that he didn't mind sacrificing sense in the process: "I knew that what I saw in the sky and falling from it was the bowels, heart and lungs, the guts of the child of winter . . . It was by this grey-dying and violent birth-giving light of the winter dusk, taut with pain and the presence of danger, that the regal paradox of Christmas was ushered in."[1]

But for the most part the prose is sturdy and straightforward – and occasionally graced with surprising metaphors that work very well indeed – supplying the reader with dates and names and a running timeline of highlights and activities but withholding much in the way of deeply personal insights. Poole doubts that the book would've been much richer if Chambers had tackled it during a period of better health, because then, "he would've seen it as getting in the way of his painting. At least I believe that's what he would've thought."

As incomplete an account as the autobiography may provide, it nonetheless remains the primary resource for anyone interested in Chambers' life and career and it's unquestionably good to have as much text as we do rendered in his own distinctive voice. And any reader who's familiar with at least some of Chambers' paintings or takes the time to really study the reproductions that turn up on every other page, will be able to construe much more than he tells us in words.

For instance, there are only two paragraphs that are solely devoted to his wife Olga, telling how he met her in Spain ("and we began going places together," he vaguely explains), giving some of her family background, recounting their decision to get married in London and rounding it all off with, "and [we] began our continuing adventure in married life." It might seem that in this act of narrative opaqueness the artist is saying, "Sorry, dear reader, but I really don't have much to say about my wife." But when you notice that elsewhere in the book Olga turns up 17 times in paintings, sketches, photos and film stills (more than anyone else except Chambers himself) you realize, well, of course, he was primarily a painter and that was the only medium where he felt he could come close to adequately representing her importance to him.

It's the same with his children for the sake of whose provision he willed himself to live far longer than anyone thought possible. References to his sons John born in May of 1964 ("When he could stand we would hear him first thing in the morning, scrape, scrape, scrape. We opened his door and there he was, with his beautifully shaped head and an enormous smile, standing in his crib. He had shunted his crib from the corner over to the door and waited quietly for the door to open.") and Diego born in November of 1965 ("He was very quiet as a baby and sometimes when he smiled, his eyes made you think he was smiling to make you feel good.") are similarly slight and few but they too frequently turn up as subjects in his art.

In other sections of the book a disproportionate amount of attention seems to get expended on less likely subjects. The most pronounced of these appears very early in the autobiography where almost three full pages are devoted to a story about a family day trip by rail to nearby Port Stanley in his tenth or eleventh summer. I have come across no paintings or sketches by Chambers of that Lake Erie port – unlike that stretch of Lake Huron to the west of Grand Bend that he returned to again and again and which featured in no less than three major paintings. So why is Port Stanley given such a large write up in his book?

One sure reason why it made such a big impression on him is because it was the first beach he ever knew. Port Stanley was the playground of his earliest youth so his experiences of it were primal and indelible. Also, I expect he was able to write so much about it precisely because it wasn't a place he'd ever grappled with as a visual subject. He hadn't already captured its essence in the medium at which he excelled – in a sense it was virgin territory – so here he gives it a much fuller treatment. And most importantly, I believe, the story he tells about that particular outing to the beach encapsulates something essential about the animating principle – or the conceptual dynamic – behind a number of Chambers' most accomplished and best-loved paintings and manages to express that principle in a far more engaging way than in his voluminous journalistic scribblings about style and technique.

The 1940s were the boom years for passenger travel on the London and Port Stanley Railway which, in an era well before universal car ownership, quickly and cheaply linked landlocked Londoners with their nearest beach about 20 miles due south. In 1943 (which would be around the time of this outing) an all-time record of 1,705,233 passengers was recorded on the then electrified line.[2]

A few times over the course of a summer, Chambers' parents, Frank and Beatrice, would pack up a picnic basket and take Jack and his sister Shirley (older by one year) down to the beach on one of the first morning trains and not return until dusk. (In addition to an annual stretch at a Baptist summer camp that his parents sent him to, this was the extent of the young Chambers' outings for the summer holidays.)

Chambers recalls the highlights – universal and particular – of such a journey. There's the rattling, swaying railway cars with all the windows pushed wide open to let in the breeze; the stomach-evaporating thrill of crossing a high and narrow bridge over a murky river ("It seemed that just by leaning out the window to look down you would tip the train over"); the sudden crush of trees and shrubbery slapping against the car as it glided through backyards coming into the Port Stanley station; and the urgent rush to change into his trunks and hurl his body into the lake and keep it there for as much of the day as humanly possible.

The choppier the water, the higher the waves, the better Chambers liked it and the more his mother would get worried. On calmer days she'd worry more about her husband than her son. In the mid to late afternoon if the water's surface wasn't too rough, Frank would swim so far out it seemed he was trying to cross over to Cleveland and Beatrice would fret all the while and have stern words with him upon his return to dry land.

The sun and spray-saturated day would be punctuated a couple of times for considerations of nourishment. First they would execute a quick raid on Mackie's for Orangeade and ice cream and in the early-to-mid afternoon, they would take the considerably shorter train trip on the Incline Railway (a five cent return journey) that transported them 100 feet up the near cliff-like face to the luscious grass and cool shade of Inverie Heights or Picnic Hill from which they could look down on the now-silent shoreline to which they would soon be returning for the final stretch of their day-long holiday.

By late afternoon when everybody's shadows started to lengthen and the sand on the beach no longer burned the soles of his feet, Chambers' rapture would be intermittently haunted by the knowledge that soon things would have to wind down and the fun would end. "The fading of the light made the evening sad, and I looked forward to getting back home and remembering the sunshine and the water when everything was right."

If the train ride down to Port Stanley was a transport of ecstatic anticipation with all his senses soaking up every detail and impression en route, then the trip home was a dreary trudge in dimming light that was best ignored as much as possible. On this one particular day, however, things didn't play out at all as he had anticipated. The crush of passengers waiting for the seven o'clock train was so great that night that there wouldn't be any seats left if the family all stayed in line to flash their tickets to a conductor before getting on board. Chambers suggested that he could hold seats for the rest of the family if he could just get inside one of the cars and his Dad helped, as surreptitiously as possible, to push him in through a window to do just that. The car was already filling up but the boy was able to find one long unoccupied seat and planted himself in the middle with his arms protectively stretched out to either side, defying incoming passengers so that they had to look elsewhere for a place to perch.

Then the train started to lurch and pull out of the station. "I sat still, thinking they would suddenly appear through all these people and take the seats I had saved. But they didn't come and now the train was moving along. Someone sat down beside me and I shifted to the window. Then someone else sat down and all the seats were gone. It was a miserable ride to London."

But here's the key thing: it was also an adventure. Fearing imprisonment for the crime of not having a ticket – or perhaps he'd be turfed off the train and forced to walk back home – Chambers had to explain himself to the intimidating conductor who was making his way through the car collecting tickets. Then when the train finally pulled into London he had to reiterate his whole horrible dilemma to another uniformed man at that station. This conductor told him to wait on the platform for the next train, assuring the nervous kid that with any luck at all, his parents and sister should be on that one.

"It was now very dark and I had never been out like this so late at night. Finally my waiting paid off and mother, dad and Shirley came off the next train into the station. It was good to get home. The incident of my parents missing the train actually stretched the day in terms of importance. Formerly, the day had seemed over when the water and sunshine had come to an end. But my solitary ride to London had made me remember the evening as being more important than the fun at noon."

Chambers expended gallons of ink in his journal and in published essays on the need to stay awake at all times, to always endeavour to let down your protective guard so that the shield that has been built up by past experiences won't cut you off from fresh insights. When we expect nothing, most of us see nothing. When we think we know something all too well, we may think we recognize it for what it is but in truth we've stopped perceiving it at all. As in the old Psalm (118:22) that presages the coming of Christ – "the stone the builders rejected has become the cornerstone" – that thing which we carelessly assume is not what we're looking for, is not what we want . . . that same discarded and disregarded thing may well turn out to be the most needful and the most transformative thing of all if only we can make the effort to perceive it afresh.

As an artist Chambers would wage a lifelong campaign to circumvent expectation and jettison assumption so as to let pure perception break through and here in this story from his tenth or eleventh summer – though he does not say as much (indeed, coming right out and saying it would, I think, be a violation of his style) – I think he means for us to see that idea taking form for the first time in his life. The principle is the very same. What would routinely be a purposefully ignored part of the day from which he expected nothing but disappointment and disenchantment, had, by this simple twist of circumstance and events, become instead the highlight of the whole outing and one of the most lavishly rendered incidents in the story of his life.

One calls to mind the uncanny revelations that are operative in so many of Jack Chambers' most sublime paintings – the half dozen or so stone cold masterpieces upon which his reputation will stand or fall away – all of them rendered in the style he called "perceptual realism" and later, just "perceptualism." At first blush we might wonder why has he perversely chosen subjects so dime-a-dozen common that most people and most artists wouldn't even be inclined to look at them? A stretch of highway on an autumn morning . . . Two boys in their bathrobes watching television . . . A sand dune on a hot summer afternoon . . . Such questions, of course, contain their own answers. Jack Chambers wasn't 'most artists' and early on he discovered the great rewards which can accrue to us when we resist that first lazy impulse and take the time to really focus on the unexamined, the ignored, the taken-for-granted.

In an interview with his good friend, Ross Woodman – a professor of the Romantics by day at the University of Western Ontario and otherwise a passionate art collector and widely regarded critic whose musings did much to bring coherence and attention to the work of at least two generations of London artists – Chambers spoke about that moment of crystallization in which all of his perceptualist works were conceived. It was "that instant when the world is in focus but not moving . . . that moment before the names go on the objects . . . where one feels that he has stepped off the conveyor belt of time momentarily and actually glimpses the world in pause."

"There really is no isolated object in the world, unless that object is singled out for special attention," Chambers wrote. "Otherwise everything co-exists in the world in relative equality. The painting that is good will have that special equalizing concentration through its entirety. It will have a unified co-existence of parts, in which no one aspect is given extra special treatment. I am not referring to the uniformity of mono-coloured surfaces as examples of unity in painting – I'm speaking of the spiritualized co-existence of things fertilized by the perceptual moment, and whose harmony in turn excites vision and makes the painting sing."[3]

What uniquely equipped Chambers to bring that "special equalizing concentration" to every square centimetre of his canvases, to make them "sing" in that utterly unique and accomplished way which was his trademark, was his classical training which he alone of mid-20th century Canadian artists had taken the time to acquire by travelling to Europe to study and starting all over from scratch. Once Chambers had received his fatal diagnosis, Ross Woodman said "that life, breathing, perceiving was a kind of miracle [for Chambers]. Everything had the quality of one last look."

This is unquestionably so in that those celebrated paintings seem so utterly saturated with longing and love. But it is usually the case when a painter takes those long, last looks that his images have become softened and blent as he readies himself to fade away as well. This is not so with Chambers in those perceptualist masterpieces which form his surest legacy; all but one of which (*401 Towards London*) were painted after his diagnosis. The world on which he gazes one last time is all so sharp and bright and uncannily tangible – so exuberantly youthful. His was a long apprenticeship that brought him to the age of 30 before he felt himself truly ready to begin his life as an artist. He had no way of knowing (though it often seemed in his moody restlessness and his sometimes abrasive drive that perhaps he had sensed it all along) that his life would be almost two thirds over by the time he felt primed and ready to strike.

8

A SOLITARY ARTIST IN TRAINING

IN THE VERY FIRST line of his autobiography, Jack Chambers precisely lays out the co-ordinates of his arrival on Planet Earth. "On Wednesday March 25, 1931 at 9:45 a.m. in Victoria Hospital, London, Ontario, with my first gulp of air, I came into possession of a mother, Beatrice, a father, Frank, and a sister, Shirley, one year less sixteen days my elder."

Chambers was born in the depths of the depression and for the first few years of the artist's life, his welder father was having a hard time finding enough steady work to keep their upper storey apartment in an East London house afloat. When Jack was two his family went to live with his paternal grandparents in their free-standing house in the eastern-most block of Dufferin Ave and it is there that Jack's first solid memories kick in. His grandfather Richard Charles Chambers – also a welder and metal worker with a glorious, white Kaiser-style moustache who had been a British sergeant-major posted in Ceylon when Jack's father was born – maintained an extensive garden where he grew vegetables, fruits and berries and flowers; especially peonies which Jack would burrow his face into for the scent and then pull away in a fit of sneezing.

Hay fever would also plague the young boy on his less frequent visits to his maternal grandparents, the McIntyres, in their far more substantial house on a 100 acre farm southwest of Alsia Craig. Perhaps because of that infrequency and the sheer scale of the place his memories of the farm and their house seem particularly vivid and painterly: "I remember . . . waking in the morning in the small bedroom upstairs where the window looked down on the orchard. The sun was bright and sharp and put everything in motion. The calves ran bawling to the wire fence and thrust their muzzles into the milk trough. Downstairs, the separator was turning out milk and cream into separate pails, and there was fresh baked bread, butter and honey, fried eggs, sunny-side up, cold pork and relish, fried potatoes, and milk for drinking and for porridge, all on the table in front of the window that looked up the road for miles."[4]

Chambers bonded with the McIntyres' mutt, Brownie, who didn't hold it against him that he was a city kid and would endlessly fetch him sticks or anything else he threw. And in his grandparents' front parlour – a room reserved for funerals and the reception of important visitors – he made some of his earliest observations about the power of light and shade and colour. A bank of fir trees at the front of the house meant that no direct sunlight ever penetrated that always cooler room that always smelt of furniture polish. Looking through the blue and crimson stained glass panels in the big front window out onto a landscape and a world suddenly submerged in those tones was so intoxicating that it made him lose his balance. Decades later he commemorated those early experiences with colour and light in works like *Regatta* and *Madrid Window* that were overlaid with transparent panels of similarly shaded red and blue plastic.

In his fifth year Jack's family struck out on their own again, this time heading across town to Byron Ave. in southwest London. With all of their gear loaded and piled into the back of a borrowed truck, Jack was nervous about whether they'd make it through the train underpass at the northern foot of Wortley Road without losing any furniture. At their new home, the power still hadn't been switched back on, and Jack remembered dining in the dark on moving day with his very favourite dish (and surely there can't have been too many other five year olds in all the world who harboured this preference) – fried liver. Because they were renting the whole house on Byron Ave. and not just an apartment – and also, no doubt because of his more adventurous age now that he was five – Jack took ownership of this new neighbourhood in an unprecedented way.

There was a tall maple tree in the back yard that he would scramble into the upper reaches of on windy days for the pleasure of being buffeted about. A few blocks to the east were the public pool and tennis courts and playing fields of Thames Park, which the south branch of the Thames River ran through. And a block and a half to the west of that was the much wilder area known as the Coves, a forested system of ravines and ponds, fed by the western branch of the same river. In addition to swimming and diving in the pool and getting up to games along the river with homemade spears and slingshots and B-B guns, the young Chambers also knew the satisfaction of putting food on his family's table.

"Sometimes in winter the ice covering the coves was so transparent that you could see the bottom and the brown foliage there," he wrote in his autobiography. "I captured a two-foot pike in an ice pool beside the coves' bank. He was in there under the ice with hundreds of multi-coloured little fish. He had only to turn to his left for breakfast and his right for dinner. I broke the ice and scooped him out. Even at close range the B-B's from my gun bounced off his shining forehead. He made five lovely baked steaks which we ate next day."[5]

Early one evening cycling home across the York Street Bridge Chambers watched, horrified but engrossed, as firemen in a rescue boat hoisted a lifeless blonde-haired boy, about his age, out of the Thames River with a pole, hooking him under the left arm so that his right arm and waterlogged clothes heavily drooped off him and his wet hair was smeared across his face. The poor boy's whole physical attitude was sharply reminiscent of pictures he'd seen at Sunday School and the incident would always be recalled whenever the adult Chambers encountered some old master's painting of Christ being taken down from the cross.

Victoria Public School where he began his formal education that fall was situated just a few doors west and around the corner. Chambers would never be a particularly good or eager student, always preferring to find stuff out in his own way and at his own pace, largely following the dictates of his own curiosity. For most of his kindergarten year, he was laid up in bed with pneumonia and what he vaguely called "a variety of childhood diseases." His grandfather presented him with a birthday present of a book filled with pictures of puppies and kittens; a book he spent so much time looking at while feeling sick that he got rid of it once he'd returned to full health lest it drag him back down like some sort of fever-embedded anchor.

As a result of missing so much of his kindergarten year, Chambers largely missed out in that crucial period of initiation into a more regimented way of life which his more steadily attending colleagues underwent. This would turn out to be a gift of great value, leaving him with a marked streak of independence. Chambers never would develop into a very convincing – or convinced – team player. He didn't learn to submit to the will of the group and maintained for the rest of his life a sturdy ability to draw back from herd movements of any kind and consider instead how he would prefer to approach things. Taken all in all this would prove to be a strength though there would be instances, particularly in his last decade when death loomed and he sought to synthesize his beliefs and aspirations in a sprawling perceptual journal that he entitled *Red and Green*, when he would give a lot of attention to some pretty arid and/or loopy philosophies that a better informed and trained mind would have shunned.

"School was never my favourite pastime," he wrote. "If I liked my teacher I could cooperate and get things done. If I didn't, it was mischief time and drudgery. Learning things was never a game or a challenge for me. School was waiting between recess and the summer holidays."

Chambers had mentioned to his grade three teacher that his mother had a collection of tiny silk replicas of all the national flags of the world. His teacher asked him to bring those in, which he did, and he then was sent to the front of the class to give a little presentation about the collection. He froze up. "Just tell them what we discussed," the teacher said.

"I said to her in front of the class that I didn't remember our discussing anything and she blew her top. I didn't cry but I thought she was crazy. I told my mother while we were doing the dishes that if I were God she would be in Hell for sure. "Good heavens!" my mother said. "Don't talk like that." "I would," I said."[6]

Much more to his liking was Miss Blackwell, his teacher for grades four and five, who "didn't take it seriously when I made mistakes". Miss Blackwell had noticed Chambers' affinity for art and got him to draw scenes on the blackboard with coloured chalks to supplement her history classes. When one of his classmates expressed particular approval of Chambers' rendering of Captain Cook, not only was his head not turned by the compliment but that was the very instant when he suddenly detected what was wrong with the work which he abruptly rubbed out and did over again to his own satisfaction.

His grade six teacher goes unnamed and unremarked but for grade seven he had Miss Dunston, another favourite, who encouraged him to draw and paint and held on to two of his coloured drawings for 35 years, giving them back to him in the last year of his life while he was writing his autobiography. "Perhaps the most special thing about these works," he commented, "is that she allowed them to exist today."

By the time he was in the senior grades of public school, it was clear that Jack was not only winning recognition from his peers for his artistic abilities but that he was also interested in pushing himself to see how much better he could become, that he was starting to see himself as an artist in training. Teachers throughout the London school systems would keep an eye out for particularly talented 12 and 13 year olds and suggest that they might want to enroll for the special art classes held downtown at the London Art Museum on Saturday mornings throughout the school year and taught by Albert Templar.

The financial cost for these was minimal but the sacrifice involved for someone of Chambers' disposition was considerable. We've seen how little he enjoyed the classroom environment generally and how much he loved to run around outside shooting and poking at things at will with nary an adult supervisor in sight. For him to willingly give up his one free and unregulated morning of the week (on Sundays he'd be hauled off with his family to Baptist Church) is a strong indication of how central art-making had become to his own sense of himself.

Chambers would be accompanied on these outings by a neighbourhood friend, Val McInnes, who attended the nearby Catholic School, St. Martin of Tours. The two boys would keep up this practice through their high school years as well, often visiting each other's homes on a Saturday afternoon after art classes to view each other's works in progress and later travelling around London and even hitch-hiking out to Arva on sketching tours.

In his final year of public school (and his final year on Byron Avenue) Chambers informed his parents that what he really wanted to try his hand at was oil painting and that he'd love it if they could get him a decent set. An art competition was held for all grade eight students at Victoria School every year and Chambers had so distinguished himself as a developing artist that he seemed the shoo-in to win top prize. When the winners were announced, Chambers learned that he had come in second, behind a lad named Dick Sherriden.

His self-confidence was such that Chambers wasn't particularly crushed by this second place showing but he was temporarily puzzled. Then all was revealed. Clearly, somebody had had words with somebody.

"After the announcement Mr. Collier, the art teacher and judge, called me into the office. First prize was a book. Second prize was a box of oil paints. He gave me a big knowing smile and I felt that life could have some very pleasant and unexpected surprises after all."[7]

Chambers' paternal grandfather had died when he was nine years old. About a year after that, as her own health and memory started to decline and she needed constant looking after, his grandmother had come to live with them on Byron Ave., taking over the young boy's bed, and then she too died in his grade eight year. With the passing of both paternal grandparents, the Chambers family then came into possession of the Dufferin Ave. home and moved back in there for keeps.

With that move Chambers commenced his high school career back in the east end of town, cycling several blocks further east to Highbury Street each day along Dundas Street, past the Kellogg's, McCormick's and Coca-Cola factories, to Sir Adam Beck Secondary School. There Chambers finally came under the influence of Selwyn Dewdney (1909-79), an art teacher who knew about art as a passion and a way of life and not just a pastime.

In addition to his skills as a painter, muralist, illustrator and mapmaker, Dewdney was also a novelist and children's writer and, in association with the Royal Ontario Museum, a pioneering researcher in the Indian rock paintings of the Great Lakes. After the Second World War Dewdney and his wife Irene started up one of Canada's first Art Therapy programs at London's Westminster Hospital for veterans in the south end of town. In his first novel, *Wind Without Rain*, Dewdney outlined in lightly fictionalized form, the crisis of principle that led him to resign his teaching position at Beck immediately following Chambers' grade nine year. (In a nutshell, it had to do with the school's shabby treatment of a Jewish fellow teacher who refused to lower his academic standards so as to pass a larger cohort of his students. When that colleague was sacked, Dewdney resigned in solidarity with him.)

Dewdney's resignation didn't mean that he and Chambers fell out of touch, however, because by then Selwyn and Irene Dewdney had already become friends and mentors of Chambers (almost a second set of parents; these ones a whole lot more art-savvy than Frank and Beatrice) and would remain so for the rest of his life, welcoming him into their home as a frequent dinner guest and buying a number of his earliest works and showing by rare example how, with dedication and adaptability, a life devoted to art could be lived even in an environment as apparently indifferent – if not hostile – to all non-utilitarian pursuits as London, Ontario.

For his second year at Beck, Chambers' art teacher was a Captain Pritchard who again enthused about and encouraged his work but that relationship never became as significant as the one with Dewdney. Chambers was concentrating so intensely on his art by this point that his other studies were suffering. In fact art class and (strangely enough) phys. ed. would be the only classes at which he excelled. He knew his own worth as a developing artist (that year he submitted an abstract work to a regional competition at the downtown art gallery and was accepted) but he couldn't quite believe his success at athletics.

"I trained at high jump, broad jump, pole-vaulting and running," he writes in his autobiography, striking a note of amused mystification. "My ability was only mediocre but I liked doing it. The fact that I was not yet five feet in height didn't help my performances. At the WOSSA [Western Ontario Secondary School Athletics] track meet that year I won the juvenile championship. As I pushed my bike home I was pleasantly shocked. "Is it really true?" I asked myself. I haven't checked, but I'm sure statistics would show that the juvenile performance that year of 1945 was probably the poorest on record."[8]

But in his more academic subjects, things weren't going so swimmingly. In fact he was bombing out and was called down to the office late in grade ten and offered the scholastic equivalent of a no-fault divorce: "They told me at the office that I would pass, but that I wasn't to return next year . . . To me, it was a mystery that I passed either year."[9]

Banished into academic exile Chambers next found himself (rather like Br'er Rabbit being tossed into the briar patch in the *Uncle Remus* stories) demoted to the one place in the world he most longed to be – H.B. Beal Technical School – where he studied art in the city's only properly outfitted art department with dedicated teachers like Herb Ariss, John O'Henly and department head, Mackie Cryderman. In his second year there Herb Ariss started up a special art training course for war veterans, a group that Chambers was thrilled to sit in with as they brought so much more ability, experience and gravitas to the proceedings. Though the major emphasis was always on commercial art (to get the Board of Education to fund such a department in the first place, they had to at least pretend that this was a sensible occupational training program that would outfit students to find gainful employment), the teachers cast their tutelary nets extraordinarily wide, offering classes in life sketching with actual models and still life painting classes.

Looking back on his time at Beal Chambers wrote, "I was really in my element there and thought of the art department as a continuation of what I was doing at home. School for the first time was furthering my education."

Chambers' life outside of school hours intensified as well. He struck up long-lasting friendships with other artists-in-training like Murray Stephens, Jill Kraemer and Bob Hedrick, and in their spare time they'd pose for one another and head out on sketching parties to nearby locales along the river and downtown (including the Queens Ave. Convent of the Sisters of the Precious Blood) and in the rolling fields of Arva just north of the City. They'd also challenge one another and exchange ideas and enthusiasms. Chambers was introduced to the large Central Library (situated just one floor below the big London Art Museum) and started to burrow his way through their art department, devouring glossy illustrated books about newly discovered heroes such as old masters Rembrandt and Master Mathis or Grunewald as well as more contemporary artists such as Vincent van Gogh and Francis Bacon.

In May of his grade 11 year, Chambers left school – perhaps for good, he thought – when he landed a job at Marley Signs. But there he quickly discovered just how boring and unchallenging work could be in the field of strictly commercial art. He rarely even got to design the signs but would just be left to carry out dreary lettering assignments. The limited opportunities afforded him there persuaded him to return to Beal for his final year of grade 12 where he graduated in June of 1949.

With his summertime earnings as a clerk at Simpson's department store socked away (significantly, at this time, he was not looking to more art-related work to raise his financial stake; perhaps because he found the misuse of his talents more threatening to his well-being than to put those talents aside for a stretch) he impulsively travelled to Quebec City where he lived for about a month with the intention of "filling my days solely with what I thought were the disciplines worthy of an artist." He chose to travel to Quebec because he wanted both to taste a different culture and to get beyond the range of family, teachers and friends and see what he was capable of when answerable to no one but himself.

He was not encouraged by the result of this experiment in living the artist's life. "My inadequacies became painfully prominent now that my whole day could be given over to painting." Rather than face that pain or wrestle with those inadequacies he found himself frittering away more and more of his time at a nearby pool hall where he would play snooker for hours at a stretch (according to Greg Curnoe he was an excellent player and would hustle to earn pocket money) and order up copious quantities of beer which he was still too young to buy in Ontario.[10]

It was during this post-Beal period that a new note of uncertainty creeps into Chambers' musings. His dispiriting term of work as a sign painter – his boss' demeaning assumption that filling in letters was all he was qualified to do – seems to have checked the youthful and teenaged cockiness that had sustained him so far. He now seemed to perceive just how great was the distance he had yet to traverse before he would attain any real mastery of his talents. As happy and challenged as he had been at Beal, he now sensed that the education he acquired here forward would have to be something that went much deeper.

In May of 1950 he won first prize in the category for artists 30 years old or under (winning out over a number of considerably older contenders from the Ontario College of Art in Toronto) at the Annual Western Ontario Exhibition at the London Art Museum for his arresting stylized painting of a pot of Easter lilies sitting on a chair. Chambers' childhood friend Val McInnes accurately described *Lilies* as "subdued and monochromatic, but the painting simply glowed."

It could've been a serious boost to his ego yet Chambers recalled, "When they gave the prize to me for *Lilies* I felt that one of these days I'd have to move on and get proper training. There were things I tried to and couldn't do, and I didn't think that what I was looking for was to be found in Canada or the USA. Actually, I didn't know what I was looking for, but whatever it was it didn't seem to be close by."

Intrigued by an exhibition the previous fall at the London Art Museum of *A Canadian Artist in Mexico*, a show of work by Leonard Brooks who had been living and studying in San Miguel d'Allende for the past two years, Chambers next set his sights on Mexico. Just like William Kurelek, and in the very same year, 1950, Jack Chambers made an ill-prepared trip south to Mexico with the intention of attending (or at least checking out) this very same art school and arrived there in August (a few months before Kurelek) only to learn that the school had been disbanded and that all of the big name artists mostly famous for their murals – Jose Orozco, Diego Rivera and David Siqueiros – had given up teaching through any school and gone their separate ways.

Unlike Kurelek who had hitch-hiked down to Mexico, Chambers took the bus and lived on it for the five days it took to traverse the USA. At their first rest stop on the Mexican side of the border, Chambers initiated himself into the glories of Mexican cuisine by ordering up a bottle of Mexican beer and four tortillas which really was a bit excessive. Thanks to his usual lack of research before setting out, Chambers somehow had the false impression that tortillas were delicate little things like small pancakes and that nobody could possibly eat just one and be satiated. Luckily his 19 year old constitution was up to the challenge and he was able to wolf down all four before clambering back on board the bus.

Whereas Kurelek stayed on in San Miguel for five months at a greatly inferior school that had been hurriedly cobbled together as a kind of substitute, Chambers moved on to Mexico City where he was briefly enrolled at the Escuella de Bellas Artes but with not much better results. As with his month in

Quebec City, Chambers was frustrated by his inability to get much done and nothing being offered at this school helped him to effect a breakthrough:

"I could only go so far with my work. I had the energy to work all day but I didn't know how to. I could only go so far with what I was doing and then I felt I was wasting my time, coming to the same dead end again and again."[11]

In addition to experiencing his very first earthquake, which set cars rolling back and forth in the street below his tiny one room apartment situated on the roof of a boarding house, Chambers was also more subtly moved by the Mexican landscape and wrote about it in a way that contrasts interestingly with what he had to say later about the landscapes of Europe and Spain:

"The Mexican countryside that I saw was quite spectacular. There were the arid desert vistas of the low regions and the lush, semi-tropical vegetation of the mountains. Both had their presence and their beauty but both made me uneasy. There was a raw newness to the landscape similar to that of North America. It was as though the dominant spirit in the land came from things of the land itself . . . the presence of non-human elements ruled the space."[12]

After a few months Chambers decided that this school was not what he was looking for and he returned to London by the New Year. Once he was back home he read more about the work of Jose Orozco and regretted – but only slightly – that he hadn't sought him out when he was down there as he felt Orozco's paintings represented the very best that Mexico had to offer. "His was very good work," Chambers acknowledged. "But I was not interested in style as such, nor in what one man had forged for himself out of his own experience."

This again bespeaks his lack of research while preparing for his Mexican foray. And we shall see that he didn't learn from this mistake and prepare himself any more carefully for any of his future travels. Such a slapdash approach towards a potentially life-changing experience (an experience which he had slaved and sacrificed to attain) sits oddly with Chambers' tireless perfectionism as a painter and his pronounced tendency to carefully monitor and analyze his every action and expound upon its significance. Why would this otherwise thoughtful and observant artist, hungry to improve his practice and consider fresh approaches, not prepare his way more carefully so that he could take advantage of whatever resources were available in Mexico?

There were a couple of reasons in play here. One was that he was such a loner that he didn't want to appropriate – or put himself in a position where he might be tempted to appropriate – any other artist's stylistic tricks. He wanted to come by his own perceptions and approaches honestly and not be thinking in the back of his head, "Well, this worked for Orozco so perhaps I'll give that a shot and see if it can work for me as well." Chambers knew that any artist had to mine his own experiences and come up with their own perceptions if their work was to have sufficient vitality and originality as to be worth doing.

But even deeper than Chambers' concerns about being stylistically influenced by other artists was his conviction that he still hadn't been properly educated. Chambers didn't really have a style yet and indeed was a little leery of developing one. While his most widely regarded perceptualist works are unmistakably the work of the same hand, Chambers turned that hand to so many radically different styles and media over the course of his career that it undoubtedly cost him something in terms of easy or immediate recognition.

Style was a secondary concern for Chambers. Bidden or unbidden, he felt that it would come and the only stylistic battle he foresaw might have to do with the struggle to repress whatever style he developed as much as possible, so as to contain it and not let any techniques, tics or shortcuts he developed get in the way of a worthy or honest representation of his subjects. Style was something he had no intention of deliberately striving to attain. As he wrote in his art-maker's journal and scrapbook, *Red and Green*, "Before the camera was invented a painting style was the unavoidable compensation for the lack of accurate visual information to the painter."

And later on in that same journal he wrote: "Style at its purest is unavoidable. Unavoidable style is a man's thumbprint, his physiological, mental and spiritual hallmark. It is an impress truly and wholly his own. It is the tracks and gestures he makes following his light. It is distinct from thinking-up a signature, devising a sign, inventing a deviation with the purpose of distinguishing his work from all the others as an aim in art . . . an aim that leaves him looking like the many. Emphasis on such a sign or the 'way' a thing should look is normally a natural secondary value, subsequent to perception."[13]

The goal Chambers was pursuing at this point in his development was something much more elemental than style. Just after that preceding comment about missing out on meeting Orozco, Chambers wrote that at this time he was after "Something like basic training, some visible standard of ability which was craft and not art. I longed to see the simple excellence of good craftsmanship." And as a place to attain that bone-deep grounding in craftsmanship which he saw as the prerequisite to good art-making, Mexico – like Canada and the USA – was too new, too raw.

Eventually he would set his sights on the Old World, on Europe, and pull his plug out of the mid-20th century zeitgeist almost completely, focussing instead on getting an education in classical art. But he still had two more years of productively flailing about in London before he would be ready to make that leap. He tried different traditional styles, most notably in a series of portraits of himself and others, and placed work in local exhibitions where he did not win any prizes but did receive at least one astutely perceptive review from *The London Free Press'* resident art critic, Lenore Crawford, who said of his three portraits in a February, 1951 group show at the London Public Library and Art

Museum:

"The general impression given is a backward look to the techniques of Rembrandt and El Greco, with their accompanying expressions, a complete forgetting that the French Impressionists and Post Impressionists had existed and also a lack of any influence by the Group of Seven. The show, as a result, makes promises of new things in Canadian art in the next decade."[14]

Chambers' routine at this time was to alternate a few months of labour at factory or construction jobs (and there was even a two-week stretch where he worked as an optical lens grinder) with a few weeks of intensive art making. Tiring of the 'off-or-on-ness', the 'either-or-ness' of that arrangement (and dismayed by the fact that he had to don his worker's hat for three or four times as long as he got to don his artist's hat), he hatched a plot to see if there wasn't some way of getting the qualifications for much better paying work that could even out that disparity or perhaps even allow him to wear both hats at more or less the same time. To that end he decided to go to university in the fall of 1952 to earn a general arts degree. He drew unemployment insurance for seven months while he crammed to attain the four grade 13 credits and five years of French that he needed to top up his high school diploma before he could even set foot on campus.

He also added to his list of extracurricular experiences at this time by spending two nights in jail as the result of trying to creep in through the second storey bedroom window of a young woman he'd escorted home one summer Saturday night. Some neighbours, reasonably enough, assumed this lug climbing a trellis and scampering over the verandah roof must be trying to break into the house and phoned the police who turned up with guns drawn just as he was about to climb in through her window. One of the cops called up to him: "Come down or I'll shoot."

Chambers wrote, "I was so angry at being interrupted that I refused to answer any of their questions."[15] The next day being a Sunday, there was no business conducted in the London courts so he rotted in the holding tank for another full day, as he not so patiently waited to be officially charged. On the Monday morning Chambers was handcuffed to another inmate who was up on a robbery charge and hauled off to court where his tethered friend, quite jovial until then, broke down in tears of remorse at the sight of his wife.

Luckily, Chambers' girlfriend was also on hand at the courtroom hearing and clarified matters quite quickly, explaining that contrary to appearances, this had not been a case of break and enter; they had in fact been out on a date and the suspect here was merely trying to prolong their time together. She was as nervous as a kitten and Chambers felt sorry for having made her go through this public spectacle which wouldn't even have been necessary if he had explained his actions to the policemen at the time of his arrest instead of sulking like some sullen Lothario thwarted in his amorous quest.

By summer's end, stuffed to the brim with his lately acquired knowledge and a new facility for speaking French, the 21-year old Chambers landed in the back of Ross Woodman's freshman English class at the University of Western Ontario in September of 1952. Woodman recalls:

"The steadily accumulating force of his silent presence came to a head one day at the end of a class when he approached me with some poems, which he said were written by a friend who would be interested in my opinion. I instantly assumed he was the 'friend' and my reading of the poems confirmed it. I suggested that he consider publishing them. Much later, some of them appeared in James Reaney's *Alphabet*. Emboldened by my response to the poems, he invited me to his house on Dufferin Avenue in London to see some of his paintings. I recall portraits of himself and his sister, the self-portraits painted sitting on the edge of his bed gazing at his reflection in a bureau mirror no more than two feet away. Apart from a small closet, there was no room for anything else. My sense of him in that room was like my sense of him in the classroom: constricted energy waiting to explode."[16]

Ross Woodman quickly came to recognize that Chambers did not possess an academic mind; that he was constitutionally incapable of flourishing in that compartmentalized way that the classroom demands and wasn't surprised six months later when Chambers impulsively (and, Woodman understood, necessarily) bailed out of university without even seeing his first year through. Again, nearly a full year's careful planning and studying had gone in to meeting the requirements just to attend. All that plus six months' worth of increasingly spotty attendance were thrown out the window when he decided to quit. And this time the educational authorities would not be dispensing the compensatory award of an unearned pass if he would just promise to stay away and never darken their door again.

Once he had quit university, Chambers' disparate energies reconvened once again as he took on three different jobs simultaneously (all of them conveniently situated within blocks of each other just north of the downtown core) and he worked flat out from March to September of 1953 with one single aim in mind, to get himself over to Europe. In his autobiography Chambers described his timetable during these six months, exulting a little in the energy he now had to burn in furious pursuit of this goal:

"From 8 a.m. till 5:30 p.m. I worked in a factory across from a restaurant. [in a 1970 interview with Lenore Crawford in *The London Free Press* he calls the factory, an "auto parts place".] From 6 p.m. till 9 p.m. I waited on tables at the restaurant. [This he identified as The Latin Quarter.] Between the restaurant and the factory was the post office. [This would be the one then situated in the beautiful old Federal Building at the northwest corner of Richmond and

Queens.] I worked there from 9:02 p.m. to 11 p.m. By September I had saved over a thousand dollars without sacrificing any of my favourite pastimes, including painting."[17]

The night before Chambers headed off to New York City to board a Greek ship sailing to Naples on which he had booked a tourist class berth, he hauled all of his paintings out of his parents' basement and took them over to Ross Woodman's house for safe keeping. "He asked me to look after them until he got back," Woodman explained.

Asked about the quality of those early paintings, Woodman said, "It was very mannered, stylized work, heavily influenced by other artists. I'm not sure that I thought it was good. The intensity was the most striking thing."

I asked Woodman if he felt at the time that going to Europe was the right thing for Chambers. "Yes, it was a good move. I didn't know what was going to happen. But I could see from what he left with me – the crucifixions and all the other kinds of paintings he was doing – that he was seriously involved in that kind of work and Europe was the place to be."

The last major painting Chambers finished before leaving Canada was the numinous and eerie *Self-Portrait No. 2* from 1953 which depicts the artist with the sloping shoulders and elongated neck, limbs and hands – as well as the cool blue halo – of an El Greco (1541–1614) saint. In many ways the painting is, if not blasphemous, then certainly brash, and yet it intuitively signals not just the eight years he would immerse himself in Spain and the work of its master painters like El Greco but also his conversion in just four more years to the Roman Catholic faith.

9

EUROPE WAS THE PLACE TO BE

IN A LENGTHY INTERVIEW published by Coach House Press in 1967, Woodman, pretending that he didn't already know the answer, asked Chambers why he had chosen to leave Canada. "Indifference," Chambers answered. "The part of Canada I knew was utilitarian, puritanical, indifferent to anything that was not a 'safe job' and a 'proper living'. It was a question of survival. I worked, saved money and left . . . I left Canada with no very clear idea of what I was after or where I was going, but with a determination not to have forced on me what I didn't want."[18]

Incredibly, after his Mexican standoff where he'd arrived in a strange country with no solid contacts in place to help him make his way (and so missed out on opportunities) Chambers repeated that maddeningly laissez-faire approach in travelling to Europe. In one of the more preposterous passages of his autobiography he makes a not very convincing attempt to explain his state of mind just before embarking on his leap into the old world:

"Being at school had never taught me to gather information. I probably doubted that there were such places as Italy and Rome. Such places only existed in books. So when I set sail for Europe, I set sail for a strange place whose name I knew but about which I had no information, or if I had information, it had no relation to this adventure or to a destination."[19]

This passage really does strain credulity. Are we to believe that he can book himself passage to Italy but he has no idea at all what to expect when he gets there? Then why would he choose it as a destination as opposed to, say, Iceland? I think what he has ingenuously expressed here in a form so exaggerated as to be almost a parody, is his long-held distrust of authority of any kind and his determination to avoid whenever possible any sort of mediation in his encounters with life and the world. This radically independent approach would for the most part serve him well but at this juncture I think we see it in its most tiresome form where it actually threatens to do him damage.

He kept mostly to himself during his Atlantic crossing, reading a lot by day and walking the deck in the evening when he loved to watch "the sinister phosphorescent life light a trail in the wake of the ship". He made friends with a German family who were travelling on to Rome once they arrived in Naples and Chambers travelled there with them, absorbing his first impressions of the older European landscape as it flashed by the train window. That "rawness" of the North American and Mexican landscapes which had made him feel so "uneasy" was not a problem in the old world. In Europe everything had been thoroughly man-handled: "The landscape was wonderful. It did not feel new nor simply self-possessed. Something of the humanity of centuries had rubbed off on it. It was not threatening."

In Rome his shipboard friends helped him secure lodgings and then they carried on north to Germany, leaving Chambers with a few tips and suggestions about how to make his way and what to check out but otherwise completely on his own in a strange land. Chambers stayed on in Rome for a couple of months, going out for extensive sketching walks each day, taking in the streets and piazzas with their spectacular fountains and the riversides and the racehorses going through their paces down at the Villa Borgesa, and then returning to his tiny rented apartment each night to work on half-length self-portraits and still lifes. While he doubtless absorbed a lot of details and fresh scenes during his daytime rambles, he wasn't making much use of them in his evening routine which was identical (even down to sitting on the edge of a bed as he sketched out his likeness in a mirror) to that which he pursued back in London. Perhaps it was still too early. Regarding his stay in Rome, Chambers wrote another one of those-too-naïve-to-believe paragraphs in his autobiography:

"One day I came up a long, modern looking avenue. It looked new and clean and only for pedestrians. At the end of it I could see a huge domed building and huge pillars enclosing a large circular plaza. It was immense. St. Peter's Cathedral and the work of Raphael. [These likely would have included his immense 16th century masterpiece, *The School of Athens*; for most people, a highlight of any tour of the art treasures of St. Peter's and The Vatican.] I didn't care for Raphael, but I went inside the cathedral and stared up at some wall paintings. It was dark and cold inside and the ceiling was very high. I never saw the ceiling. I came out. Years later, it came to me: Michelangelo; the Sistine Chapel. But then Rome was behind me and I had missed that part of it."[20]

Ross Woodman at first seems inclined to believe that Chambers really didn't know what he was missing during his flying visit to perhaps the single greatest repository of classical art in the Western world. "He's the only person I've ever known who went into the Sistine Chapel and never looked up," Woodman told me incredulously. But then he added a few more words, suggesting that perhaps there was more going on here than ignorance. "I was outraged at the way he treated Europe initially. How could anyone go into the Sistine Chapel and not look at the ceiling? How could you do that? When you're in there, everyone else around you is looking up."

His agent and good friend, Nancy Poole, believes the oversight (or should that be undersight?) was more loaded than that. "Visiting the Sistine Chapel and not looking up," I asked her. "What was Jack expressing there?"

"His orneriness," she replied, with a weary sort of growl in her voice.

In a 1973 interview with Avis Lang, Chambers recalled how belligerent he could be when it came to acknowledging other artists, saying that when he was younger and was asked whose art he liked, he would often answer, "Nobody's but my own."[21] Nancy Poole remembers him dropping into her gallery on some sort of business when another artist's work was being displayed and disdainfully sniffing the air; "As much as to say, 'Why do you bother with this?' Oh yes, he had all the necessary arrogance that an artist must have."

And we've also seen repeated instances of his wariness about allowing himself to be influenced by other artists, dead or alive. But after five years' intensive study of art at various schools, not to mention his freelance plundering of glossy art books from the London Public Library, is it even remotely credible that Chambers could've stood in that space and not known what was overhead? If indeed he didn't look up, I, like Poole, believe it was an act of negative will, not ignorance.

Chambers had travelled to Europe because he felt that his art education was incomplete and lacking any sort of classical foundation but for the first few months over there, he wasn't taking any sort of action to address or correct that. At least to start, his modus operandi seemed to be to hurl himself into the deep end of Europe and drink in whatever impressions came his way by purest happenstance and then worry about digesting those or putting together some sort of plan for getting that education once he'd seen a few things for himself and acclimatised himself to the place.

And speaking of matters climatic, towards the end of November in Rome, Chambers' Canadian-made inner barometer was out of sync with his environment and he felt a powerful physical need to experience snow and cooler weather. Following up on another contact he'd received from his German shipmates, Chambers headed for higher and more northern ground by travelling to the outskirts of the town of Graz in Austria.

There he lived in utter old world rusticity for about a month with a woman named Bertha who owned a ramshackle two-storey farmhouse outside of town where she lived with her two teenaged children, her mother and her aunt, all of whom she provided for by teaching English. Chambers took over an unheated out-kitchen to use as his studio and finished a number of paintings and sketches there, including a gentle 1953 graphite sketch of Bertha from behind, her hair held in place by a kerchief tied under her chin, which was given to the Art Gallery of Ontario by the Chambers family in 2007 and featured in that Gallery's 2011–12 retrospective. The artist earned his keep by chopping wood and cleaning the floors and helping out when the town butcher came around to slaughter two of the goats that Bertha raised. This was an experience that made a very deep impression on his mind and was vividly recalled in his autobiography:

"The first one he smacked on the forehead with the butt of an axe. I have never heard a sound like the one this stricken kid made. It was a very high-pitched scream of absolutely pure and helpless surprise. As a witness I felt that something in me had been violently assaulted. The butcher took the other kid into the shed and there was no sound except the smack of the axe. Later, we took the butchered animals in a box on a sleigh to have sausages made at a shop downtown."[22]

One calls to mind here Chambers' mesmerised boyhood sighting from the York Street Bridge of a drowned child being fished out of the Thames River. And one also looks ahead to the use he would make in his paintings and his films of creatures that are put down as nuisances or slaughtered for food or religiously sacrificed for the expiation of sin. Of course, any thinking being finds death troubling and compelling but with Chambers that dark fascination seemed to run even deeper. Indeed, he confessed in a 1971 article by an anonymous writer from *The Sarnia Observer*, that he had long found death strangely attractive.

"I can say that from my very early teens, I had the feeling of death being something that I really looked forward to. That wasn't that I wanted to end my life, but it was something that was going to come at some unknown moment and it was going to be a completely different, altogether 'other' experience."[23]

A few years before that, when a CBC TV film crew came to London in 1966 to film a report on the city's lively arts scene, Chambers (along with Greg Curnoe and James Reaney) was part of a coterie of artists and hangers-on who assembled around a table at the York Hotel for an interview with host William Ronald. In one rather jarring segment of their conversation, Chambers coolly gazed at Ronald (an abstract artist of some reknown and decked out in an ascot) and asked him matter-of-factly: "Do you think a person should have the opportunity to die on TV? . . . A lot of people don't want to die alone, so this is an opportunity to die observed by all your fellow men."

By early January of 1954 Chambers' inner barometer had been restored to some sort of equilibrium and deciding he had had quite enough of winter, he said his farewells to Bertha and her kin and boarded a train for the sunnier climes of France. He fell into conversation and played a few rounds of chess with a priest, who, hearing that Chambers was looking for a good art academy, recommended the one in Vienna. "'Where is that?' I asked," wrote Chambers. "He pointed back the way we had come. 'It's here in Austria,' he said. Once again I had suffered from a lack of information. 'Well, we're going the wrong way now,' I said, and we played some more."

Chambers may have been unaware that Vienna was in Austria or that the world's most celebrated religious mural was situated just over his head while visiting the Sistine Chapel, but as his train pulled into Cannes he tells us, "I knew that [Pablo] Picasso lived in Vallauris. It is a village a few kilometres above Cannes. Perhaps he'll teach me something, I thought, and I walked up to Vallauris."[24]

Arriving at the great man's walled villa in the evening, Chambers was informed by the porter in the gatehouse that Picasso was away in Nice. Chambers wasn't sure he believed that and rented a room in Vallauris for the night, returning to the estate the next morning before nine with a package of freshly purchased sausage to distract the Great Dane that patrolled the grounds. Throwing the meat to the dog, Chambers scaled the wall at the back of the house and knocked at a screen door.

For a 1970 Saturday feature for *The London Free Press* (at the time of his first retrospective at the Art Gallery of Ontario, a show which had travelled from the Vancouver Art Gallery) Chambers recalled his encounter with Picasso to Lenore Crawford: "In a couple of minutes Picasso came out in his underwear and sort of said in French, 'What the hell are you doing here?'"

More frightened of Picasso's demeanour than the Great Dane's, Chambers haltingly tried to summon up enough scraps of French language to let the older man know that he was an aspiring artist just over from Canada in search of a good art school. This seemed to soften Picasso's wrath and the older artist laughed a little, saying, "Go to the school in Barcelona," and "Come back later this afternoon and we can talk."

Then, incredibly (and Crawford's account makes this much more clear than Chambers' own retelling of it in his autobiography) Chambers did not return in the afternoon for that extended talk with Picasso – an opportunity most aspiring artists would've killed for: "But I told him I was in a hurry. So I went down to the train station. I think I must have felt I was closer to where I was going and I wanted to keep on."[25]

Nor did he take the older artist's advice. Yes, he took the train to Barcelona and stayed there for two days but he never bothered to check out the school that Picasso recommended. Then, on a bit of a whim, he took a boat ride over to Majorca where he marvelled at the lushness of the grass that seemed to cover the island like a carpet.

So if he didn't take his advice and didn't even take up the great man's offer to return for a more extensive conversation, then why did Chambers go calling on Pablo Picasso at all?

Nowhere else in his writing does Chambers cite Picasso as an influence or a figure he particularly looked up to or might wish to consult for advice. But at that time Picasso unquestionably was the best-known living artist in the world; simultaneously the most famous and the most notorious, the most admired and the most reviled. On reflection I have come to consider Chambers' assault on Casa Picasso as a kind of bookend to his snubbing of the world's most famous classical artist in the Sistine Chapel. In his autobiography Chambers presented the 'visit' to Picasso as a kind of homage being paid but I find it hard to construe it as such considering that he, in effect, broke into the place, caught out the old man in his underwear and then stood him up, rejecting his invitation to return for a private audience.

Indeed, as Ross Woodman said, the way he was treating Europe was utterly outrageous. Within three months of setting foot on European soil this aggressive little upstart from London, Ontario had managed to beard the world's foremost artistic lions – both ancient and modern – in their very own dens. Now, with these little gestures of defiance out of the way, would Chambers be able to stop flitting about and get down to acquiring that classical education he'd crossed an ocean to find?

At Majorca, Chambers told Lenore Crawford, "I lived in a cove where in winter there were just a few fishermen and myself. I'd bicycle into town and get provisions and it was in Majorca I ran into a storekeeper who sold me a brochure with illustrations and photographs in it of The Royal Academy [the Escuela Central de Bellas Artes de San Fernando] in Madrid. When I saw that I knew that I had got my sights on what it was I hadn't been able to see before. So I was Madrid-bound from that minute and I left Majorca almost immediately."

In mid-march of 1954 Chambers handed over the rent for a nine-foot square room in one of Madrid's poorer neighbourhoods in the north end. He would make the odd trek to other countries and regions of Spain but he would continue to rent that tiny room for the next eight years. He finally had a home base and found he had about two months to prepare himself to take the two-week entrance drawing exam at the Escuela Central in early June; an exam which only 40 of some 350 applicants would pass. Chambers signed on for a cram course at a private drawing academy run by a friend; a course that was geared specifically to the Escuela Central's expectations. He augmented these classes by going day after day to a museum of plaster reproductions, El Casson, to sketch full-size reproductions of ancient Egyptian, Greek, Roman and Renaissance sculptures. At first Chambers thought he was making much more progress than he actually was:

"I considered [the El Casson] a real service and used it daily. I had no idea that this method exists and was required practice. I carried on my approach of starting somewhere in the middle and working out. Often there would be insufficient space on the paper to get the whole object in. My forms would be incomplete; my shading tones were varied but produced no volumes. Some parts of the drawing were obviously more worked than others. Still the sense of being myself seemed preferable to the impersonal, angular and schematic lines on the drawing paper of others around me. I felt that they had either lost their soul or had none. My sense of myself was a tough hound to lose. If I lost the sense of my own worth, what would be left? I still had not understood that all this impersonal schematic scaffolding was the means one used to get to a desired end. I had as yet little inclination of what that desired end could be since I didn't possess the means of approaching it."[26]

Aspiring students took the entrance exam in what were called 'shifts' – groups of about 40 students who were gathered into a room with easels set up and when an obscuring sheet was grandly yanked away from a cast figure sculpture (for Chambers' shift it was a figure by the 4th century BC Greek sculptor Praxateles) they set to work to earn their place in the school. Chambers was so confident of success and so ignorant of classical practices that the only tool he used throughout the examination was a piece of charcoal. All around him other Academy applicants made use of "the required aids: sandpaper to point the charcoal, a string with a weight on the end with which to arrive at an absolute vertical plumb line, various cloths and difuminos [paper cylinders] for shading, and soft erasers." Watching the progress of the other applicants over the course of the two weeks, Chambers came to realize well before the examination's end that he wasn't half so qualified as these other aspirants and, indeed, he did not make the cut.

Conferring and joining forces with another student, an English girl, who also failed to win a pass in one of the other shifts, she and Chambers decided to take the entrance exam at the Escuela Superior de Bellas Artes de San Carlos in Valencia. Those exams were being held in August and – provided they passed that one, of course – they could then have their matricula transferred to the Escuela Central in Madrid where they could start taking classes in late October. In preparation for the August exam in Valencia, Chambers went back to El Casson and sketched plaster casts from the moment the museum opened its doors, until closing time and he now brought with him all the artist's tools he'd formerly eschewed:

"I put my precious feelings aside and bore down. By August I had the method under control. Now that I possessed some technique, the possibilities opened before me. Two weeks later, I came back from Valencia and enrolled as an official student in the academy."[27] Chambers doesn't tell us whether his compatriot in this ingenious plot to use one school's exams to win entry to another school, made the cut as well.

Chambers studied and worked at the Escuela Central for the next five years. Always there was a three-hour painting class first thing in the morning and a two-hour drawing class every night. The afternoons were taken up with two other classes and over his time at the Madrid school these included modelling in clay, anatomy, art history, pedagogy, techniques, design, engraving, mural painting and restoration. Over his first winter at the Escuela, his money started to run low and he took on part time work, three nights a week, teaching English at Madrid's Marigold Institute.

Chambers' battle to put aside his own 'precious feelings' wasn't won in a single stroke. Sometimes he worried that by submitting to this strict artistic regimen, he might actually be brutalizing his own sensibility and replacing his own genuine inspiration with cold-blooded systematization. Conceivably, he feared that he might end up at the end of his classical education as a remarkably adept hack. Usually he understood that what he was doing was expanding and tempering his set of skills and that this was a good thing to do; that at the conclusion of all this training, his soul would still be there quite as intact as it ever was, and he would now be equipped with more and better ways of expressing it than ever before.

But then he'd forget that for a while and find himself kicking against the regimen that most of the time he knew he wanted and needed. Even well into his second year, his old wilfulness and personal preferences would still erupt from time to time and get in the way, holding him back from progress and truly fruitful development. He gives a humorous description of one of his later breakthroughs in his autobiography:

"Then it happened in the painting class one morning. My paintings, though very finished, lacked the rich impasto and bold colouring of some of the better students. A substitute professor walked in one day when we were at work on the portrait of some gypsy facsimile, and said to me, 'Get some colour into it.' He took my brush and began to mess around with my work. You sonofabitch, I thought, you'd better come up with something good. He didn't, but he made me conscious again of my being precious about my work. I had learned by now that the violation of this preciousness was not an abandoning of myself, of my feelings for my work, but that it was a stretching of my capabilities to encompass more. From that morning, and for the next two years, painting became an exercise in trial and error. I would take a painting to the point where I had learned something, then I would paint it out and start again from what I had learned. It took me a good two years to work out some kind of system whereby I could achieve consistent results. Upon such results I would wipe out and build further."[28]

It undoubtedly helped him stick to his path when he received his first grades in the spring of 1955 and was awarded two first class marks and a sculpture tuition scholarship. Then that fall, Montreal's Elizabeth T. Greenshields Memorial Foundation awarded him $900 in their inaugural scholarship – nine tenths of the stash he'd raised to initially come over to Europe – which greatly eased his budgeting difficulties for at least the next year. The Greenshields Foundation would top that up the next year with an additional $500 and in the summer of

1956, Chambers earned $500 from a sale of his own works that he organized in Stoke-by-Clare, England, where he'd lived and worked from July to September.

Chambers had originally written to the sculptor Henry Moore to see if he needed an assistant. Moore already had all the assistants he needed but instead of just saying 'no', he very kindly put Chambers in touch with a painter in Suffolk who offered him room and board and the use of a studio for three pounds a week. Chambers taught art classes to a group of local amateurs while there and at the end of his season in England, mounted a show and sale in a 14th century monastery to which amateurs and professionals alike contributed. Chambers got to meet Henry Moore, John Nash, Graham Sutherland and Michael Ayston – all of whom contributed works to the show and thereby greatly increased the amount of attention the show received. Feeling positively flush by the time he got back to Madrid and the Escuela Central, Chambers was able to give up his teaching gig at the Marigold Institute.

But then he took on something else that surprised a lot of the people who knew him best. Jack Chambers joined the Roman Catholic Church:

"About this time, I took steps to answer my need for some spiritual discipline. I found that a lot of my energy was being used up on pastimes that did nothing for my peace of mind and nothing to further my work. One of the reasons I became a Catholic at this time was that moral rules provided me with a tangible spiritual discipline that I could work at, in much the same way that the academy provided standards to direct my anxieties into specific problems to be solved. I set about trying to put my house in order. However, in adhering to moral rules, I was working on the assumption that the returns from such a discipline would purify my vision. I believed that serious obedience to the rules governing spiritual growth would have the effect of gradually cleansing the so-called window of perception. The glory of the existing world would, in the process, be revealed and passed into the work. If one sought first things first, the rest would come of its own. But this discipline did not pursue as its end the love of God, but rather it pursued, through the laws of Moses, the love of art."[29]

As the above note makes clear, Chambers' primary motivation in becoming a Catholic was – like just about everything else in his life – artistic. He saw the Catholic Church as an agency that would help him to push himself harder, perceive more clearly, and to hone his skills. As he told Dennis Young in a 1970 interview, "Catholicism to me was one way of putting a harness on the horse and getting the animal to work for an end. It was a way of harnessing a lot of energies, a lot of anxieties."[30]

Publicly Chambers downplayed any sense of great moral urgency behind his decision to join the Church. One gets the sense from what he wrote and said in interviews about this period that perhaps he was drinking a little too much beer again and not doing such a great job of marshalling his resources and time but that he wasn't overly concerned about the state of his soul. However, to his closest friends he was more forthcoming. He did indeed harbour a very serious moral concern at this time.

Three of his oldest friends, Val McInnes, Susan Downe and Ross Woodman, all recall Chambers telling them about an experience he'd had in Spain in 1956 that shook him to the very core of his being, making him question what kind of man he was or might become if he didn't get the kind of help that the Church could uniquely provide. Susan Downe spoke to me about a conversation she and Chambers had where she took issue with him – thinking surely he was being a little melodramatic – when he told her it had been absolutely 'essential' that he join the Catholic Church:

"At the time – it's hard for me to imagine because I don't ordinarily do this to anybody – but I really quizzed him on that. I thought that didn't seem to fit at all for him. But he said, 'Lookit, I was wandering around half starved, half drunk, and one day I almost pushed a passed-out bum into a river to drown. He was passed out . . . he was on this slope just above the river . . . I almost did that. I almost killed somebody.' And that got his attention. And so he said he joined because he needed the discipline."

In 1957, as the result of a call she made to the Escuela Central looking for an English-speaking student who could act as a chauffeur and guide to Spain's national museum of art, the Prado, Chambers had met Peggy Walker, a wealthy, wheelchair-bound American woman who did work for the World Health Organization. She took an interest in Chambers and bought some of his earliest paintings and employed him again as a chauffeur in 1960 for a two-month inspection of leper colonies in Spain; a tour of duty that was bracketed by sight-seeing jaunts in France and Portugal.

Chambers picked up two scholarships in 1958, the State Prize for figure painting and the Paular Scholarship for landscape painting. The latter prize constituted three month's all expenses-paid residency in a small palace that had been converted into dormitories and studios in Segovia, about 60 miles north-west of Madrid. He would call that long summer in Segovia, "my most enjoyable months in Spain," and would tell Lenore Crawford in 1970, "Even now when the spring or fall comes around my nostalgia is for that place."

In addition to a well-appointed room and studio space, Chambers recalled, "The food was first-rate home cooking and abundant. After breakfast everyone made his way out into the landscape to paint until noon. Then lunch, siesta and back outside again. During those three months I really came to love the Castilian landscape."[31]

Not too surprisingly, the next summer after wrapping up his final year's study at the Escuela Central, he longed once again to get out of Madrid and back into the Spanish countryside. At the recommendation of a painter friend,

Jose Luis Balaguero, he travelled to the town of Chinchon, 30 kilometres south of Madrid and based himself there for the final year and a half (including two winters) of his residency in Spain. If the landscape around Chinchon was just as ravishing to his eyes as that around Segovia, the accommodation was decidedly inferior:

The house he and Balaguero shared was entirely constructed of cement. The interior walls had been whitewashed but the cement was soft and crumbly, meaning the place was dusty during dry spells and exuded damp throughout the winter and during rainy spells. The whole town was perched on the side of a hill and cement retaining walls were in place to prevent the different buildings from collapsing into one another. During one doozer of a thunderstorm a neighbour's retaining wall came crashing down onto their plot.

Chambers and Balaguero split their house into two sections, so that each had their own clearly defined living and studio space. Balaguero was primarily around through the summers and would otherwise come and go, leaving Chambers on his own for long stretches of time. When Balaguero was around, their life together tended to be very convivial and was regularly punctuated with day long feasts that took a day to prepare for and – because of the quantity of wine consumed – a day to recover from.

Chambers himself was travelling back and forth to Madrid a fair bit himself, particularly on weekends, to visit with his wife-to-be, Olga Sanchez Bustos, whom he met at a birthday party early in 1959. Born the fifth of six children to Spanish parents living in Argentina where her father had business in the timber trade, Olga lived in an Argentine boarding school run by a convent of nuns from the age of six to eighteen and then when the family came back to Spain she lived with her younger sister, Margarita in a residence that was also run by nuns. In those first months and years after joining the Church, one can only assume that Olga's Catholicism was part of her strong and immediate attraction to him even though her faith – not to mention her housing arrangements – made the prospect of Chambers being able to scramble over a roof and slip into her bedchamber decidedly slim.

As marvellous as the place was in the summer, during the winters, life in Chinchon could get a little grim and this was reflected in some of the dark and menacing paintings that Chambers surprised himself by producing at this time. "The winters were miserable in the house. There was no heat and the cold was bitter. Perhaps the unliveable conditions of the place contributed to the kind of paintings that began to emerge. They were bleak and were born behind my eyes. They owed almost nothing to the reality of sunshine and fresh air. They proceeded from regions within me of dark and brooding emotions. It was as if, after five years of training, I had acquired a means whereby these emotions in objective forms could step up and be noted. Before, without the means to escape me as things in themselves, they had simply caused confusion and a disturbing desire to be."[32]

Not helping his mood at this time, Chambers was back to teaching amateur painters – Air Force wives mostly – at the American air base in nearby Torrejon. Sarah Milroy speculated that the recently converted artist was also troubled at this time by God's silence. While he would later claim that he had only joined the Church for the sake of his art and not his soul, we know that between his love for Olga and his concerns about his own capacity for evil, there was something much more personally urgent at work in his religious identification than a desire for professional advancement. Perhaps during those dismal Chinchon winters, Chambers had dared to ask God for help with more than his painting and felt that his prayers were not being answered.

There certainly is something unmitigated and merciless about his paintings from those Chinchon winters. In his talk at the AGO at the time of the 2011-2012 Chambers retrospective, poet and author Christopher Dewdney (the youngest of Selwyn and Irene's sons) remembered being creeped-out as a young boy by one of these 'behind-the-eyes' paintings that his parents displayed in their house. Heavy on blacks and greys and browns, works such as *Man and Dog* (1959), *Flying Saint* (1960), and *Surrealist Composition* (1960) featured anguished, strangely proportioned and grotesquely over-muscled human and animal figures, a fierce dog with bared teeth, leering skulls and another face completely covered in gauze wrappings like a mummy.

By February of 1960, Chambers was more than ready for a change of scene – even though it couldn't have been a much happier one – when he was yanked out of his studio for two full months to act once again as chauffeur and translator with Peggy Walker on her W.H.O. tour of Spanish leper colonies. It was at this time that she bought *La Trilla*, a farm scene with two hefty plough horses front and centre being harassed by a dog; a painting Dennis Reid identifies as "probably the most upbeat image" of the gloomy Chinchon works. With the money from that sale on top of the chauffeuring gig, Chambers was able to give up the lease on his tiny Madrid apartment (really just a room) and buy a far more substantial flat of his own on the outskirts of the city.

Chambers spent the month of June with his family when Frank and Beatrice came over to visit his sister Shirley who had married and was living in Germany. The family toured through Germany, Switzerland and Bavaria (where Chambers adored visiting the palaces built by mad King Ludwig) and then came back to Spain via Italy where he visited the Biennale in Venice. While he loved Venice, the 30th Bienalle left him cold with its faddishness and sensationalism: "The Biennale looked like a carnival. Personalities were obviously laying claim to as much or more attention than the pavilions and getting it."[33]

As it turned out Chambers would only get to live in his new and more commodious flat for a year. In April of 1961 he was suddenly called back home to London, Ontario by the dismal news that his mother was now apparently dying. One imagines he must have derived some consolation from the memory of all the time he'd shared with his mother and his family just ten months before when they visited Europe. When Chambers left Madrid for Canada he thought he'd be back in Europe within the month. As it turned out his mother didn't die for another 15 months. But even then, except for vacations and a trip to sell off his Madrid flat and arrange for Olga to join him in Canada to wed and start their life together, he never would return to Spain to live.

Though he did not know it at the time, didn't even see it as a possibility, Chambers was about to move back to Canada for keeps. Much to his surprise, that 'puritanical' and 'utilitarian' land for which he had felt only 'indifference', had – like Chambers himself – changed for the better in the eight years he'd been away.

So what did Chambers get from Spain? Ross Woodman told me, "He had gained a vision of European training and what it meant to be an artist."

Nancy Poole told me, "I think Spain was terribly important. He saw a completely different way of life. He saw the light of the Mediterranean, which is quite different from here. During his time at the Academy he met other artists in varying degrees of advancement and one of whom he knew had great talent. [This would be the Madrid realist painter Antonio Lopez Garcia who reciprocated Chambers' admiration and influenced him as overtly as any artist would; particularly in his *Portrait of Marion and Ross Woodman* from 1961.] It was terribly important to him to have that kind of atmosphere as well as the great art that he had all around him."

"He went from being a raw Canadian to being a more knowledgeable human being about art and music," Poole continued. "You cannot be in Spain without learning about that. And cuisine. What does anybody learn when they go to Europe? I used to try to go every year to, as I said, refresh my eye. Our cities are incredibly ugly and the old cities are very beautiful. Architecture was important. And space – park space, avenue space – space was important. The demands of the people were different from a new country such as ours. All of that was important to making Jack Chambers."

According to his own account in that 1967 interview with Ross Woodman, Chambers said that in Spain, "I learned how to draw: not that anyone comes forward and tells you how to do it, but you learn by working a lot and observing those who already know how. The main thing for me was getting oriented, starting with a beginning, constructing the figure gradually and developing it from one stage to the next: discipline. Another thing was the gradual change in my own taste and sensibility. I underwent a series of births.

"The Castillian landscape was always impenetrable for me. It was something I desired to become by entering it but never could or never did. The land-scape was always a beautiful mystery: human odour seemed to reside in it so that a vista of several miles in that clear and machineless light seemed a particle of torso under a microscope. The hills were rubbed bare by wool and hands had touched every inch of them. There was an organism within an organism that appeared as landscape. But I knew I was not inside."

He had matured, he had seen a lot and made friends (and met a wife-to-be) who would sustain him for the rest of his life. He had unquestionably devel-oped skills and techniques as an artist and started to make real progress. He had won a number of prizes and scholarships, including the Paular Scholarship in Landscape Painting in 1958, and just one month before returning to Canada he landed his first one man show at Madrid's Lorca Galeria de Arte. But in spite of all these positive achievements and inroads, Chambers was beginning to realize that Spain was not a nut that he would ever be able to crack.

10

THE FACES OF LONG LOST FRIENDS

WHEN CHAMBERS left London in 1953, no artist in town had a studio of his own. That was starting to change by 1961 when he returned. Greg Curnoe's studio was up and running by then and other artists would soon step forward as well, determined to make a go of it in this indifferent burg.

"They all had the idea that you could live in London, you could be a painter and you could make a living," Nancy Poole said. "And certainly Greg and Jack proved that that could happen. You have to be ruthless to be able to do that and they did."

Chambers' old friend and mentor Selwyn Dewdney was running the Artists' Workshop and gave him work there teaching children and adults. In addition to his early champion Ross Woodman, poet (and later playwright) James Reaney was now teaching up at the University of Western Ontario as well. Originally from the Stratford area, Reaney came to London after a thankless stint of teaching literature to agricultural diploma students ('aggy dips', they were called for short) in Winnipeg. Back in a region of the country for which he felt a very strong attachment and identification, Reaney started up *Alphabet* Press to print fine art editions of poetry and a semi-annual arts magazine and asked Chambers to do the exquisite pointillist ink illustrations for his 20-page poem, *The Dance of Death in London, Ontario*.

If there was a defining centre to the burgeoning London art scene at that time, it was Greg Curnoe. Characteristically, he warmly welcomed Chambers back to London and exhorted him to give the city another chance. Throughout his career Curnoe was unfailingly encouraging to other artists of every stripe and never entertained dark thoughts of infringement or jealousy. He was always trying to expand the range of artistic goings on in his home town and to this end, with Chambers and a handful of other London artists (Brian Dibb, Larry Russell, Tony Urquhart, Bernice and Don Vincent) he opened the first of London's artist-run art galleries, the Region Gallery, in November of 1962, which would be succeeded by the 20/20 Gallery in 1966 and then The Forest City Gallery which still operates today.

Curnoe said that on his very first visit to his studio, Chambers seemed determined to shake off the old world and re-immerse himself in the new, re-questing that Curnoe play him some rock 'n roll records and particularly tak-ing note of Fats Domino. Curnoe made that comment in 1989 at the Toronto International Experimental Film Congress where all of Chambers' films were being shown for the first time in years. Some snippets from that talk give us a peerless glimpse into how Chambers appeared at that time to one of his sharp-est observers:

"Jack Chambers was one of my best friends for a period of about fifteen years. He was a complex person, perhaps the most complex person I knew. His complexity took the form of great personal privacy. His closest friends didn't know what he was doing and important personal decisions and actions would be taken without their knowledge."

This insight would be seconded by Chambers' good friend, Susan Downe, a retired bio-energetic analyst and poet and writer who was crushed when she didn't receive an invitation to Jack and Olga's wedding on the last day of August in 1963. "He compartmentalized his friendships and so for example, I wasn't asked to that wedding. I expected to be. We were already close friends. He'd told me all about Olga so I felt I was already part of the wedding. I was greatly saddened by that but Jack didn't seem to notice."

"He was a good actor," Curnoe continued. "And this, combined with his sense of humour and his willingness to use his sense of humour anywhere, added to the complexity of his personality, and to the varied reactions and per-ceptions people had to him and about him. And I was no exception. It was hard to know when he wasn't serious."[34]

One of the most jarring examples of Chambers' knack for catching people off guard and confounding them – is he being funny or is he just really creepy? – is recounted by art historian and curator, Dennis Reid, at their very first meet-ing:

"Jack Chambers had a memorable, if somewhat unusual, personality. I first met him in the fall of 1966 when I was a graduate student in art history at the University of Toronto. The encounter took place in the men's washroom on the sixth floor of the building that housed the Department of Fine Art. I was using one of the two side-by-side urinals when a stranger came in and engaged the other one. I finished first and, brought up well by my mother, crossed the room to wash my hands. The stranger came over while I was still scrubbing, stood by the sink until he had caught my attention, then declared in a clear, strong voice, 'My dink is clean.' Taken aback, I couldn't help staring at his face, where, after a couple of seconds, I thought I saw just the hint of a twinkle. Then he turned and walked out."[35]

When considering Jack Chambers, Curnoe said it was helpful to keep in mind Oscar Wilde's dictum: "the true artist is known by the use he makes of what he annexes and he annexes everything."

"Jack was very generous," Curnoe said. "He was always able to laugh at himself. He did not suffer fools gladly and was impatient with social events unless they were of some use to him . . . He had the moves of a natural athlete. He was always sniffing and had a lot of allergies. He had acquired some Spanish figures of speech and always inserted 'no' as an Ontarian would use 'eh'." Perhaps his European experience also explained why he habitually and uniquely called Curnoe, 'Gregor'.

Particularly touching somehow is a segment from Curnoe's talk which shows us Chambers not as a smooth operator or an enigmatic joker or even as an artist but in an utterly unguarded moment of enthusiasm: "Jack and I watched a lot of hockey games together," Curnoe said, "and we attended a lot of closed-circuit boxing telecasts of heavyweight matches at the London Arena and London Gardens. We both followed George Chuvalo's career with anguish. During those bouts, Jack would pound me on the shoulder as things got exciting."

These two artists, Curnoe and Chambers, always regarded as the reigning titans of the London art scene, made a fascinating tag team. They were so utterly different in both their talent and nature – Curnoe the affable, shaggy, lightning-quick cartoonist and iconoclast and Chambers the more private, saturnine, ever-thoughtful classicist cum realist – that they posed no threat or competition to one another and therefore got along like nobody's business. They could even work on the very same subject and in the very same room (most famously in their contemporaneous paintings of Victoria Hospital) taking their sightings on the very same day from the roof of Curnoe's studio just across the river from the hospital, and not worry about ripping each other off or getting in each other's way.

I asked Nancy Poole: If that circle of fellow artists hadn't been here – Jamie, Selwyn, Greg – do you think Jack would've stayed here or do you think he would've returned to Spain?

"I've never thought of that," she admitted. "No. I think he would've stayed because he really felt love for the landscape of Middlesex County. Whether this is a genetic thing or not, I don't know but this is what he used to talk about. His horizons were very limited and that I realized when he went to Banff and he couldn't believe the Rockies. He knew nothing about the west and he was just overwhelmed by it but there are no paintings from there. He tried but no. But he loved south-western Ontario – the landscape – and I understand this because I do too. And remember he spent a summer in the south of England so he was acquainted with that wonderful landscape as well. But to answer your question, I think he would've stayed here. I think he felt deeply rooted in south-western Ontario."

And yet he didn't when he left, I pointed out.

"That's right. But that was the young man questing," Poole said. "This was different. Jack was different. He had changed."

Chambers thought he needed classical training to equip himself to master any project. He painstakingly crossed an ocean and gave up almost a decade of his life to acquire such skills and then discovered that while he had the techniques down cold, he was cut off from his own wells of inspiration. He could paint classically but he couldn't conceive or be inspired classically. For that he really did have to come back to the city and the people he'd jettisoned a decade before.

A couple of years after returning to Canada, Chambers told *The Toronto Star's* David Cobb that maybe there was a sort of artistic birthright that could only be tapped into in the place where an artist was born: "I'm interested in building up an alphabet of my own . . . in a realistic way that doesn't go back to the old stuff of a few years ago . . . Spain's a country with a golden age of art, a full breast to draw on . . . It was one of the things I envied most about their painters today, this continuous flow of tradition behind them all, and I think the best new realistic painting will come out of Spain . . . You're suckled off your own I suppose . . . If I'd been born in Spain, I might have been able to do it justice. I'd have felt it belonged to me. As it was, in that clear landscape with its browns and greys, I was a stranger and forever in a vast hurry."[36]

In his account from the autobiography of his return to Canada, Chambers writes of his quickening sense that maybe London was where he was supposed to be after all: "I had returned to Canada via New York, and took the N.Y. Central railway to St. Thomas and then a cab to London. It was while riding a city bus uptown that its slow smooth ride spoke to me of opportunity and comforts I could not expect in Spain. It was a feel for the place that produced my intention to stay on in London. It was also my home town, and there were spaces here along the river and in the landscape that had become mine years ago and continued to be so. The memory of such places multiplied the longer I remained so near them, and the images wedded to their presence surfaced in me like the faces of long lost friends. At this time, I discovered my own past, that of my parents and of their parents, in the likenesses preserved by photographic magic. I dug up all the photos I could find from both the McIntyre and Chambers sides of the family. I was to use these photos soon in my paintings."

Perhaps buoyed by his recent exhibition in Madrid, on his return to London via New York City, Chambers made an overture to a dealer there and was included in an opening group exhibition at the Forum Gallery in the Big Apple that fall and even sold one of his works, *Red Mount and Flowers* (1960) to the astute American collector, Joseph Hirshhorn.

Setting up his first London studio in Selwyn Dewdney's Artists' Workshop space (in a second storey on Dundas Street across from the Armouries) Chambers' first Canadian paintings in eight years were (not so surprisingly) drenched in Spanish influences. Though it was obviously a period of transition for the artist, there was nothing tentative about his approach or the speed with which he produced new work.

Dennis Reid describes one of the most spectacular of his 1961 paintings: *Slaughter of the Lamb* (1961) as the closest of these new London paintings to the work he was doing in Chinchon. "It evokes the traditional Spanish Easter slaughter of lambs in a hallucinatory explosion/implosion of creatures, land forms, and symbolic flowers and seeds, an almost overwhelming array of Spanish experiences, all intensely recalled, and all neatly contained within a finely crafted frame that is integral to the work."[37]

That same year he was commissioned by his subjects to paint the *Portrait of Marion and Ross Woodman* [Plate 5]. The likeness of his friends is excellent but their pose (standing next to each other behind a fence and looking straight out at the viewer) rather inappropriately calls to mind Grant Wood's *American Gothic*. (I say 'inappropriately' because it's hard to imagine anyone less likely to wield a pitchfork than Ross Woodman.) Rolling out behind the Woodmans is a stylized but unmistakably Spanish landscape of bare (except for one perfectly round fruit tree) undulating red, brown and orange hills underneath a narrow banner of dusky sky revealing a pale and waning quarter moon.

Visiting the Woodmans in the 1970s, Marion would always point out the weird positioning of her left hand with a somewhat crabbed baby finger that rests atop the fence. The source photograph for this work was actually a snap of the couple standing behind a high-backed wooden chair, with Ross's arm around Marion's shoulders and Marion's hand gripping the top of the chair. Chambers never liked what he was able to do with Marion's hand and quickly snapped a photo of Ross' mother's hand as she leaned out a car window and he used that hand (and that wedding ring) instead of Marion's for the finished painting.

Also because of the way Chambers had built up his gesso on the wooden panel on which he painted this portrait, there's a slight protuberance in the inner corner of Marion's left eye which, in certain lights, appears like a teardrop just waiting to cascade. Ross Woodman wrote in a 1969 article for *ArtsCanada* that the Spanish idiom of the portrait initially struck him as an "invasion" but that this soon passed and the painting ultimately "had the effect of stirring our life in the direction of art."

Chambers was ferociously productive during his first months back in Canada and soon established a relationship with Toronto dealer Av Isaacs who featured Chambers in a four-man show at the Isaacs Gallery in January of 1962. He also showed locally wherever he could, even placing work in the Annual Western Ontario Exhibition where he'd won his first big prize more than a decade before.

The plundered family photographs started turning up in Chambers' 1962 paintings such as *Messengers Juggling Seed* and *McGilvary County* and the 1963 ink pointillist work *Sunday Morning No. 1*. Again, the physical likenesses of his human subjects are superb, showing what a wonderful draughtsman Chambers had become. And the landscapes now are distinctly those of south-western Ontario. As befits departed spirits, these dead Canadian relatives occupy their landscape in a strangely un-integrated way – they "retained properties of levitation," is how Chambers described them – appearing at times almost like cut-out figures superimposed onto or even floating above the fields of south-western Ontario.

Matters familial were much on Chambers' mind not just because of the death of his mother in August of 1962 and the flood of photographs and memories that such a milestone unearths but because he was getting ready to start up a family of his own. At the same time as Chambers was artistically commemorating those who had gone before him, he was preparing the way to continue that line into the future.

Ross and Marion Woodman accompanied Chambers back to Madrid in the spring of '63 to sell off his flat and pop the big question to Olga. "Spain is an intensely Catholic culture," Ross Woodman told me. "And Olga was raised in that world and came out of a convent school and was deeply and profoundly Catholic without having to be or do anything about it – it was just the way it is. And we spent our visit with them there just going church to church to church, looking at crucifixes and some of them were very, very moving and all of them had stories attached to them about various miracles and how they cry on certain days and all of this was taken quite seriously."

Chambers returned to Canada an officially engaged man in June and Olga Bustos followed him here late in mid-August, their wedding taking place in the Lady Chapel of London's St. Peter's Cathedral Basilica on August 31, 1963 – one year after the death of his mother. Their first son was born in the spring of 1964.

Chambers' own Catholic fervour was waning at this time. Some say he'd stopped thinking of himself as Catholic at all during his time back in Canada up until the diagnosis when he returned to it with great urgency. I asked Nancy Poole what it must've been like for Olga to be yanked out of all that cultural, familial and religious grounding to come to Canada and marry Chambers.

"I would think it was simply ghastly," Poole replied. "He got her from the airport and brought her around for me to meet Olga. And I was relieved when I met her because her English was quite good. And I thought, 'Okay, that's not going to be a big problem.' And of course the next stop was at the Dewdneys. And thank God for Irene because she just took Olga under her wing completely."

Susan Downe was also on that tour of stops where an excited Chambers took his just arrived bride-to-be to show her off to his friends, though Downe recalls her English-speaking skills as being a little more perfunctory: "They visited here the first day she was in Canada and she had very little English and she was just so graceful as she always was. She never made a thing out of being uncomfortable. She had marvellous manners. [laughs] She learned English from Jack which meant that she said 'dese,' 'dose' and 'dem' quite a bit. His parents didn't talk that way so I don't know why he took that up. Olga stayed very close to Jack and close to home. Jack encouraged me and I'm sure other women – Irene [Dewdney] would be one – to make friends with her. She made friends in the Spanish-speaking community, I suppose partly through St. Michael's."

In 1964 Chambers was featured in a second group show at the Forum Gallery in New York City. Susan Downe and her husband went down to that show (as did Greg Curnoe and the Dewdneys) and she picked up a pointillist drawing, *Olga with John and Cornelia*, for $325. Olga's his wife, of course, John is his infant son (being held in Olga's arms) but 'Who is Cornelia?' I asked Susan Downe as she took me for a tour of the drawing.

"She was a Vanderbilt and she married a French man. Jack never knew her but he loved what he knew about her. For example, every time one of her sons would bring home a fiancé she would have her to lunch and she had this long rope of pearls and she would snip off a couple of feet for each new daughter-in-law. This is Olga. This is little John and this is a boy from the little village in Spain where Jack lived and this is his dog. We went to the opening of that show on Madison Avenue and it was a great lark. There was a garbage strike going on and I remember the garbage piled up in the streets. And I bought it there and I had to agree to let it go to other shows and then I got it back later on."

Olga with John and Cornelia would be developed three years later (at the beginning of Chambers' 'Silver' period) into the much larger colour-muted painting, *Olga Visiting Mrs. V.* Shortly after receiving his fatal diagnosis, Chambers told Susan Downe that he might want to buy back the drawing, "He came here one day after the diagnosis and he said, 'I want you to sell me that back,' because he wanted something to leave the boys. So I said, 'Let's talk tomorrow.' At that point he didn't have a great body of work yet. He still had the big ones ahead of him. I thought about it and since he'd said it was for the boys, I said, 'If you die and you don't have something else to give the boys, I'll make sure the boys get it. If you live and have a lot of work, I have no intention of giving it up.' And as you can see, I didn't have to give it up."

No matter how engaged he was in the studio, now with a wife and a son to provide for, Chambers found it necessary to beef up his income by accepting every teaching gig that came his way. He wouldn't receive his first Canada Council grant until 1965 and then would subsequently be awarded some sort of Council prize every year for the rest of his life. Two stories about Chambers as a teacher indicate that these tutelary duties were undertaken with a bit of an attitude and half a heart.

Greg Curnoe recalled that, "In the early 1960s the head of the art department at the H.B. Beal Technical School in London was seriously hurt in a car accident and Jack Chambers was hired as a substitute teacher. On his first day, another teacher introduced him to the class by saying, 'This is Mr. Chambers. He is teaching in place of Mr. Ariss. Behave yourselves and let's not have any problems.' When the other teacher left, Jack said, 'My name is Jack, and that guy's a bit of a prick, isn't he?' He and the class got along very well but the other teacher was not amused."[38]

Victoria-based textile artist, Carole Sabiston was living in London in the fall of 1964 and told me about taking Chambers' oil painting course at H.B. Beal Technical School in the evenings: "So I went along and got signed up. I was all excited. I was what . . . all of 24 years of age? It was in one of those upper floors, crammed with easels and for the six or eight weeks or whatever it was he brought in a model, fully clothed, usually wonderful characters, male and female, and they just sat there and dozed. He'd probably just paid for their dinner or something. I don't know. So we'd set up our easels and get to work. There were a few of us young 'uns, shall I say, who were really keen to work on our painting. But there were a lot of retirees who were there to do a picture to put over their fireplace and so they'd bring in calendars of a snow scene or sunset or something like that. Jack was very sweet. He never lectured us. He just went around and said, 'Oh, that's nice, Mrs. So and So and dah dee dah.' He might say, 'You need a bit more orange here,' and he'd pick up their brush and dab some orange onto it. Or with a snow scene, he'd say, 'A little bit of blue and that white would be nice here.' When it came to the few of us who were young students who really wanted to learn, when we'd say, 'Can you give me a little bit of criticism?' he'd only say, 'Oh, you're doing just fine.' He would not do it. He didn't want to be there. I could tell that. And it was much easier for him just to putter around and put dabs of orange paint on little old ladies' paintings. He didn't want to discourse with us at all. And why should he? Because he had his own mind going. I can see that. I don't think he was a born teacher. The only reason to do that was for the money."

Unlikely as it seems (in that it was a commission and not a work he instigated on his own) I think the first time Chambers managed to pull together what he could do with both landscape and human figures into the same frame was in his 1963 portrait for Nancy Poole. In his talk at that 1989 film symposium, Greg Curnoe tells a wonderful story about another of Chambers' portrait commissions from around this time that didn't go so well, though the artist managed to charm his way through to a less than disastrous finish:

"In the 1960s he got a few portrait commissions, which helped him to earn a living. Nobody sold many paintings in those days. One commission I remember was for a retiring dean at the University of Western Ontario. Jack worked from a photograph in which the dean looked slightly ridiculous with a lopsided grin and a noticeably crooked tie, a striped tie. The portrait was very faithful to the photograph, and some of us wondered how he would ever get the university to accept it. Tony Urquhart, the resident artist at the university, was with him when he went to the meeting that was to examine the portrait. And to this day, he doesn't know how Jack managed to sell them the painting. It was hung in a closet until Jack became better known, at which time it was taken out and displayed more prominently."[39]

Poole had taken a drawing course from Chambers a couple of years earlier through the Artists' Workshop and described herself as "a most inept student." But she considered her first meeting with Chambers to discuss the possibility of a portrait which would ultimately be entitled *Summer Behind the House* to be her real introduction to the man:

"I remember the formal, initial meeting which I think was at the Artists' Workshop. And of course that was arranged through Selwyn Dewdney because I said to Selwyn, 'I would like to have a portrait done of my daughter and me and who would you suggest? I want a London artist.' And he suggested Jack Chambers. I had seen a work that he had done at the Dewdneys' before '63 – a work that he had won a prize for, actually – but I really wasn't familiar with any portraiture. But of course he didn't do portraits. No good artist does. So we spoke and he said 'no', he was not interested in doing portraiture, even though I knew he needed money. And then he came back and said, 'Do you have any statues in your garden?' And I said, 'No.' He was big on statuary at that time – I think that came out of his Madrid background. So he said, 'Well, let me come and see the landscape.' So he did and of course he was sold because the field behind our house was really lovely."

Poole, her daughter, Andrea, and their dog, Betsy, took Chambers out into the open field behind their home at the northernmost end of London – a field that has since been developed and includes the site of the elementary school named after the artist. Chambers took a lot of photographs and agreed to undertake the commission.

"In terms of giving Jack that first commission," I said to Poole, "it almost sounds, for lack of a better phrase, like a pig in a poke."

"It was."

"When did you know you had something special?"

"I didn't see anything until it was done. It was a beautiful summer, a beautiful July. He'd come every morning at the same hour, set his easel up in the same spot and paint outside all day. Then he would put a thing over it, carry it home and work on it at night. At the same time he was working on a bigger edition of the landscape with a portrait of Olga. [*Olga Near Arva*, 1963] It's the same landscape but it's longer and deeper. It's superb. These are the only two works to the best of my knowledge that were done in the open air. And in my opinion you can see it. The painting gives off light. And so does *Olga Near Arva*. This was the man's genius. I was thrilled. My mother was dying of cancer at the time and she was at our home upstairs and it was a dreary November when he finished this and I took it upstairs and all she said was, 'It's like sunlight coming into the room.' And she was dead right. And that thrilled Jack because there was nothing more authentic than my mother saying that."

In 1964, just before John would begin to crawl (which could prove dangerous in their second floor apartment on Cathcart Street in South London) Chambers moved his young family into a home of their own on Lombardo Ave. (named after big band leader, Guy) at the other end of town. "The house was a two-storey red brick with three bedrooms upstairs and two bedrooms in the basement. It was in North London and had a lovely fenced-in backyard, big with lots of shade. I was looking for a house we could afford, something around $8,000. We certainly couldn't afford this place, which cost almost three times more than I felt I could cope with. So we bought it."[40]

The house was just a few lots north of Gibbons Park (one of the largest and most glorious of London's riverside parks) situated within easy walking distance of the University of Western Ontario and the homes of his two professorial friends, Ross Woodman and James Reaney, as well as Susan Downe who remembers, "That began another phase of our friendship including our children because our son Bill was born about that time too. Those bad boys played together for years and were best friends. They used to go between our houses by going on the roofs between our houses. I found that out later from neighbours whose shingles were falling off."

Chambers' description above makes it sound like the move to Lombardo Ave. was recklessly imprudent but it was actually quite fiscally shrewd on his part as he was able to defer a lot of the costs of carrying a mortgage by renting out the basement bedrooms to student boarders. In terms of its suburban uprightness and the tony cachet of the neighbourhood, Chambers' home was quite unlike that of any other London artist. Greg Curnoe, for instance (and at about the same time) made his first real home out of a derelict printing factory in a working class neighbourhood and largely undertook the building's conversion himself. The move was one more way – like his more discreet appearance and his smoother demeanour – that Chambers set himself apart from his more overtly bohemian colleagues in the arts community.

And then midway through 1964, right around the time he started to shoot the first (and gentlest) of his avant-garde films, *Mosaic* (a slightly surreal meditation on birth and death and the fragility of life which wasn't finished and released until 1966) Chambers' painting style began to radically change. The colours were no longer as bright or were isolated to one section of the canvas or were done away with altogether. The images became flatter and expressed less volume and depth. As Chambers himself put it in his autobiography: "The light areas and the shadowed areas . . . were not modelled but were reduced to outlined shapes which I then treated in different ways."

Early on during this period a dulling oil wash, usually apricot in colour, was laid over all or part of many of the paintings, damping down their brilliance and obscuring finer details. Then a whole series of paintings were produced where the primary colour tone was supplied by a lead-based aluminum paint sprayed out of aerosol cans. These became known as the 'silver paintings' and while they have their champions, none of these works has the appeal or the accessibility of his earlier, more colourful work nor of the perceptualist paintings that would start to emerge in all of their glory toward the end of the decade.

In the lead essay to the catalogue for an exhibition of Chambers' silver paintings and films at Museum London in 2011, Mark Cheetham argues that their comparative unpopularity is unjustified: "In composing art history," Cheetham writes, "an all too common distortion is the selection of only a very few works – perhaps at best a period or a style – in an artist's life to stand for her or his work as a whole. Even the most famous . . . are often thought of only in terms of their largest donations to an imaginary art bank . . . Chambers' work before Perceptual Realism suffers from such an occlusion. By focussing attention on the silver paintings, I aim to turn the tables on the selectivity of history and show that Chambers should be remembered for more than his achievements after 1969."

Cheetham concludes that essay with this enormous and startling claim: "The aluminum paintings underscore the important role of touch in perception. Chambers is rightly remembered for the transcendent domestic subtleties of his perceptual realist paintings, but in his silver paintings and in his films, he could more boldly command our attention and turn it to the world around us."[41]

Certainly a revered perceptualist painting like *Sunday Morning No. 2* is minutely concerned with "domestic subtleties" but even it has much to show us about "the world around us" and how it looks; whereas the sublime landscapes and seascapes such as *401 Towards London* and all of the Lake Huron canvases are entirely concerned with the outer world. But Cheetham is right; the best perceptualist works (domestic or not) are indeed "transcendent"; they open us up to other worlds and other realities in a way that the silver paintings and the films do not.

If I talk about the silver paintings together with his collage-like, narrative-free films – *Mosaic* would be followed by *Hybrid* (1967, which intercuts images of flowers with the faces of napalmed Vietnamese children), *R34* (1967, about a day in the art-making life of Greg Curnoe), *Circle* (1969, a compilation of a few seconds of footage of his backyard shot for 365 consecutive days from the very same vantage point) and *Hart of London* (1970, his major opus about, to quote Kathryn Elder, "the challenges of artistic expression . . . the schism between us and nature . . ." and "the transience of life") – I only do so because Chambers himself saw the paintings and the films as very much connected.

"I've been working with aluminum paint lately," Chambers told Ross Woodman in their 1967 interview. "My use of colour had become too subtle – silver is a refreshing neutral from the tense calculating that goes into controlling colour effects. There's something translucent about silver; it has a built-in light effect. The painted surface changes when you move. It's a light medium – an optical medium. I observed that silver gives a positive-to-negative image reversal depending on the source of light or where you view it from."

Asked if his experiments in the silver paintings grew out of his interest in film-making, Chambers replied, "There is a direct influence. These silver paintings are instant movies."[42]

Though Woodman has considerable regard for the silver paintings, he was nonetheless upset at the conditions in which they were created and the threat those conditions posed to someone with Chambers' history of respiratory complaints. The silver paintings were mostly produced in 1966 and '67, and just the year before, "In 1965," Nancy Poole wrote in the introduction to Chambers' autobiography, "Jack was seriously troubled by weakness in his lungs, and spent several months in the Tubercular Sanitarium in London."

"There he was in his studio, not wearing a mask, spraying lead paint onto a board and choking on it," Woodman told me. "And he was just out of the hospital with TB. I couldn't stay in there very long without choking but everybody said, 'That's Chambers'."

Interviewing Nancy Poole, I raised the subject of the silver paintings and then hemmed and hawed a bit, trying to elicit her opinion of them without disclosing my own. With typical directness, she cut to the chase: "They leave you cold?"

"They do."

"Of course. They leave me cold too. I had a tough time as his dealer. I did sell the *Madrid Window* and that particular buyer was content. She had a most astute eye and she was buying Chambers. She knew what she was doing. But for me those paintings were experiments."

If I was relieved by Nancy Poole's frankness, thinking, 'So maybe it isn't some failure in myself that I can't get on board with the silver paintings,' then I was lifted into the uppermost stratosphere by what Susan Downe had to say about how the artist himself felt about them:

"I remember the day Jack came over with the silver paintings and lined them up over there. And we just looked at them and he said, 'I'm doing this to just keep going because they bore me silly. I've run out of ideas.' He was just keeping it going, hoping that his interest would be restored."

I don't believe Chambers would've shared that opinion with just anybody and I don't believe he always felt that way about all of his silver paintings – though he did similarly (if a little more gently) downplay their importance in a 1973 interview with Mavis Lang, saying they were, "pretty well an intellectual exercise, almost an optical exercise, and so they didn't last that long."[43] But one cannot read extensively in his own writings about art-making and be in any doubt that he – as well as his broader public – considered his perceptualist works to be his supreme achievement.

Ross Woodman wrote that, "Chambers' films are what he himself called 'personal' films. He began making them at a time when he felt the need to escape his professional commitment to painting, which he believed was now blocking the flow of his own feeling by arresting or freezing it into the resolution of purely painterly issues. He was becoming disturbed by the acceptance (not reflected, of course in sales) of his art (partly because he was 'realistic') by a society he still believed was 'utilitarian, puritanical, indifferent to anything that was not a 'safe job' and a 'proper living,' and therefore fundamentally rejected everything for which he as an artist stood."

A little later in that same essay, Woodman writes, "Chambers believed his art was encouraging people to take up a temporary and aesthetic residence in a world of illusion that allowed them to avoid the necessity of 'self awareness'. He was playing into the hands of the real enemies of art . . . Chambers' films explore the dynamics of the act of perception. They are attempts to wake up an audience that he feared his paintings might now be putting to sleep."[44]

If Woodman has faithfully described Chambers' attitude toward his public here and at least partially expressed the motivation behind making less immediately accessible paintings and totally 'out there' movies, there seems to be an unmistakable note of animosity in play; a resentment of anyone who might be so gauche as to try to enjoy Chambers' art for the wrong or unapproved reasons.

With their jarring edits and soundtracks, their crude assembly that combines found film stock with footage that Chambers shot himself (such as the slitting of a lamb's throat with blood spewing everywhere in the climax of *The Hart of London*), their superimposition of images on top of each other so that everything becomes a bewildering mêlée, and the numbing repetition of certain clips or the optic reversal of them so that they are projected in negative form, Chambers' films never set out to do anything so bourgeois as to attract or beguile a viewer, let alone tell a readily graspable story. For most people – either because of the tedium they evoke or the graphic horror of certain scenes – they are an ordeal to watch.

With no concessions made to conventional forms or public taste, Chambers' films are a kind of 'cinema of cruelty'. They are the filmic equivalent of what the French cultural theorist Antonin Artaud (1896-1949) sought to accomplish with his so-called Theatre of Cruelty. Indeed Artaud sounds eerily (and arrogantly) Chambersesque when he writes about the need to shake his audience out of their safe state of illusion that "lies like a shroud over [their] perceptions."

While Chambers might present his filmic goals in an aggressively challenging way to Woodman, he presented himself in a far more placid light to *London Free Press* art critic Lenore Crawford: "But Chambers continues to spend most of his time painting, and he says his film-making is chiefly "a kind of relaxation – like the piano is for somebody else.""[45]

The films may indeed have 'relaxed' the artist by giving him a holiday from painterly concerns but that wasn't the effect his films had on most viewers who saw them.

"I remember being transfixed by *The Hart of London*," Nancy Poole told me, recalling the special screening that took place in 1979 for the Canadian High Commissioner and other guests and functionaries at Canada House on Trafalgar Square. "I hated it but that was just a normal response. I knew how powerful it was . . . I haven't looked at Jack's films for a long time. I haven't looked at them since that appalling moment in London, England when everybody walked out of the screening room except my daughter and me. I'll never forget that."

"I might have more use for some of them if I saw them again," Poole continued. "Older, wiser, perhaps. But for me the genius of the man was his ability to paint light and space. And like all the good artists, he wanted to do it all. He wanted to be a sculptor, he wanted to carve . . . He was quite obsessed at one point about doing wood carving. This was another way of expressing himself through film and I'm told they're considered masterpieces and well they might be. I do not consider myself to be a judge in any way."

Young kids are less reticent about passing judgement, even when they don't intend to do so. Susan Downe remembers taking her young children with her to one such screening in London: "We went to see *Circle* at Althouse College or somewhere on campus and my children came with me and Bret was sitting beside Jack. And this film, you know, doesn't have a lot going on in it, and Bret leaned over and fell asleep on Jack's shoulder."

And while Chambers' films do still get screened at experimental film symposia from time to time, the number of people who are interested in seeing such films is both miniscule and highly specialized. Another reputed 'giant' of the avant-garde film world, Stan Brakhage, has said of Chambers' *Hart of London*,

"It's one of the greatest films ever made." Brakhage puts it in his top five of all time. It's high praise indeed but the circle in which such praise counts for anything at all is a tiny little coterie that relates to movies in a most eccentric (if not downright inhuman) way.

Consider that one of the most recent screenings of *The Hart of London* took place on December 17, 2010 at the Anthology Film Archives in New York City in a program organized by Jonas Mekas and actually given the title: "Jonas Mekas Selects Boring Film Masterpieces." The other titles included in that series (and get a load of the length of some of these epics) were *Empire* (dir. Andy Warhol, 1964, b/w, 485 min.), *Sleep* (dir. Andy Warhol, 1963, b/w, 321 min.), *The Human Condition* (dir. Masaki Kobayashi, 1959, b/w, 574 min.), and *Solaris* (dir. Andrei Tarkovsky, 1972, colour, 165 min.).[46]

I remember the late London filmmaker and historian, Chris Doty, telling me how disgusted he was at Jack Chambers' reckless disregard for the earliest news film archives at London's pioneer television station. In recounting the story of how Chambers was given access to those archives and how he treated that cache of irreplaceable film while scouting out footage to use for *The Hart of London*, even his good friend Greg Curnoe suggests there is cause here for complaint.

"Jack approached CFPL-TV, the local television station, about getting some old film stock and stripping it to do some experiments with painting on film. He was very interested in Norman McLaren's work in that area. At some point, he got interested in the images on the old stock. He then asked for permission to use some of their old news footage. He was given permission by the station manager over the objections of the news director, who felt the film files of the station were a historical archive.

"CFPL used reversal film exclusively at the time, and copies from reversal film lose a lot of quality, so Jack was allowed to go into the original rolls of film in the files, which were organized chronologically. He took out sections which he edited together at the station. He would give the edited clips to the lab man, Hank Lane, who would print them. Jack would edit more original film into the second-generation print and it would be reprinted again. He would do this through several generations of prints. The quality gradually became more and more degraded. He was using specific material in this manner – for example, car accidents involving particular models, specific London street scenes, a deer running up a city driveway, etc. Because he took the film out of various cans, cut it up, removed sections and rolled the film up again unspliced he badly damaged about five years of original news footage from the early days of CFPL-TV. Whether the film that resulted from this work is of more significance than the local history contained in a TV station's files is another question; one that will have a different answer for you or for the local historian."[47]

In terms of both his working methods and the results he achieved, there is far more consensus and much less complaint when we leave behind the silver paintings and the films and turn our attention to what was produced when Chambers once again took up his brushes to show what he could achieve with colour and light.

11

THE PERCEPTUALIST MASTERPIECES

NANCY POOLE BELIEVES that Chambers' silver period was a sort of necessary rest stop between those two other periods – his first years back in London and the perceptualist period that arrived with *401 Towards London* [Plate 6] in 1969 – when he achieved his finest and most accomplished work: "I'll tell you I used to have a theory and I don't know how good the theory is. And I never would've said a word to him about it. I had a feeling. Look at *McGilvary County*. It's awash with colour. This is the same [points to *Summer Behind the House* over her mantelpiece], *Olga*, all of them. And then suddenly – snap – like that. I think that he was just permeated with colour and had had enough. I don't think it was a case that it was easier – could have been – but I think it was a case of he just couldn't bear any more colour. He had started *401* before the sword of Damocles and for me that is the single purest work that Jack has because he's returning to colour and there's nothing there to impede anything. After that the sword of Damocles is there. I remember in one of the shows we had I was standing with Ross Woodman and I said, 'Ross, I want you to look and confirm what I'm seeing, that there is a distinction in *401* that none of the others have. All his colour talent has come here and it's pure, pure, pure.' Ross agreed. And Ross had a good eye. But after that there's something that's coming between the painter and the work. Now, I am not a spooky person. That's why I say you have to look to see this – that there is this brilliance in *401* that isn't quite there in the others. That is not to downgrade in any way the others because they're superb. But there is a brilliance in *401*. In between – what I call the grey period or the plastic period, the non-colour period – that's just giving that part a rest and it came flooding back with *401*."

What could be duller, you might think at first, less rewarding of our attention, than to gaze upon a near-empty stretch of highway 401 cutting across a south-western Ontario landscape with the back of one truck in the foreground and three smaller vehicles in the distance, two of them moving away from us? (401 *Towards London No. 1* 1968–69) How could such a banal and impersonal scene – white lines on tarmac delineating lanes and shoulders, some sort of flat warehouse complex off to the right, a farmer's field off to the left – be painted in such a way that it simultaneously takes your breath away and lifts your spirit with a sense of limitless possibilities and freedom?

Part of the answer is Chambers' unparalleled skill in mixing and manipulating his paints so that he perfectly captures the luminous blue and white tone of a crisp autumn morning. Another part of the answer is his peerless and painstaking accuracy as a draughtsman by which he imbues a usually ignored scene with such precision and resolution (imagine paying that much attention to the mud flaps on the back of a tanker truck?) that it can only be called love.

"At first glance it seems to reflect the anonymity of modern highway construction," writes Dennis Reid in *A Concise History of Canadian Painting* "but soon reveals a particularity of place and time that, in an unexpected way, is deeply moving."[48]

And then there's the sheer, awesome scope of the thing. Here the commuter's usual low and stunted perspective, locked into his lane and preoccupied with the traffic ahead and behind and to either side of him, is elevated and widened to heroic, God-like dimensions. The top two thirds of the canvas on the right side and three quarters on the left are taken up by that massive banner of cool autumn sky, the horizon's southward tilt down toward the Great Lakes magnifying the sense of space yet further by suggesting the very curvature of the Earth. If you imaginatively straighten out that horizon line to a flat perpendicular, you'll find that the painting actually contracts a little, pulls in a bit from the sides.

Chambers first saw this scene in his rear view mirror during a drive to Toronto on a cool morning in October of 1968. He was heading east and moving up a slight incline just beyond the Delhi turnoff to Highway 59, and fleetingly glimpsed the scene, out of the corner of his eye almost, and was electrified by the vision. He pulled over at the top of the hill to take a long hard look and, not having his camera with him, he scribbled down quick notes, recording the precise time of day, the approximate air temperature, his own feelings – anything at all that would help him to recall, to re-vision that moment when he was so suddenly assailed by the glory that had been captured in his rear-view mirror. Three mornings later when the weather and the light seemed comparable, he headed back out to the scene of the revelation with his camera and stood on the Highway 59 overpass to photograph the scene below. The only overt 'adjustment' he made to this photographed scene when it came time to paint it, was to change the white lettering on the green Ontario highway sign in the lower right quarter to read "59 WEST/LONDON" instead of "59 SOUTH/DELHI".

401 was soon followed by what might seem an even less promising subject – the artist's two young sons, John and Diego, decked out in their Dr. Denton pyjamas and housecoats, sitting in armchairs to either side of a portable black and white television in a suburban living room that is drenched with early winter morning light. In *Sunday Morning No. 2* (1968-70) [Plate 7] the light flooding in the window behind the elder child almost washes out the image on the TV screen of a gentleman wearing an Alpine cap and suspenders.

"Kids watching tatty crap on TV?" you might ask. "What a yawner. What's to see here?" Absolutely everything, as it turns out. As a painter who had already displayed his mastery at capturing the fiendishly elusive qualities of light in the previous year's painting of the 401, he doubles – indeed triples – down on that accomplishment here; catching not just the blondish light inside the room but the harder, snow-reflected light of the suburban streetscape outside the large picture window, and the nearly washed-out skim milk-glow faintly emanating from the black and white TV in the corner of the room.

Because that big window faces east, the rising sun casts a slanting rectangle of that harsher exterior light onto the softer-toned plaster behind Diego (whom Chambers was known to call 'Diablo' when he misbehaved) sitting in his chair. The shadowed lines of the window pane which punctuate and frame that brighter projection shift ever-so-slightly to the right as its glow is cast onto the protruding glass surface of the framed Greg Curnoe stamped-ink and relief-print work of four shattered and taped hockey sticks that is hanging above Diego's head (*Hockey Stick Blades from West Lions Park, London*, 1965). And that very same projection of exterior light also turns up, though this time miniaturized and concave, on the upper right quadrant of the television screen.

The title, *Sunday Morning*, the profusion of different treatments of light, and the three silvery cut-out Christmas stars hanging in the window lend the scene a church-like aspect so that however mundane the subject may initially seem, we are irresistibly invited to deeper levels of contemplation. And that is when this painting of the artist's two sons in that light-dappled room, as exquisitely and precisely rendered as an old Dutch interior by Vermeer, becomes an almost heartbreaking vision that somehow expresses both the improbable miracle and the cruel brevity of life itself.

In his essay, *Past the 401: The International Classicism of Jack Chambers*, Mark A. Cheetham quotes Chambers talking about the moment he conceived *Sunday Morning No. 2*: He had happened upon his sons in the living room, Chambers said, "with the sun and . . . (snaps his fingers) . . . there it was, there was something, right? So . . . I made up my mind that the next Sunday morning that I came down or Saturday morning . . .and there was a bright light like that again . . . I would get it."[49]

Chambers' admission here that it could've been a Sunday or a Saturday morning when he snapped the source photographs of his boys glued to the telly (and we also learn in Cheetham's essay that Chambers went outside to photograph the neighbourhood scene that would be framed inside the big front window) may well address a nagging little question I've always had about this painting, namely: "So what the heck is that image on the TV screen all about?"

The jolly looking gent wearing Alpine gear – unless he's a member of the Von Trapp family warbling out a stirring hymn – looks more like a denizen of the Saturday morning TV wasteland for kiddies than anyone likely to turn up in the more sober programming featured on a Sunday morning. In my experience (about ten years before the Chambers boys, I grant you) you never made a point of hauling yourself out of bed for an extended cathode ray bath on a Sunday morning. What would be the point? All those sermons and hymn sings and dreary discussions of current events would just send you right back to sleep.

Chambers painted and sketched at least four different scenes of his favourite Lake Huron beach. For *Lake Huron No. 1* (1970–71) and *No. 3* (1971–72) he faced the water; from the level of the beach in the first one, beautifully capturing the white-capped waves as they roll in, and in *No. 3*, from just behind and below the top of a dune so that you get two lines of horizon running clear across the canvas, one of parched beach grass and stunted shrubs on the top of that dune, and then above that the brilliant line of undulating ultramarine denoting a calm lake.

For the other two, he completely turns his back on the lake and faces the dune instead, magically evoking the lake just as powerfully by implication, by looking in an unexpected direction at a scene whose every element and contour unmistakably bespeak the unseen. *No. 2* (1971) is a sketch which served as a preliminary exercise for *No. 4* (1972–76) [Plate 8] – a painting (one of his last major works and one of my favourites) – in which we see sparse shrubs and clumps of beach grass along the face of the dune and one larger, gnarled bush on the top. The shape and posture of all this plant life bear the signs of perpetual struggle to stay rooted in that sandy, windswept soil.

There are two staircases that are situated perhaps 100 feet apart on either side of the scene, running down the lake-ward face of the dune to the beach. One is constructed out of dried-out wooden boards that have been weathered grey and the other is made of glistening metal; both of them bearing their characteristic signs of existence in this place where for eight months of the year, they must absorb the full force of that other un-depicted force of nature – the sun.

As with his painting of the 401, this scene is crowned by a towering expanse of clouds – these ones more widely and evenly dispersed but not so voluminous or substantial. These ones mottle the sky – all of it – but feel thinner, wetter, hotter and more static. Except for that one lonely bush perched on top of the horizon, the sky in *Lake Huron No, 4* completely takes up the top four fifths of the canvas in a way that almost seems to curve out toward and over top of the viewer. One is incredulous to read the small print and learn that the painting is perfectly square; not taller than it is broad which your senses insist.

How does he accomplish that illusion? Sarah Milroy wrote of this painting: "Chambers spliced together two photographic sources – one of the dunes, another of the sky directly overhead – and then compressed them together in one image, which gives us the dizzy sense of being rocked back on our heels. The rug is pulled from under us, but it is a blissful fall. The picture imagines the threshold between one world and another, a breathtaking roller-coaster ride into the wild blue yonder."[50]

For all of Chambers' perceptualist works, using a camera and photographic images was indeed central to the process but before any photographs were taken, something was required that was even more central yet – there had to be the perception; what Chambers often called the 'vision', welcoming the religious overtones that word brings. Therefore Chambers did not regard himself as a photo realist or what in the '60s was sometimes called a 'hyper realist.' He did not slave to recreate the likeness of a photograph through paint. He was after much bigger game than that. His quest was metaphysical. "Perception is the intelligible brilliance within us, when our soul and the soul of things become present to one another," Chambers wrote in one of his later musings in *Red and Green*, his mammoth artist's journal. "It is the intuitive unfolding of both the self and the other in one embrace."[51]

We have seen in our discussion of how *401 Towards London* came to be, that three days passed between conceiving the painting and photographing the scene that inspired the conception. With *Sunday Morning No. 2* we know that a number of weeks passed between the conception and photographing the scene. In both those cases he already knew what he wanted; the 'vision' had already been received, so the photo or photos wouldn't be providing that. Rather, as he said in an interview, the photograph, "would remain faithful to the appearance of things" and that faithfulness would prevent him when it came time to execute the painting to not let his own tricks of "invention and style" do anything that would "super-cede" the original "experience" or vision.

In his autobiography he expounded further on the limited role of the photograph. "You must know what you want and make the photo give it to you. Duplicating the photo as an end in itself and as a display of technique has nothing to do with the purposes for which I require its aid, and of course nothing to do with art. That must be clearly understood when speaking about photos, and tracings, and copying, and art . . . [these] are labour-saving devices that hasten the appearance of the end I seek – an image of my own vision."[52]

He reiterates this point in one of his chapters in *Red and Green* about realism and the use of photos – which he insists on spelling 'fotos' in that book. "Nature cannot be imitated or 'transcribed' without first being taken apart and put together again. And the same goes for the foto as well. The foto is always subsequent to and as a result of perception: the camera's view is never the substitute for vision."

Chambers went on to say, "Perceptualism is a result of perception. It is an example of how one's vision has been expressed in paint . . . I don't mean hallucinations or images of the imagination. I mean that faculty of inner vision where the object appears in the splendour of its essential namelessness . . . the names and games of the perceptual mind are inoperative during the perceptual moment. Inspiration has taken over the mind."

Chambers often reiterated this idea of 'namelessness' in the visionary moment of perception. It was a pre-verbal, pre-logical, instance of glory breaking through. The only word that needed to be uttered at such a moment was "wow".

"Then where does the painting come from?" Chambers asks in his autobiography. "In my case I am convinced that the inspiration always belonged to the object. . . The object is invested then with the experience of inspiration and is seen with the heightened awareness of visionary recall. It is by means of this experience influencing the objective presence of the thing, that painting seeks to ascend to an excellence of being that is both visible and invisible. The invisible property in the wholeness of vision is the source of unity in the painting. The visible property of the painting describes the act of seeing that occurs after inspiration, while the miracle of the object's appearing still persists."[53]

Sometimes while perusing the thick tangle of Chambers' analysis of his own artistic practice, one feels a sudden burst of real comradeship with Chambers' London artist colleague Murray Favro who told Bill McGrath, "that whenever Jack talked about his art, I couldn't understand a word of it."[54]

Armed with the photograph that would prevent his own tricks of style and invention from messing with the appearance of things, Chambers would lay out a mathematically precise grid over the photograph which he would then transpose with pencil onto his canvas or, quite often, his treated plywood boards. (Unfortunately a seam is clearly visible in certain lights on *401 Towards London* where two of these boards have been joined together.) This grid allowed Chambers to exactly reproduce the larger image one tiny cell at a time. It can be a little jarring to see some of these original photographs and compare them to the well-known paintings. Aside from scale, so much appears to be precisely the same . . . and yet . . . and yet . . . in some uncanny way there's just so much more going on in the paintings; so much more has been invested.

One of Chambers' muted oil paintings from the silver period, *Antonio and Miguel in the USA*, was included in a grand exhibition of works displayed at Ottawa's National Gallery of Canada from May to September of 1967, entitled *300 Years of Canadian Art: An Exhibition Arranged in Celebration of the Centenary of Confederation.* (The show then went on to the AGO in October.) On August 23, 1967, J.W. Borcomon, the National Gallery's director of exhibitions sent out a form letter to all the living artists whose work had been included in the show. It read as follows:

Dear _____

The exhibition 300 Years of Canadian Art, to which you have contributed, contains such important material for an understanding of the development of Canadian art that the National Gallery has decided to use it as a basis for producing a slide library of Canadian art in sets containing approximately 2,000 titles. These will be produced in sufficient quantities to meet the needs of museums, schools, universities and other educational institutions (distribution will be restricted to such institutions).

We should be most grateful if you would grant the National Gallery of Canada permission to reproduce in 35 mm colour slides, for educational purposes, the following works executed by you: _____

If you agree would you please sign in the appropriate place and return the copy to us. If we have not heard from you by September 15, 1967, I shall assume that you are willing to authorize the National Gallery to reproduce in 35 mm slide form the work referred to above.

Sincerely yours,

J.W. Borcomon

Today, the gall of this proposition seems staggering but back then, it was utterly routine; it was business as usual. There is, of course, no mention of paying the artist anything to use his image. Equally unspoken is the assumption that the artist should be honoured to be included because his work will be put to use by educators and curators across the land. Particularly irksome is the bit where the artist is told he will have to pipe up if he objects to being taken advantage of in this way; that his silence will be construed as consent.

Chambers was not silent. He answered this form letter with a form letter of his own which he sent out to J.W. Borcomon and 130 other Canadian artists – basically, every artist he could think of and dig up a mailing address for. The response to Chambers form letter was so immediate and pronounced that the National Gallery suspended their great slide project.

Chambers wrote: "The prompt reply from these concerned artists showed me that we had in Canada a nucleus of discontent over the way artists were being taken for granted, and that this number could be increased, particularly as grievances were spelled out and solutions to them proposed . . . For example, copyright payment to the artist was his right by Canadian law, but most of us did not know this even though the National Gallery accompanied any purchase of an artist's work with a form letter in which he was asked to sign over his copyright to the National Gallery. It should have been obvious but nobody was asking questions. Also, there was the question of rental fees to artists for exhibiting their work in public galleries."

For someone who could barely organize his own passage to Europe 14 years before, Chambers had become formidably adept at researching an abstruse issue, organizing his findings and putting forth a powerful argument that others found compelling. "Every other profession in society was organized long ago in the business of 'fair exchange: payment for services'," he wrote. "All the persons connected with an exhibition of an artist's work, from the gas station attendant who filled up the truck that transported the works, to the museum janitor, the office staff and curator, are paid a fee or salary. The artist is the reason why the others have a position and a wage, yet the artist is the only one who receives nothing."[55]

Though it would take a few years to become fully operational (and require input and refinement from other artist leaders like Tony Urquhart and Kim Ondaatje) Chambers' form letter to J.W. Borcomon and 130 artists marked the birth of Canadian Artists Representation (CAR) which had 1700 members by the time of Chambers' death and has greatly improved the prospects for all Canadian artists, ensuring that they receive fair payment whenever their works are exhibited or reproduced.

Victoria artist Carole Sabiston could speak for many Canadian artists when she says, "And of course I joined CAR which Jack Chambers started. I thought this sounds interesting. What does a 25 year old know? Not much. I was a loyal member for a long time. I thought he's doing something for Canadian artists."

Asked if she thought Chambers might have paid a price for starting CAR; if he offended certain parties in the upper echelons of the art establishment (as Nancy Poole told me, "The National Gallery never bought directly from him, from us, never.") Sabiston answered, "I can see that completely. How dare these minions working in their little ateliers with a bit of paint demand to have money for their work? No, I can see that. Jack was very important in what he accomplished there in his incredibly quiet way."

Earlier I quoted a snippet from Bill McGrath's paper to The Baconian Club in which he wrote that fellow artist, "Murray Favro said that whenever Jack talked about his art, he couldn't understand a word of it." Here, after discussing what Chambers accomplished by setting up CAR, is the place to put the second half of Favro's comment: "But when Jack talked about business he was very clear and tough-minded."

That tough-mindedness was at the fore again in March of 1969 when, after a period of comparatively slower sales and lower prices (ie: his silver period) Chambers informed his Toronto agent, Av Isaacs, that in London he would be exhibiting his work at Nancy Poole's Studio while Isaacs could continue to represent him in Toronto. Fourteen months later, Poole sold *Sunday Morning No. 2* for $25,000 (the highest price paid at that time to a living Canadian artist) and then topped that five months later by selling *Victoria Hospital* for $35,000. Isaacs wasn't about to compete with that and told Chambers he wouldn't charge the new, much higher prices he was demanding. But by that point, Poole had opened the Toronto branch of her art dealership and thus became Chambers' exclusive agent.

Also influencing his drive for higher prices was receiving the diagnosis of acute myeloblastic leukemia in July of 1969. As Chambers wrote: "Now that my capacity to produce was in jeopardy, I was forced to turn my attention to a more practical value: the amount of money the work was really worth. I had to arrive at a price for my talents that was not so low as to insult the work itself nor so high as to be impractical . . . Once a price was set, there was no turning back. That was it. Many artists may think, 'I'll charge what I want.' But if you are not prepared to stand behind your decisions in the knowledge that you are wholly and truly justified in your price, you may price yourself completely out of the market. I decided what I was worth, set my price, directed my agent, Nancy Poole, and she found a buyer. The majority of my work, however, sold in the public sector to private clients. I am happy it is so because one need never seek favour nor tremble at the possible changes in the personnel of our public galleries or purchasing institutions."

In her recently published memoir, *The Past . . . Comes Back* (2012), Poole claims that Chambers was instrumental in leading her to become an agent. "I didn't know it at the time," Poole told me. "Which is fascinating. I only discovered that in the last two years. It's funny. You don't really know the path you have followed until you go back and retrace it. At least, that's my experience."

I asked her why she thought Chambers aimed her in that direction. "What did he see in you?"

"Why did he select me? It was because, one, he knew I had connections. Two, he knew that I wouldn't be dependent on my earnings from him to make a living and therefore it would be pretty smart on his part to use me in that way. He then learned that I perhaps brought more than just connections and the ability to sell. But that is what it was in the beginning. He saw me as a way into people with money. I was a good manager. And that was our relationship. He trusted me. I missed him when he died because we had just a great, trusting relationship. I knew that he was never going to produce anything but what I would be proud to present and try to sell at the prices that he was putting on. I knew that I wasn't cheating anybody with what I was doing. I think he saw me as a good manager and maybe he saw me with a good eye but I don't know that because naturally he was only concerned with his own work."

There was a remarkable confluence of factors operative in Chambers' life as the 1960s tipped into the 1970s that – briefly on the national level and more lastingly at the local – turned him into a very powerful media legend, a figure of unassailable accomplishment and virtue, the kind of upstanding man you could safely name a school after; a sort of Pablo Picasso crossed with Terry Fox. While his new and rising fame was welcome to the extent that it justified his rising prices, it also tended to isolate him somewhat as an artist.

In the case of the perceptualist paintings that he was producing at this time, nobody with eyeballs (however untrained) could deny that this fellow could paint magnificently. Lots of excellent painters produce a lifetime's work without ever being acknowledged by a particularly broad public but Chambers was yanking all spotlights onto himself in this period by becoming spectacularly and unprecedentedly successful. As *401 Towards London* (1969), *Sunday Morning No.2* (1970) and *Victoria Hospital* (1970) rapidly succeeded one another in reaping higher and higher prices, national media of all kinds – from Pierre Berton's and Roy Bonisteel's television chat shows to glossy weekend newspaper supplements that were inserted into newspapers all across the land – came clamouring for interviews and features.

After a few months of such coverage, you might have expected a reaction to set in. Sure, Chambers is good but is he really the best? Aren't there a lot of other artists we should be considering as well as this guy? Are anybody's paintings really worth that kind of money? But in the face of his leukemia diagnosis any such notions of cutting Chambers down to size became unthinkable.

His friend Greg Curnoe expressed his displeasure to Chambers about the way in which his incredible new prices were skewing the market for other artists. Curnoe knew Chambers well enough to risk that kind of criticism and Chambers knew Curnoe well enough that he could reply with a wry wink that he really didn't see how Greg would be able to "stay mad at a dying man".[56] Post-diagnosis, such frankness from anyone became increasingly rare in Chambers' life.

By dint of his terminal illness Chambers had now ascended onto the plateau of the critically untouchable and would remain there for the rest of his life. But his new conspicuousness and success exposed him to other kinds of pests that most garden variety artists would never have to contend with. In a February 1971 feature article in one of the national weekly newspaper supplements (somewhat depressingly entitled, *What makes Jack Chambers Canada's top-priced painter?*), writer Alan Walker talks about the famous paintings and the famous prices and his famous illness and then a different kind of commercial reality rudely intrudes:

"Chambers was still talking about his health when someone knocked at the door. The irony to come would be called unbelievable even in fiction, but, in truth, the man at the door was also interested in talking about Chambers' health. 'How d'ya do, sir, Ted Tomlinson is my name, from Manufacturers Life. I enjoyed the article about you – congratulations on the big sale. I sent a letter to you, and your phone number is, heh, heh, unlisted, and I didn't know where your studio was, so I decided the only way to get to see you was to drop by the house. If you're busy right now . . .'

"'I am busy,' Chambers said politely.

"'Well, I'd appreciate it if you'd give me a call – here's my number,' and Ted Tomlinson, Supersalesman, thrust a business card into Chambers' hand."[57]

One can see where Mr. Tomlinson got the idea. Unlike a lot of artists at this time – long of hair, flamboyant or slovenly in their dress, visibly excitable or contemptuous – in appearance the clean shaven Chambers was quite zipped up and did actually look like the kind of man who might be interested in buying life insurance. The portrait of himself that is featured in *Grass Box No.2* from 1970 depicts the artist in a proper pair of slacks and loafers and a long-sleeved shirt pushing along a motorized lawn mower. The image he projected of himself was far more redolent of Ward Cleaver than some impulsive denizen of Outer Bohemia who might challenge your conventions or pee on your rug.

With death now sitting on his left shoulder, Chambers felt a new urgency to work things out, both to do whatever he could to amass some sort of nest egg that would provide for Olga and the boys after he died and to come to a new understanding about matters of ultimate importance. His old sketching partner from his childhood in South London, Val Ambrose McInnes had kept up his study of art all the way to the university level and became a priest of the Dominican Order and was the head of Judeo-Christian Studies at Tulane University in New Orleans, Louisiana. The two men kept in touch intermittently, sometimes getting together when Father McInnes visited London but during most of that period through the early to mid '60s, Chambers was so caught up in his own art and his family and the wider arts explosion then underway in London, that he didn't have much use for the Church he had joined with such urgency in Spain and seems even to have been a bit embarrassed by how completely he'd lapsed as a Catholic.

That started to change after receiving his fatal diagnosis and when Fr. McInnes made an overture to Chambers over Christmas of 1969, Chambers eagerly invited his old friend to come to his house and celebrate Mass there on Christmas Day. The relationship deepened then with more frequent visits and a correspondence which Fr. McInnes quotes in his book, *To Rise With the Light*, about Chambers and the vexed art project he commissioned the artist to undertake. Originally conceived as a painting, when Chambers became too weak to undertake that they decided to make a limited fine art print on a subject Father McInnes brought to Chambers' attention – the British army officer turned priest named Henry Edward Dormer who had died in London in 1866 during a typhoid outbreak when he was ministering to the sick and poor and became London's only candidate for sainthood. Indeed, the painting-cum-print was devised as a fund raiser to aid the cause of Dormer's beatification.

Chambers didn't get down to serious work on the project until perilously late in his life and according to Nancy Poole and Olga Chambers, the project wasn't finished to the artist's satisfaction. Very near to death, he was reported to have said that the snow on top of Dormer's gravestone (around which a group of young Catholics are standing in homage) looked like icing. He refused to sign off on it. According to Fr. McInnes and Rudolf Bikkers whose shop, Editions Canada, was in charge of the printing, things had proceeded far enough that they felt certain Chambers would have wanted it printed. Prints were made but never signed and bad blood existed thereafter between the two arguing parties. Other than Fr. McInnes (who included a small reproduction of the print in his book about Chambers) I've never heard anyone make very grand claims for the work. It is definitely lesser Chambers; whatever distinction it has derives from its status as final Chambers.

The other major unfinished work, and the largest, is *Lunch*, which he began in 1969 and toiled at intermittently and without ultimate success for the next five or six years. Chambers knew he had accomplished something very special with *Sunday Morning No. 2* and he originally conceived *Lunch* as part of that series, and planned to call it *Sunday Noon*. Its titular downgrading to the more perfunctory, *Lunch*, would seem to indicate that he knew this one was somehow – and fundamentally – flawed.

Susan Downe told me that it was her son Bill who snapped the source photograph for *Lunch*. His mother recalls how miffed Bill would be with Chambers' abruptness when he was looking to clear the house of extraneous young pests at meal or bed times, barking at the boy: "Hit the road, Bill." The boy wasn't sent packing on the day he took the photograph, however. He stayed to lunch and there is an unoccupied place set for him at the table between the artist and a potted Easter lily that is set on the floor. The presence of that lily next to the empty chair caused some po-faced critics to speculate on possible allusions to divinity – was that place at the table set for Jesus Christ? – inspiring much mirth among those who know the mundane truth.

Gillian McKay, an editor at *Canadian Art* magazine, deftly outlines some of the problems with *Lunch*: "It shows Chambers seated at the dining room table with his family (it is the only painting that unites all four of them), and includes a potted Easter lily, two wine bottles and an empty place setting. The references to the Last Supper and the compositional parallels to *Sunday Morning No. 2* (*Lunch* is set at the opposite end of the same room, looking out on the snowy backyard instead of the front) suggest that Chambers intended to evoke the spirit of Holy Communion. Sadly, on this occasion, there was no epiphany in the family church. John and Diego look bewildered and isolated in a room whose unfinished walls, ceiling and floor are as drab and claustrophobic as a cardboard box. Their frozen-lipped parents gaze only at each other. The large blank on the floor where a Persian carpet was supposed to be destabilizes the composition, making it appear as if the table could slide right out of the picture. Chambers claimed he could never make the elaborate carpet work – his friends recall that he laboured on it for days, only to paint it out. At least that was the reason he gave for abandoning the project. Perhaps he knew it was better left unfinished. *Lunch* is about what cannot be fixed, even by a virtuoso."[58]

I asked Nancy Poole why she thought Chambers never finished *Lunch*.

"That is the great question and I think the great answer is because the bloody rug drove him crazy. Every time I walked in to his studio and it would look wonderful and I'd say, 'Terrific.' I'd walk in next time and he'd painted it out. He was never really happy with it. I think this is the simple explanation."

Poole then offered a less simple and more multifaceted explanation which I think is probably much more pertinent. "I promised Olga that I would never sell it. I never tried to sell it but then it was unfinished so it wasn't a big problem. But I know this about the man; that if he had painted it the way he wanted it, then as far as he was concerned, it would be finished. He couldn't care less. There was no sentimentality about, 'Oh, I don't want this portrait to go.' Nope. That meant dollars and I would've been called right away. 'It's done, get on with it. Here's the price.' And also remember he was trying to build up a body of work so that was challenging him and taking time from what he could do."

If Chambers' two great post-diagnostic goals were to provide money for his family and accomplish the finest body of work that he was capable of, then *Lunch* was doubly doomed as it would assist him in fulfilling neither.

Fr. McInnes quotes long sections of letters Chambers wrote to him during his last nine years that sound unlike anything else he ever wrote, that sound like the urgent musings of a devout and faithful Catholic. In one such passage which Chambers had asked Fr. McInnes to read out at his funeral, Chambers wrote: "Perhaps even with the sickening failure of my life, and as I see how I fail each day, these failings in faith may become the seeds of humility disposing me more to God's love. I ask God through Jesus Christ to crush my will and mill it into the brightness of His love."

We have seen before Chambers' marked propensity for tailoring what he had to say to his audience, or not saying anything at all. Obviously this is something we all do to an extent but as Chambers' friends Susan Downe and Greg Curnoe have remarked, with Chambers this tendency was particularly pronounced. At about the same time as he was lamenting his failure and unworthiness to Fr. McInnes, he told the writer Susan Crean that being diagnosed with leukemia had actually helped him to focus and get down to work. "To have all the seats in the theatre to choose from provides you with a problem, eh? But if one seat is left, you jump into it and watch."

Nancy Poole – not the most sympathetic person with whom to discuss matters Catholic but she did know the man – answered my question about how Catholic Chambers ever became with this terse appraisal: "Well, let me tell you. Don't ponder too long. To whatever degree he thought it was good for him – that's how Catholic he became."

12

FIGHTING FOR HIS LIFE

DURING THE NINE years that he lived with his fatal diagnosis, Jack Chambers looked into any sort of dietary or spiritual regimen (no matter if it might strike others as a little flakey or contradicted his Catholic faith) that held out any prospect of prolonging his life for as long as possible. Chambers did ask Fr. McInnes what he thought about him resorting to the ministrations of the Indian teacher and healer, Satya Sai Baba, and McInnes replied that wherever his friend found good, God would be there.

His friend and close neighbour Susan Downe recalled: "The most time I spent with Jack was post-diagnosis, partly because I was studying Reichian theory at that time and Jack was very interested in that. We talked maybe two or three times a week. I'd go over there, he'd come here, we'd go over to the park and walk around talking about it. I think he might've felt more desperate and maybe even hysterical except that he was so focussed on living until the boys were older. His intention was huge. He had plans and he carried them through. I would say that most of the time I knew him well he was pretty darn focussed. He had pared his life down to the essentials. Olga . . . Well, maybe even his work first, then Olga, the boys and his friends. Oh, and he was trying to get healthy. You'd better move that right up to minus one. Outside of those, he didn't waste any time or interest.

"Early on he was reading all about vitamins and was taking half a cup of pills three times a day. Olga juiced all the time and all the water he was drinking came from natural springs. He brought back a suitcase full of laetrile from Mexico and he was stopped at the border. Laetrile had a reputation for being efficacious in halting leukemia and cancer. I think Bill Poole [Nancy Poole's lawyer husband] went down to get him out of the pokey at the border but he couldn't bring the laetrile through. There was a clinic there. I would've gone if it was me with cancer. I don't think he was trying just anything but if it passed his internal idea of being worthwhile, he'd go after it. He had an imagination that could go beyond the traditional, conventional medical model in London, Ontario. He knew about things. I don't think he was flighty about his search. I think he was quite focussed.

"And his idea of 'worthwhile' would include something like Sai Baba. He went to see Sai Baba a couple of times in India. When everybody gets there, they're welcomed but the men go here and the women go there and they live in separate communities for a number of weeks and then after a while someone will say, 'Sai Baba would like to see you today.' So by the time they go in to see the guy, they're kind of indoctrinated to the weather, a little bit of the culture and so on. The first time Sai Baba said to him, 'You will be well.' Which just took a load off Jack's shoulders and he came back. Then the remission ended and Jack went back again and he asked Sai Baba, 'Did you mean I'd be well in my body? Would I be alive when I'm being well?' And as I recall he got a kind of enigmatic answer that time, though I don't remember the words."

Chambers' travels in search of medical and spiritual healing took him on trips to the United States, Mexico, England and India to visit clinics, gurus and assorted healers. The whole grim process may have appeared to lack dignity or philosophical coherence but as Nancy Poole pointed out with some vehemence, at the end of his last day – a day that had been delayed for far longer than any-one could've predicted – Chambers had certainly beaten or at least extended the crummy odds he'd been handed with his fatal diagnosis:

"He was clever, cunning and he survived for nine years with that blooming disease," Poole told me. "And he produced the body of work that he set out to do and made enough money that he at least left Olga and the boys so they could stay in their home. Not many artists could have done that."

It obviously wasn't coincidental that Chambers started to compile his massive artist's journal *Red and Green* at this time. To call *Red and Green* a journal is a little misleading. It's more like a commonplace book as the great bulk of its pages are comprised of snippets (some very large indeed) by other writers. While many of the passages contained in the book concern themselves with artistic practice, far more of them have to do with the dynamics and the implications of perception and meaning. Chambers thought *Red and Green* was of major importance and tried to get it published to no avail. While publishers expressed polite interest, none of them were prepared to bankroll the printing of so sprawling and esoteric an opus as this.

Art critic Sarah Milroy, ordinarily a major fan of Chambers who has written multiple essays on the artist that are loaded with insight and enthusiasm, can't disguise a note of exasperation when writing about *Red and Green*:

"In the 1970s, art itself became his religion and he the high priest. He obsessed until he died over a project he called "Red and Green: A Journal," a collection of writings and quotations explaining the complex underpinnings of his style. He ransacked local libraries and bookstores, devouring works on everything from Catholic mysticism, Hindu Vedanta and Buddhism to the more extreme fringes of Theosophy and the occult. Whether the brilliance of the

Jewish theologian Martin Buber or the arcane Madame Blavatsky, all got tossed in the crazy salad that is "Red and Green." The febrile, declamatory tenor of his own thinking comes through in his journals: 'Be awake! Be present! . . . We are existing in one another – we are one. We are everything we see – one substance, one energy – one space.'" [59]

Following the death of Olga Chambers in June of 1991, author and curator Tom Smart was given a pile of three ring binders by John Chambers who hoped to fulfill his father's wish and see *Red and Green* published. Twenty-two years later in the summer of 2013, Smart published his 175 page gloss of *Red and Green* subtitled *An Artist's Inquiry into the Nature of Meaning*. Smart credits himself not for writing or editing but rather for 'decrypting' *Red and Green* and forthrightly admits in his introduction that Chambers' journal, "cannot be published in its full original state because it is an immense sequence of hundreds of quotations from the writings of others. The work of clearing permissions to reprint all those excerpts would take a lifetime."

Far more indulgent of Chambers' frenzy of clipping, gluing and speculating than Milroy, even Smart sometimes lets a smirk of incredulity slip into the mix: "Blavatsky was very influential on Chambers as he struggled to add nuance to his definition of perceptualism. He relished quoting her, if only to capture the strange ways she articulated principles that were analogous to perceptualism's – even if her ideas skirted the edges of reason. For example, Chambers cited a passage about stars being 'intelligences' inhabited by spiritual beings who exercised influence over other beings . . . . In this dense mosaic of quotations, Chambers' reader is often overwhelmed, adrift, wondering why he is collaging all these frequently divergent ideas. It would seem that his purpose was no less than codifying all of nature and its modalities."[60]

Just as frequently quoted in *Red and Green's* pages as Madame Blavatsky is Jane Roberts (1929-84) a New York-based poet and psychic who first contacted a ghost (or, if you prefer, a 'discarnate ascendant master') named Seth via her Ouija Board in the early 1960s and spun many bestsellers out of the books that he dictated to her about the true nature of reality and the purpose of life. *Red and Green* isn't made up of wall to wall nut-jobs. Some first rate writers and thinkers like Arthur Koestler and Jacques Maritain are also given their say but it's all so wildly and indiscriminately compiled that one is not compelled to shout 'Eureka!' so much as to mutter, 'Bibbity-bobbity boo.'

Confronting his fatal diagnosis, it is small wonder that Chambers' fevered curiosity as reflected in *Red and Green* so frequently zeroes in on enormous metaphysical questions and matters of "meaning, redemption and eternity". But having gone to the trouble of joining the Catholic Church some fifteen years before, one can only regret that Chambers did so strictly for the discipline and structure it could provide for his art and, "not" as he said "for the love of God".

None of us can speak with any certainty about how we would handle a diagnosis such as Chambers', as none of us is fit to speculate on the authenticity or depth of another man's faith. It's at least as perilous to presume to judge another man's faith as another man's marriage. If you do not know it inside out, then you do not know it, period. But leafing through the cacophony of contending theorists and quacks listed in Tom Smart's index of cited writers in *Red and Green*, it is hard to suppress a sigh of frustration.

Why would Chambers take the musings of Seth so much to heart and not Jesus Christ or St. Paul? Why Madame Blavatsky and not St. Augustine or St. Thomas Aquinas? It seems such a shame that he apparently could not, or at least did not, let the Church he'd elected to join play a larger role in providing him understanding and comfort as he endured the protracted crisis of his final nine years of fading health. Over the past 2,000 years the Roman Catholic Church has had, to say the least, a lot of experience with art and death and has developed some truly sublime strategies for wresting meaning and salvation out of just the kinds of challenges Chambers was facing.

Sometimes Chambers' own writing in *Red and Green* can be full of good painterly sense, such as in this excerpt in which we also learn why he selected that particular title for his journal; that tints of red and green can act as agents of distinction and clarity to assist both painter and viewer in the all-important act of perception:

"For some time it has seemed to me that all colours in painting can be derived from a red-green basis. That is, in mixing colours to effect an illusory distance on a flat surface, red and green can be used as basic ingredients to create polarity between one colour and another, since red and green are themselves complementaries. Two colours in a given area, black for instance, can be intentionally separated from one another while still remaining black by adding a little green to one and a little red to the other, but not enough in either case for the black to look like anything but black when seen alone. This complementary approach to organizing colour maximizes our control over the subtle effects of distance and the obvious ones. For example, the vertical gradation of values in a sky from light horizon to darker zenith can ascend straight up like an elevator using the analogous approach of mixing a little white with blue at the horizon and less white with blue at the top. The up-and-in concave effect of real skies can be achieved by alternating light blue-pink at the horizon to darker blue-green in the middle to blue-purple at the top or by any number of such alternating red-green steps required to produce an up-and-in effect."

As I say, almost anyone – and certainly any aspiring artist – could read the passage above with profit. But in numerous excerpts such as this next one, with its promiscuous lumping together of artistic, psychological and spiritual concepts, one hopes that Chambers' words at least meant something to him.

Certainly, if I put on my thinking cap and really squint up my brain I can dimly apprehend a few stray traces of sense here but frankly it's hardly worth the effort of wading through all his leaden and didactic verbiage:

"Perceptual experience is the perceptual phenomenon one step removed to its first 'materialization.' It is the flow into the 'simple' senses and into consciousness of perceptual nourishment. Perceptual experience is the re-emergence in the flow of an emotion of a 'high-light' of the world at a particular visual point before me. 'Simple' experiences are those encounters that occur in consciousness through the five senses. Perception is the gestalt 'sense' of the simple senses themselves – the 'spiritual unity' of these simple senses. The perceptual in-swing travels via the simple senses to the mind – to that part of the mind – or arrives in such a manner for perception to occur. Then the out-swing as emotion exits via the brain to the simple senses again which structure the exterior world. As an intentional out-going art, that is, as an inner light structuring outer matter, perceptual experience is crafted by means of a discriminating dialogue with what was seen."

What kind of painter writes this way? A plugged up painter, I suspect, who is perhaps a little too intelligent and analytical for his own good. And a lonely painter whose reputation has become so exalted and even saintly that he no longer gets to hang out with colleagues who'll call his bluff, puncture the balloon of his self-seriousness and call him back down to earth. And also perhaps a weakened and exhausted painter who is leery of taking intuitions and impulses for a test drive because the craft of his art-making has become so elaborate and demanding that he can't just dash off an exploratory probe on a whim to see what the potential might be, lest he saddle himself with another un-resolvable *Lunch*.

In December of 1977, against the advice of his doctors, a greatly weakened Chambers returned for his second and final visit to Bangalore and Puttaparthi, India (his first visit, lasting three months had commenced in January 1975) to stay once again at the compound of Sai Baba. This would have been the visit when he received an enigmatic answer from his guru to the utterly pathetic question: 'Did you mean I'd be well in my body? Would I be alive when I'm being well?' While there he produced his last pictures – a series of often brilliantly coloured but blearily delineated landscapes and still-lifes executed in coloured chalk and graphite on newsprint; beautifully described by Ross Woodman as, "frail as the breath from which they were drawn."

For this second visit, his already shaken health collapsed further and he couldn't endure the Spartan conditions at the compound for even a month. Back home in London, family and friends became frantic at the seeming likelihood that he might die, all alone, in India.

Susan Downe remembers: "Olga and I were with each other day and night because Jack was so sick in India that he was dying in a hotel room. A maid I think found him and he was so weak that he couldn't lift his head from the pillow. There was an order of nursing nuns who took care of him until he was better. Olga and I were phoning India but there was a huge storm some place and it kept disconnecting and I remember Olga shouting into the phone, 'Don't hang up!' We never did get through that night. But he came home from that trip [indeed, Olga went over to retrieve him] and he lived a little longer."

At this point in our interview, Susan Downe appeared a little exasperated at the sketchiness of her memory and sadly added: "I wish I'd kept more notes. He was such a big figure in my life. I never thought I'd forget anything."

In early January of 1978, almost immediately after returning from India, Chambers was admitted to Victoria Hospital where he died on Thursday, April 13. Nancy Poole wrote in her memoirs about his final hours: "Olga, Irene Dewdney and I were with him in his final hours in a small private room in the old Victoria Hospital, that same hospital where he had been born and that he had painted a few years earlier. I had been summoned from a Board of Governors meeting at the UWO with the words, 'Mr. Chambers is dying and Mrs. Chambers would like you to come' . . . Everything that happened that day from that moment remains clear in my mind. When I entered Jack's room Olga was sitting on Jack's far side holding his right hand, and Irene was leaning against the south wall by the window. I sat facing him and took his left hand in mine and then noticed the nurse who was standing at the head of the bed who occasionally put a suction instrument in his mouth. The room was dimly lit, quiet and the atmosphere peaceful as was his dying at about six o'clock. He was conscious almost to the end."[61]

Acknowledging the roles the Dewdneys had long played in Chambers' life as surrogate, art-savvy parents, Poole said of Chambers' three bedside graces, "When he was dying there was the mother, there was the wife, there was the manager. It was an interesting scene for those few hours."

In Greg Curnoe's brief and affecting reminiscence of Jack Chambers at the 1989 screening of all six of Chambers' films at The Toronto International Experimental Film Congress, he expressed dismay that Chambers, whose reputation (like Curnoe's own) once seemed unassailably secure amongst all the London artists who had made such a big impact in the 1960's, was somehow disappearing.

"I have been overcome with sadness as I write much of these things. I remember how close we were and how his becoming ill changed everything. I still can't believe that he had such bad luck. It is very good to see this event taking place because I am afraid that we have been losing track of Jack Chambers and his work. His paintings are rarely seen and his films almost never. And, of course, he made all these things to be looked at."[62]

Even back in 1989 Curnoe was not alone in his concern that Chambers was slipping away from public renown. The latest attempt to call back that ever-receding tide took place in 2011-12 (35 years after the artist's death) when Jack Chambers was the subject of a major retrospective at the Signy Eaton Gallery of the Art Gallery of Ontario (AGO) that was curated by Dennis Reid. But unlike the travelling William Kurelek retrospective that same year, the Chambers exhibition (not very engagingly given the grab-baggy subtitle, *Light, Spirit, Time, Place and Life*) did not travel to any other galleries and doesn't seem to have done much to bring the featured artist to any sort of widened or renewed public appreciation.

Realizing that many 21st century art patrons might greet the announcement of the exhibition by asking, 'Jack Who?' AGO director Matthew Teitelbaum acknowledged in the very first paragraph of his foreword to that show's catalogue that Chambers' "work has all but disappeared" from the national consciousness and that this exhibition is "a project of repositioning", to pull "back into the spotlight an artist indispensable to a history of the image in twentieth-century Canada."[63]

The Walrus magazine followed up their big splashy preview article on the AGO show by Sara Angel (which was everything that Teitelbaum and Reid could have desired for getting the word out) with alarmed coverage on their website of the washout that occurred at the media preview immediately before the show's grand opening. "Where's the Love?" asked the headline of Barry Chong's update:

"'Do we have more than four people? This is Jack Chambers, for God's sake!' These are the words of a bewildered Art Gallery of Ontario foot soldier, uttered moments before the nearly media-less media preview for *Jack Chambers: Light, Spirit, Time, Place and Life*, the gallery's expansive tribute to Canada's best-known artist outside the Group of Seven. I was surprised too – Chambers should not be a tough sell."[64]

That website article was accompanied by a photo of one of the AGO's more recent Chambers' acquisitions, the numinous and eerie *Self-Portrait No. 2* from 1953 which he finished just before he set sail for his open-ended tour of Europe. A commenter to that update on *The Walrus* website who identified himself as "Ezekiel-bones" (the first of only two commentators which, again, seems to reflect Chambers' lack of a following) chimed in with a note of stubborn incomprehension that may all too accurately describe the current state of Chambers' reputation:

"Eh, maybe Canucks aren't that interested in the art of dead old white guys that living old white dudes think is awesome? Maybe if AGO tried to dig a bit beneath the surface to what's really edgy in Canadian art, people would be more interested? I never heard of Chambers till this article – and the picture in the article is not really that interesting to me. Why are we all supposed to bow to what 'experts' tell us is real art? I personally don't like most of it in terms of just looking at it – and it doesn't give one anything to think about conceptually either. Portraits of people . . . hmm okay. Pretty boring if you ask me."

The 2012 exhibition gathered together more than 100 finished works in various media as well as a fascinating array of source materials such as note-books, letters and preparatory sketches and photographs. These works and sup-porting materials were arranged in different quadrants of the exhibition space that addressed the four great organizing themes of *Light, Spirit, Time and Place*. It should have been enough yet what one heard again and again from people with an informed appreciation of Chambers' accomplishment was that it was not.

Incredibly, this modern day retrospective had fewer pieces than the first big Chambers' retrospective at the Vancouver Art Gallery in 1970 – a show that subsequently moved on to the AGO and was mounted when Chambers was still alive and had at least seven more productive years ahead of him.

My wife and I almost had the gallery to ourselves on the day we moved through, quite late in its run, and one never heard of crowds at this exhibition to compare with those that attended the Kurelek show. I tried to get attendance figures out of the AGO but they weren't terribly helpful. The first answer I got from the AGO's Iain Hoadley was downright alarming:

"We had a total of 273 visitors during that time that the exhibition was on display. It was included with general admission so those were the number of visitors that came into our building at that time. How many actually went to Jack Chambers is unknown because we don't check tickets at the entrance to Jack Chambers but at least that's in the range of how many people were in the building and likely went through the Chambers exhibition at that time."

"So, just 273?" I asked.

"Yeh, 273,000."

"Ah. That's a little better."

"Yeh."

"So there's no way of sorting that out a little?"

"No. As I say that was our nets – that's paid attendance, that's members, that's groups and anybody that gets a complementary ticket. No further way to break that out, really."

"Why didn't the show tour?"

"We did pitch it to a few institutions but none of them responded."

I asked Nancy Poole what she made of the AGO show, strongly suspecting (quite correctly) that she would not have been impressed.

"That was a farce because really what it was about was the gallery showing off what they had acquired and asking a few of us to lend work to the show. There should have been a proper retrospective. They didn't do that but there was one there in 1970. Well, 40 years later it wouldn't have hurt them to make a major show of it. They didn't make a major show of it; not at all."

What was it missing?

"An incredible amount of work. It was missing early works, other paintings, major works. For instance they didn't have the great nude from London. They didn't have the huge *Lake Huron* from London. You see, they wouldn't borrow from any other galleries. They didn't have *Olga at Arva* from Montreal. They were missing great works that truly demonstrated his genius. All they were doing was showing off what they had. Now, that's not very nice of me. Well, it's not – because I was looking at it from the point of view of what was best for Jack. And they didn't do what was best for Jack. They should have shown all his work and borrowed from London and borrowed from Vancouver and Winnipeg and Montreal. They should have borrowed from the other institutions that had bought far earlier than they had. It was too thin. Far too thin. The great *Lake Huron*, the huge one that we have here, his nude that we have here, *Mums* that we have here."

Do you think Chambers' place is secure?

"I don't see how it cannot be. How can you deny talent of that kind? I suppose it's happened dozens of times. But now that the AGO has as much as they have, I think that probably has secured his place even though they didn't do a proper show."

What are the rules here? When could we have the next big Chambers' show?

"It all depends on the curators and the terrible thing that's happened is if you went into the universities and into the visual and fine arts departments and you said the name 'Jack Chambers', I'd hate to think how few would be able to say they'd ever heard of him. It won't be until a curator with a fair amount of clout in a major gallery – try the National (*laughs*) – comes along and says, 'We have a great Canadian artist and we haven't seen his work in the National Gallery ever . . . ' They've never . . . Someday, somehow that will happen, I feel sure, because the work can't be denied. It's there. But it will depend on a curator coming along and discovering him."

The one great delight that I found at the AGO show – and a work I'd never come across before in my life and kept returning to again and again because I found it so powerfully affecting – was his last, great perceptualist masterpiece, *Meadow* (1972–76). The scene depicted is an open field in London's Gibbons Park. Situated just a few doors south of his Lombardo Ave. home, the sprawling park was almost like a grander and wilder extension of Chambers' own backyard. It was a place he knew intimately and where he took his family for picnics and swims and where he frequently rambled about in deep conversation with some of his closest friends like Ross Woodman and Susan Downe.

Recalling that flood of paintings where he first made use of family photographs after returning to London, Sarah Milroy wrote, "The image of the meadow had long been a motif in Chambers' art, with crops of ancestors, mothers and children and exotic flora and fauna seeming to germinate spontaneously from the fecund soil."[65]

This is another south-western Ontario field, rimmed with trees and sprouting one shingled rooftop in the distance, but there are no people here. The sun is setting off to the right and great long shadows of trees all but cover the meadow; only a few streaky patches of lush grass in the upper middle and left still bathe in the brightness and warmth of the descending sun. It is a sublimely peaceful scene even though looking out on such a vista would have made the much younger Chambers a little panicky. When such a mellowing light had signalled the end of a radiant day at Port Stanley, the ten year old Chambers found that it "made the evening sad, and I looked forward to getting back home and remembering the sunshine and the water when everything was right." But contrary to his expectation, that day wasn't over yet and it suddenly opened up to a whole new adventure that taught him a lesson he would never forget.

Over the course of his life and artistic career Jack Chambers made his mark by not looking away from or ignoring those banal or dismal scenes that initially seem to promise little but which can actually reveal epiphanies if we take the time to look a little deeper and faithfully record what we find. More than any other of his paintings *Meadow* has what Ross Woodman called, "the quality of one last look" and, if the scene is a little more subdued and its details not quite so meticulously observed, it is nonetheless as beautifully and lovingly rendered as any of his perceptualist masterpieces. The painting exudes, as tangibly as the aroma of the evening-cooled grass he has here depicted, both his undimmed fondness for the world where he was privileged to live and a courageous acceptance of his hard fate that it couldn't have been for longer.

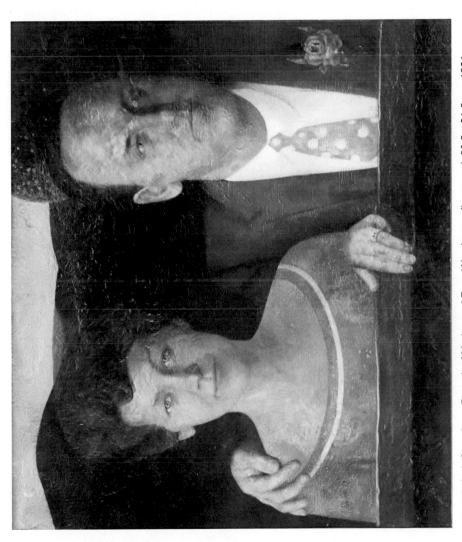

PLATE 5 Jack Chambers: Portrait of Marion and Ross Woodman, oil on wood, 80.5 x 91.5 cm, 1961. Art Gallery of Ontario, Toronto. From the collection of Ross and Marion Woodman. 98835

PLATE 6 Jack Chambers: 401 Towards London No.1, oil on mahogany, 183 x 244 cm, 1968 – 69. Art Gallery of Ontario, gift of Norcen Energy Resources Ltd., 1986, 86/47

PLATE 7 Jack Chambers: Sunday Morning No. 2, oil on wood, 121.9 x 121.9 cm, 1968 – 70.
Courtesy Loch Gallery, Toronto

PLATE 8 Jack Chambers: Lake Huron No. 4, oil on wood, 121.9 x 121.9 cm, 1972 – 76.
Courtesy Loch Gallery, Toronto

JACK CHAMBERS

Works cited in this essay:

CHP   Reid, Dennis, ed. *A Concise History of Canadian Painting*, 2nd edition. Toronto: Oxford University Press, 1988.

CJC   Woodman, Ross G. *Chambers: John Chambers Interviewed by Ross G. Woodman*. Toronto: Coach House Press, 1967.

FJC   Elder, Kathryn, ed. *The Films of Jack Chambers*. Toronto: Cinematheque Ontario Monographs, 2002.

JC   Chambers, Jack. *Jack Chambers*. London, Ontario: Nancy Poole, 1978.

JCLD   Chambers, Jack; Cheetham, Mark A., Holubizky, Ihor, Welch, Adam (essays). *Jack Chambers: The Light from the Darkness, Silver Painting and Film Work* (exhibition catalogue). London, Ontario: Museum London, 2011.

LSTPL   Reid, Dennis, ed. *Jack Chambers: Light, Spirit, Time, Place and Life* (exhibition catalogue). Fredericton: Goose Lane Editions; Toronto: Art Gallery of Ontario, 2011.

PCB   Poole, Nancy Geddes. *The Past . . . Comes Back*. London, Ontario: Nancy Poole, 2012.

PS   Prothero, Frank; Prothero, Nancy. *Port Stanley: Musings & Memories*. Port Stanley: Nan-Sea Publications, 1980.

R & G   Smart, Tom. *Jack Chambers' Red and Green: decrypted by Tom Smart*. Erin: Porcupine's Quill, 2013.

Citations from newspaper and magazine articles, website postings and unpublished papers are listed in full below.

CHAPTER 7: A TRIP TO THE BEACH

1. *JC*, p. 20
2. *PS*, p. 161
3. *JC*, p. 125

CHAPTER 8: A SOLITARY ARTIST IN TRAINING

4. *JC*, p. 34
5. *JC*, p. 27
6. *JC*, p. 20
7. *JC*, p. 32
8. *JC*, p. 38
9. *JC*, p. 38
10. *JC*, pp. 40–42
11. *JC*, p. 44
12. *JC*, p. 42

13. *R & G*, p. 133
14. *London Free Press*, 5 February, 1951
15. *JC*, p. 47
16. *FJC*, p. 19
17. *JC*, p. 49

CHAPTER 9: EUROPE WAS THE PLACE TO BE
18. *CJC*, p. 3
19. *JC*, p. 49
20. *JC*, p. 51
21. Jack Chambers Collection, Art Gallery of Ontario. Avis Lang: Interview with Jack Chambers, 23 May, 1973.
22. *JC*, p. 53
23. *Sarnia Observer*. "Young London Artist Finally Hits Success." 25 February, 1971
24. *JC*, p. 53
25. *London Free Press*. Lenore Crawford: "Portrait of Jack Chambers." 14 November, 1970
26. *JC*, p. 58
27. *JC*, p. 60
28. *JC*, p. 63
29. *JC*, p. 76
30. *LSTPL*, p. 71
31. *JC*, p. 80
32. *JC*, p. 84
33. *JC*, p. 88

CHAPTER 10: THE FACES OF LONG LOST FRIENDS
34. *FJC*, pp. 181-83
35. *LSTPL*, p. 11
36. *Toronto Star*. David Cobb: "Lines on Art." 2 November, 1963
37. *LSTPL*, p. 28
38. *FJC*, p. 183
39. *FJC*, p. 183
40. *JC*, p. 98
41. *JCLD*, p. 25
42. *CJC*, p. 15
43. *JCLD*, p. 8
44. *FJC*, pp. 46-47
45. *London Free Press*. Lenore Crawford: "Portrait of Jack Chambers." 14 November, 1970
46. *LSTPL*, p. 189
47. *FJC*, p. 184

CHAPTER 11: THE PERCEPTUALIST MASTERPIECES
48. *CHP*, p. 318
49. *LSTPL*, p. 135
50. *FJC*, p. 16
51. *LSTPL*, p. 67
52. *JC*, p. 152
53. *JC*, pp. 122 & 125
54. Bill McGrath, paper to The Baconian Club of London and The Wrinklings, 2012
55. *JC*, pp. 113-14
56. Bill McGrath, paper to The Baconian Club of London and The Wrinklings, 2012
57. *Canadian Magazine*. "What makes Jack Chambers Canada's top-priced painter?" 6 February, 1971
58. *LSTPL*, pp. 79-82

CHAPTER 12: FIGHTING FOR HIS LIFE
59. *LSTPL*, p. 82
60. *R & G,* p. 76
61. *PCB*, p. 111
62. *FJC*, p. 185
63. *LSTPL*, p. 7
64. *The Walrus* website, 14 December, 2011
65. *LSTPL*, p. 65

GREG CURNOE

13

IT CAN HAPPEN HERE

MY OLDEST BROTHER Dave was tooling around in our parents' car one autumn night in the mid '60s when he drove down Weston Street and pointed out a rather boxy and flat-roofed house to me. "That's where Greg Curnoe lives,' he said. "It used to be a factory."

"Who's Greg Curnoe?" I asked in my ignorance which was profoundly deep and total. I would have been 14 or 15 years old.

"He's an artist," said Dave, and a whole series of cosmic tumblers fell into place in my skull and the universe suddenly became more interesting. This was the first time I'd heard of an artist who wasn't dead or who didn't live so far away that I'd probably never get to see his house. The implications of this were staggering. "It can happen here," I thought. "It can happen now."

I hadn't met the man yet and grown to like and admire him as much as I would. I had yet to clap eyes on a single blessed work he'd created, though Dave told me that his own name was included in a long list of words and names and statements in one of Greg's lettered works from December of 1966, *24 Hourly Notes*; his name popping up because Dave had interviewed him for a piece in the UWO student newspaper, *The Gazette*. This very attractive and empowering idea that art could be and was being made here was an encouragement – indeed a kind of epiphany – that Curnoe provided and continues to provide nearly a quarter century after his death for more London artists of all kinds than we will ever be able to enumerate.

Unlike the other two artists examined in this study, Greg Curnoe (1936-92) was not a Roman Catholic. Indeed, he felt no attraction whatsoever to any of the world's religions, at least as a reasoning adolescent and then adult who could no longer be hauled off to Calvary United Church on Sunday mornings by his parents. According to all the reports of those who knew him best, he was as thoroughgoing a religious sceptic as ever drew breath but probably owing to his rarely-failing lightness of touch and humour and also perhaps as a mark of respect for both of his parents and particularly his mother whose faith was deep and sincere, this scepticism never emerged in his art or his conversation as animosity but only as bemused indifference or incomprehension. His friend Bob

McKenzie told me that the usual Curnoe answer for any inquiry of a religious or mystical nature was: "I don't think about that sort of thing."

In his 1984 essay, *Oregionalism: Geocentrism and the Notion of Originality* which appeared in the first issue of *Provincial Essays*, poet and writer Christopher Dewdney wrote of his friend: "Curnoe, for his part, has always had a profound mistrust of mysticism or anything that smacked of the irrational or psychological, any system of belief or theory, in fact, that supplanted logical and clearly perceivable descriptions with anything that referred to hidden realities or symbolic meanings. For Greg Curnoe, reality is inherently apparent and perceivable to the clear thinking individual possessed of common sense. Mystic concerns only confuse the issue, bringing in seemingly deliberate complications where none are necessary."

For somebody whose life was so much of a piece, who had such a rare and heightened sense of fidelity and loyalty, and for whom continuity and keeping in touch with his earliest influences and inspirations was so important, it can seem surprising that having been exposed to church as a child, Curnoe let it go so completely as an adult, never referenced religion as an artist. And yet a case is made by some brave souls that Curnoe's own religious capacity wasn't so much jettisoned as rechanneled.

In his final recorded interview with me over Christmas of 2013, Ross Woodman (then in the process of a radical reappraisal and upgrading of Curnoe's worth) said, "Greg is not religious in any recognizable sense but his dedication to and his personal identification with London struck me as religious – a Protestant religiousness. But talk to Curnoe and he would say that was sheer nonsense and I would understand that."

Woodman was his usual insightful self in identifying the distinctly Protestant flavour of Curnoe's quasi-religious devotion to London. Unlike Kurelek or Chambers, Curnoe – who read independently and widely and attained a far broader and deeper grasp of the art scene than either of those artistic compatriots – never aspired to situate himself within some larger tradition or insert himself into an established milieu. Unlike Kurelek, Curnoe never wished there was some way to release his paintings without signing them. Indeed his very particular personality was central to his art-making; both in its in-studio conception and execution as well as in its public reception.

In saying this, I am not suggesting that Curnoe was encumbered with any more ego or self-regard than any artist requires to create something and believe that other people might want to look at it as well. Curnoe was not a self-regarding fathead and repeatedly displayed a selfless concern for the welfare of other lesser known artists. Celebrity came to him early and he repeatedly did what he could to – if not push away exactly – at least broaden the range of fame's spotlight so that its warmth and glow fell upon other practitioners as well. The work he produced in the 1960s when he enjoyed his greatest celebrity as the newest sensation wasn't a patch in terms of craftsmanship and realization on the work of his maturity. But in a way that isn't true in encountering the best work of Kurelek or Chambers, some knowledge of Curnoe's personality was a necessary prerequisite to 'getting' what he was up to. This was particularly so at first but even towards the end of his life, Curnoe was still producing the occasional work whose full appreciation hinged on one's knowledge of and interest in Curnoe the personality rather than Curnoe the artist – such as a bold lettered work from 1987 that asked the questions: "WHAT IF DAILY LIFE IN CANADA IS BORING? WHAT IF I AM NOT AWARE OF WHAT IS INTERESTING TO OTHERS ABOUT MY LIFE?"

Unlike Chambers, Curnoe would never submit to any school's regimen regarding how art should be made. For Curnoe there was no such thing as a universal curriculum for an education in visual art. As long as the aspiring artist honed his craft and faithfully followed his own curiosity, he'd be all right. Yes, Curnoe made a point of knowing what was going on in other times and other places but he was determined to emulate none of it. The distinctly Protestant note that Woodman identifies is struck in the way that Curnoe always kicked against the idea that there were authorities or centres of power that needed to be referenced or deferred to. He might listen to what certain experts had to say or check out what scenes were unfolding in certain cities or countries but ultimately he would be responsible for his education and his practice. He would figure it all out for himself and go his very own way by staying where he was and being answerable to no one else, thank you very much.

Curnoe's devotion to London was the most stubborn and the most original thing about him; the most endearing, the most perverse and the most inspiring. Though he would never have phrased it this way, for Greg Curnoe, London, Ontario was The New Jerusalem – the ideal city and the only city (at least as far as he was concerned and he had difficulty seeing this might not be the case for others) where all could be fulfilled. I remember interviewing Christopher Dewdney in the mid '80s shortly after Dewdney had landed work at York University and had finally decided he really would have to leave his hometown and move to Toronto. He was deeply touched – and I couldn't help sensing, a little appalled – at how fervently Curnoe had beseeched him and badgered him to not give up on London; insisting not just that London needed him but that for the purpose of realizing his poetic gifts most fully, Dewdney needed London.

London writer and university professor Stan Dragland (who ultimately left London too but at least had the decency to hang in until after Curnoe died) spoke for literally hundreds of London artists, writers and musicians when he shared his memory of Curnoe with journalist Doug Fetherling in a memorial cover story in *Canadian Art* magazine in the summer of 1993: "I met him at Michael Ondaatje's house here in 1970, the year I moved to London. The Nihilist Spasm Band, I must say, made awful music that cured me for years of wanting to hear any more like it. Yet from such things I came to know that I could live and work in London. In all the years I've been here, Greg laboured to make an arts community, trying to fold people into it."

In that same article, Dewdney summarized the centrality of London to Curnoe's life and art: "For him, sense of place was essential, part of his empiricism. In all Greg's work, there is the awareness of 'This is my place.' That, he felt, was the only real subject. He felt that to compare what one was doing with other localities or styles was the worst provincialism. Such was the grammar of his experience: regional identity first, but conscious of what went on elsewhere."[1]

For Curnoe, there was no deprivation (indeed, there were many benefits) to living and working in a place that might be perceived as a cultural backwater. He believed that wherever an artist happened to live was fine. In fact there was more potential for a really original vision to flourish away from the usual centres. In Nowheresville an artist was less likely to get caught up in passing fads and sensations and would be better able to shut out any distracting media buzz and instead zero in on the forces in his own life and immediate environment that most fascinated him.

In a 1970 interview with Elizabeth Dingman published in the November 28 edition of *The Telegram*, Curnoe answered the mandatory 'Why do you insist on living in London?' question this way: "It's where I was born, where my sons and many of my friends were born . . . [He's not snubbing Zoe here. His only daughter wasn't born yet.] What goes on here couldn't happen in cities over 200,000. In a small city there is less privacy but more concern with people. That's how things get done. People know what you are doing. It gets around pretty quickly. There is none of the closed-up studio paranoia of 'I'll not let the guy in because he'll steal my ideas' . . . I don't want London to change too much. Probably I'm pro-Canadian because I think the only way you can progress is in a small situation. The same holds true for Ontario, for Canada. There must be resistance to the U.S. which is a centralizing force geared to commercial interests. There's nothing in that setup for anybody. I'd rather be called anti-American than pro-Canadian.

"I'm not talking about isolation. At one time nobody showed outside London, but you can't sell enough here. You have to have it both ways, otherwise you get a narrow thing. You cannot afford to ignore what's going on outside but you must not lose sight of what's first: the things within hearing and seeing distance. That's where it all starts. That's where I think McLuhan is incorrect in his assumption of the world as a village. Our culture is extremely complicated. The only one we can possibly understand is what we come in immediate contact with . . . When I came here [after bombing out at the Ontario College of Art], people said, 'Why? It's so isolated.' There is a distinct culture here as there is in regions all over Canada. It just needs articulate artists to bring it out."[2]

A big Curnoe watercolour which I saw during a studio visit in 1988 (never finished or titled and presently rolled up in a tube in his Weston Street home) featured a pair of sunglasses, a guidebook and a touristy t-shirt floating in the air over Lake Huron. On the front of the shirt were printed four place names of international importance – London, Paris, Rome and Grand Bend. The Bend, of course, is London's beach playground on Lake Huron, 40 miles to the north. But Curnoe being Curnoe, London – and for that matter, perhaps Paris as well – were winking references to the Ontario cities that bear those names. Yes, it was a joke but yes (as with most of Curnoe's jokes), on some significant level he meant it too. Curnoe believed that the operational factor in art and life is the consciousness of the perceiver: that anywhere on planet Earth could serve quite nicely as the gateway to experience and truth so long as the artist had an organic connection to that place.

British Columbia-based poet, historian and university professor George Bowering recalls in his book, *The Moustache: Memories of Greg Curnoe*, that, "Greg didn't like it when he was called a pop artist. I think it was mainly because in the '60s the pop artists were USAmerican. It was a USAmerican phenomenon and a USAmerican name. Greg said he was interested in neglected Canadian details and the stuff that was around him in his life. The pop artists were after the attention of the fickle New York gallery shoppers. He was not pop and he was not op, the other buzzword in newspapers of the time. To get him mad I used to call him pop. Jeez, he would say, and rub his nose with his knuckles. What kind of artist are you then? I'm a London artist, he would say, every time."[3]

I was delighted when I discovered that Curnoe shared my enthusiasm for N.C. Wyeth, the American painter who made his living by illustrating adventure stories for children like *Treasure Island* and *Robin Hood*. Wyeth's best work is just overwhelming in its passion and colour and ingenious structure but most educated critics and patrons won't give him the time of day because he did illustrations for books. It was also reassuring to see that Curnoe's notorious anti-American animus which struck many people (such as cultural commentator Robert Fulford) as sometimes teetering over into obnoxious bigotry, wasn't absolute.

Curnoe was never impressed by an artist's reputation in critical or academic circles. Where other artists might dash off an homage to Chagall or Picasso or Bruegel the Elder, Curnoe listed his favourite cartoon characters in *Dessin Anime*, a big, bold watercolour from 1987: "Betty B., Daffy D., Popeye, Superman, Woody W., Mickey M., Goofy, Elmer F., Droopy, Mighty M., Screwball and Tin Tin." (Again, except for Tin Tin, and, some might argue, Superman, all were of American derivation.)

For Curnoe there was no working model for what an artist's life should be. If you needed to travel the world as a beggar, take lots of mind-altering drugs, explore the wonders of homosexuality or marry a series of women whose incompatible temperaments would drive you into agonies of tortured artistic production . . . well okay, if you really must. Curnoe was utterly faithful to his first and only wife Sheila, was emotionally and practically very present in the raising of their three children – Owen (born 1966), Galen (1968) and Zoe (1971) – was refreshingly un-eccentric and un-self-preoccupied, and for all the unorthodoxy of his calling as an artist and the originality of his vision, Curnoe displayed a sober and hard-working diligence that would've paid equally big dividends in hardware store management or accounting.

Sometimes the real originals are so comfortable with themselves that they can risk appearing normal. Like a trimmer, fitter, non-smoking Peter Gzowski (whom he sort of resembled as both of them realized and joked about during interviews on Gzowski's CBC Radio shows) Greg Curnoe was unflappable; so disarmingly straightforward and friendly, so utterly self-assured that he was somehow irresistible.

Sheila told me of her first formal introduction to Greg one afternoon in 1965 at his third-floor, King Street studio. "Here was this strange character wearing braces and pants that were too short and too tight, heavy work boots and this big moustache standing in the middle of this mess . . . these colours and images . . . and I looked at the room and it was . . . this is what I wanted to do! Ever since I was fifteen, I'd thought I was going to be an artist. Didn't we all? But this guy was different. He was doing it."

Greg Curnoe's appeal was exactly that uncomplicated. At the snooty, pedigreed cat show of modern art (Should I be liking this artist's work? Should I *appear* to be liking this artist's work?) Curnoe was the guileless, bounding mongrel, the cheerful mutt, who upset all the display tables and tangled up the ankles of the judges with his leash and won every heart in the room. He wasn't posing and waiting for ribbons or trying to come up to anybody else's standards. He just made the body of work which was his to create and revolutionized everybody's perspective in the process.

It is no exaggeration to say that from here on in, the art of our region will be looked at in terms of pre and post-Curnoe. He wasn't the only artist who took part in the regionalist explosion of the 1960's but all of the critics (from the Curnoe-besotted art historian Dennis Reid to the more grudging and sometimes prickle-ish Nancy Poole) point to Curnoe as that movement's central and defining figure, the sine qua non (literally, 'without which, not') and rallying point of an entire scene. Pre-Curnoe the art of our region – even something as locally celebrated as Paul Peel's painting of the Covent Garden Market – conformed to imported, European traditions. (And Peel had to win acceptance in France before Canadians, let alone Londoners, would acknowledge his genius.) Post-Curnoe, the onus is on our artists to go digging in a local garden and come up with our own indigenous bones. Post-Curnoe, our artists can take confidence in the victory which Curnoe won: if they can make their work interesting and fresh enough, then the world and its media, even horrible old *TIME* magazine, will come to London, Ontario.

By the time of his death in November of 1992, five days shy of his 56th birthday, Curnoe was starting to iron out some apparent paradoxes in his life. For every apple cart he had once pushed over, he had set up a new fruit stall of his own. The one-time Hell-raiser and rebel had become a bearer of standards. The wild child had become the head of a family and the father figure for an entire artistic community. For instance, singled out by Nancy Poole in her history of London Art (*The Art of London, 1830-1980*, Blackpool Press, 1984) as the main force behind a 1962 'happening' which threatened to wreck the old London Art Museum when it was situated on the second floor of the Central Library on Queens Avenue, 30 years later Curnoe had become a founding member of Save London, a citizens' coalition dedicated not to the trashing of our most venerable institutions but to the preservation of London's architectural heritage.

Or try on this paradox: In 1968, the outraged (and outrageous) young artist had his virulently anti-American, 26-panel mural for Montreal's Dorval Airport yanked from the wall by the Department of Transport for fear that it might set off an international incident. The mural was positioned right by the U.S. 'Arrivals' tunnel, meaning that all the American tourists coming up to Montreal had to walk right past a depiction of – among other things – President Lyndon Baines Johnson (or someone who looked so much like him as to make Curnoe's denials less than convincing) getting his hand hacked off by a working propeller built right into the work. Some 20 years later that no-longer-so-young artist was able to sit in the studio of his Weston Street home (which the banned Dorval commission largely paid for) and tell me that, "Sheila and I talk a lot about censorship . . . what it means, particularly for women, if there are no limits to what you can say, how and where you say it. Are some forms of expression even uglier and more destructive than censorship? We kick that one around a lot."

The British wit Max Beerbohm once sketched a series of cartoons where he'd juxtapose older and younger caricatures of famous writers and politicians who faced off against themselves. These two representations of the same person would be appalled at – respectively – what rabid little twerps they used to be, or what smugly complacent oafs they were destined to become. These bifurcated cartoons were undeniably funny even if they weren't exactly fair. When you go a little deeper than that which can be construed by skimming an early page and a later page of anybody's life story, you can start to trace the various themes as they've had to develop and change over the intervening years. With even the slightest investment of empathy, it was always possible to discern the unyielding spine of personal integrity that ran right through Curnoe's life; a clear and reigning philosophy that would perhaps be highlighted or downplayed in this or that season of his life depending on the issues in play at that particular time but which did not alter its fundamental shape. In a way Curnoe's whole approach to his life and his art was neatly encapsulated in a doggerel couplet he inscribed in my wife's autograph book when she approached him at a Twelfth Night banquet at the Auberge du Petit Prince in the early '70s in her capacity as a star-struck fan:

"Roses are red, violets are blue,
Learn to paddle your own canoe."

14

GORDON AND NELLIE'S FIRSTBORN

GREG CURNOE'S CANOE was first ushered into the rushing stream of life on November 19, 1936 at London, Ontario's Victoria Hospital. (That sentence, by the way, in employing a hokey poetic metaphor, was just the kind of hooey that Greg abjured in any kind of writing but particularly in art criticism. Poet Christopher Dewdney told Doug Fetherling of the care he had to take in writing texts for catalogues of Curnoe's exhibitions: "You had to be careful writing of Greg to say nothing less than the obvious.")[4]

After a few days' residence there, he went to live in the south London home on Langarth Avenue – an English cottage-style bungalow which Greg always thought resembled Snow White's cottage in the Walt Disney movie – that his maternal grandfather had built for Greg's parents Gordon and Nellie (nee Porter) and which they had first moved into just three months before.

In her 2001 family memoir, *My Brother Greg* (published by London-based Ergo Productions) Lynda Curnoe produced just the kind of book that Greg would've loved; an unpretentious and downright account of her oldest brother's life that takes great care to situate him in his familial and geographic contexts – the two classifications from which he derived his greatest sense of meaning and belonging. George Bowering's *The Moustache* appeared the year after Greg's death, whereas Lynda Curnoe waited almost a decade before bringing her book forth. Hungrily reading both memoirs soon after their publication, I responded rhapsodically to Bowering's because here was a guy who was really on Greg's wavelength and who talked the same lingo, moved in the same bohemian circles and had an insider's access to his subject. Lynda's book in comparison seemed kind of pedestrian and stodgy, heavy on the meat and potatoes and not much sauce.

I've gone back and re-read both of them this year and was surprised to discover that my reactions to these very different texts have completely reversed over the intervening years. Now that Greg's been gone for almost a quarter century and time has marched on in its inexorable, world-transforming, detail-erasing way, I profoundly appreciate the care Lynda Curnoe has taken to fill in the background and particulars of her story. Bowering's book, a collection of quick snapshot-style memories rather than a full portrait, still works for me when he recalls certain quintessential Curnoe gestures – the ever-handy pencil parked behind his right ear, the quick knuckle rub on the side of his head or his nose when formulating a thought – or his characteristic manners of speech. Greg was always so gentle about disagreeing with you and would preface his contrary remarks with some kind of genial softener of which Bowering supplies two: "I'm not sure I agree with that," and "That's an interesting way of looking at it."[5]

But for the most part, Bowering's book no longer tells me enough whereas Lynda's book tells me just the sort of stuff I now want to know – where Greg went to school and how he got along with his teachers, what were the comics and trading cards and pop bottles he collected, how did he interact with his parents and his siblings, what were his summer jobs. No one but Lynda would risk appearing so banal as to include a paragraph like the following in her memoir of her famous brother:

"Our Porter grandparents lived only one block west of us, at the corner of Wharncliffe Road and Langarth, in another house built by my grandfather. The Porters' presence defined the neighbourhood for us, so that it seemed to belong to us. We were always walking up to Grandma's house and it was like our second home. As teenagers, Greg and [younger brother] Glen took turns mowing their lawn every week. Greg and [cousin] Gary spent hours sitting on their front porch listing the makes and models of cars that whizzed by on Wharncliffe Road, Highway 2, that linked London with Lambeth, Port Stanley and other towns to the south."[6]

As I say, all that might strike some readers as unremarkable – though that note about seeming to own the neighbourhood of his earliest youth helps to explain the enormous confidence that Greg possessed even as a child and which always drew people to him as a scene-maker. But his fellow townsmen (or at least this one) levitate with bliss at the mention of familiar London street names just as we feel a surge of nostalgic recognition when gazing at his early collage works that incorporate old LTC bus transfers, O-Pee-Chee bubble gum wrappers and cardboard Silverwood's milk lids; though secretly we wonder, "Can this work be as meaningful for anyone who didn't grow up in London handling civic trinkets like these?"

I asked Ross Woodman who moved to London as a young adult if he thought some knowledge of London was necessary before a person could 'get' Curnoe?

"I never thought that," he said. "I thought that getting Curnoe was a way of getting to London. And also a way of getting out of London in terms of what he did with that kind of material. Yeh, I can see Curnoe getting to you because you are very much caught up in the concrete, detailed life of London as a writer so your newspaper columns and articles on London would fit with Curnoe in a way I can recognize."

Sheila Curnoe has no doubt that her husband would have thoroughly approved of Lynda's book. "I supported Lynda completely when she wrote that book," Sheila told me.

"You came here from England at the age of 15," I said to Sheila. "So living with someone for whom life in London Ontario was so central, so unquestionable . . . Could you always relate?"

"It was funny. I didn't understand it at the time. We would go to 74 Langarth Street for supper with his mom and then we would get in the car. Driving home down the streets he would say, 'There's Mr. McIntosh's house and I delivered papers there. And I delivered papers there. And over there too.' And I'd think, 'Jesus Christ, do we have to do this every single time? I don't care where you delivered papers.' Now I see it differently. It was so important to Greg. These things were so important. Just this month I was driving up to Stratford with Robin and I couldn't stop remarking on how beautiful it is. The trees, the colours, the fields. I've felt this way for some time; that I am now looking at London and Ontario through Greg's eyes. And I value it so much more now. He would argue with George Bowering about how much more beautiful Ontario was than B.C. because B.C. is just over the top with its mountains and everything . . . it's trying too hard. When I look at the countryside now and I see how well we live here and all these idiots complaining about things . . . I think, 'Look at what you have here. And value what you have. He felt these things so strongly. And I think it came from the family – that rootedness. He was so unique and very special. He saw things differently than anyone else. And he was so taken with the blue colour of the Ontario sky. There's a certain blue that happens and he would have to stop everything and go out and look at it. Or sunsets. It was physical for him. He just loved it."

And on the not-so-mundane side, consider this little revelation that Lynda casually drops on page 42, citing the local origin of the colour theory employed throughout the career of an artist celebrated as a most unorthodox colourist. "In the 1920s and 30s, many young Londoners had summer holidays in nearby Port Stanley. Mum often spent hers there at Ruth Bright's parents' cottage on Bessie Street. The London and Port Stanley Railway carried trainloads of passengers to the lake every weekend. Port Stanley, on the shore of Lake Erie, had a famous dance pavilion called the Stork Club where Mum and her friends would go to dance. It also had a restaurant on the boardwalk called Mackies, distinctively painted bright orange and blue, colours Greg said had attracted him as a child and later influenced him as an artist."[7]

Any discussion of Greg Curnoe's art – whether it's about his figurative work or his lettered work, the earlier, cruder oil paintings which first brought him

wide renown or the more precisely accomplished water colours that he started producing in the later 1970's when he wasn't so much of a media darling
– makes mention of his bold use of intense colour combinations that simply
shouldn't work but in his case most brilliantly do. The end papers for the catalogue of his great 2001 retrospective, *Life & Stuff*, are the very same hot shade of
pink that I've only ever seen in two other books – one a cultural history of the
Barbie doll and the other, Barry Humphries' mock autobiography of his comic
alter ego, Dame Edna Everage, *My Gorgeous Life*. Curnoe's colour sense was
one of the most original things about him and here his sister matter-of-factly
explains that one significant origin of that originality was something he picked
up for free as a kid with a frosty glass of Orangeade.

The three Curnoe children (little brother Glen was born in 1939 and sister
Lynda in 1943) attended Wortley Road Public School and at the age of two,
Greg first met his exact contemporary – future diarist and street celebrity, Roy
McDonald – in Calvary United Church's basement nursery where they were
both members of an infantile (and decidedly non-musical) aggregation called
'The Baby Band'. It's delightful to picture these two London legends in the bud,
with over-sized heads and putty-ish limbs, slobbering all over each other and
their blocks while their parents upstairs warbled Protestant hymns.

From his very earliest years, Curnoe was a naturally magnetic leader; never
bossy or demanding but so engaged with the world and ideas that others were
irresistibly drawn to him. He was lucky in that both of his parents – particularly
Nellie, who was always on the scene as a stay-at-home mom – genuinely liked
kids and were always generously tolerant of the mess and noise that their children and the hordes of their visiting friends would get up to.

Lynda creates a sort of nostalgic panorama of the domestic/creative ferment at the Langarth Street house: "In my mind the three Curnoe children
still occupy that house and yard. They are still sleeping in bedrooms upstairs,
playing in the living-room, building constructions in the basement with their
friends. Greg, as a child, is still visible to me there in every room, crouching
on one knee on the dining-room floor, rolling and shaping his modelling clay
into cartoon figures, stretched out on the living-room carpet sorting his comic
books, or laughing and scooting about with Glen on the freshly-waxed hall
hardwood. Mental pictures remain of Greg at the supper table arguing with my
red-faced father about art, getting a job, taking responsibility. Outside on the
street, in front of the house, I remember him directing races with neighbourhood kids and, in the laneway, hammering soapbox cars together. I can still hear
his friends thundering up and down the basement stairs, to a studio where the
room was alive with music, talking and laughing. From this house and neighbourhood, Greg's life radiated outwards, until it included the world."[8]

A lot of kids don't really develop much social capacity until they enroll in school. For Curnoe the onset of formal education – temporarily at least – threatened to have the opposite effect; initially it cramped his style. School made life less interesting and dampened his social life. "Although Greg was outgoing, good-natured and friendly with strangers, he was unhappy to leave home and attend Wortley Road Public School Kindergarten," Lynda writes. "Leaving Glen at the Hodgsons' next door, Mum would take Greg's hand and walk him two blocks east on Langarth Street to Kindergarten every day, until he had the confidence to go by himself. His teacher, Miss Rhea, would meet them at the door and lead him inside. While he didn't cry over going to school, he would say to Mother every now and again, "I don't feel very well." On those days, she would let him stay home where he would lie on the couch creating cartoon figures from modelling clay. Other than absences from school for various real or imagined flus, Greg was never seriously injured or ill and was generally healthy, although throughout his life he did suffer from asthma."[9]

Sheila Curnoe paints a slightly less robust picture of her husband. I had asked her how she thought Greg would've aged, given the chance?

"He was a bit of a hypochondriac and I don't think he would've been happy about the whole thing," she answered. "He could not stand sickness. I remember him vomiting in the toilet once and – it astonished me – he was actually yelling, 'Help, help'. [laughs] And I thought, 'What have I married? How can this be? How can a grown man be yelling 'help, help'? But it happened."

What did he want help with?

"I think he wanted his mommy or something to stop the terrible feeling. He was just at the end of his rope. He didn't do pain very well. He cut himself once. He was pruning an apple tree and he cut himself very badly on his thumb and he came staggering in and there was all this blood and he was as white as a sheet. He couldn't take the sight of blood. I made him lie down on the floor and elevate his feet. He didn't know what to do with these feelings of illness and sickness or pain when it happened to other people or when it happened to himself."

From his very earliest childhood, Curnoe was always drawing and sketching. Both parents – and again, particularly Nellie who was sometimes known to whip off a not-too-shabby sketch herself – encouraged this. The Curnoe home was always well stocked with paper, pencils, paint sets and plasticene and Gordon's work downtown at *The Farmer's Advocate* newspaper (where Greg often helped out) introduced the boy early to the wonders of lettering and print and for his tenth Christmas Greg was given his very own rubber stamp set. A 1982 catalogue for his one man show at the National Gallery of Canada features some childhood cartoons he sketched of his brother and sister, the elaborate cover to a grade seven history project entitled, 'London's History' ("Satisfactory. You could be neater," his teacher wrote beneath the figure of a pioneer chopping down a tree), and a cartoon about relatives visiting for Sunday dinner with fat bottoms overflowing chairs and a speech balloon that says, 'BELCH'.[10]

Lynda writes: "Every year, the London YMCA held a Hobby Fair and Greg created some memorable art pieces for these events. One was a model of Ichabod Crane based on the Walt Disney movie of *The Legend of Sleepy Hollow*, which he and Glen had seen at the Elmwood Movie Theatre on Wharncliffe Road. The model was set in a box, which had a painted background of a graveyard and tombstones. The skinny, long-legged figure of Ichabod Crane was seated on a wild horse, which appeared to be flying out of the box. Crane's eyes were wild with fright. Because Greg was ill, at the time, Mum helped him complete the figure for the deadline."

Unlikely as it seems Lynda also recalls Greg's participation in the making of "a plasticene replica of the crown that Queen Elizabeth wore for her coronation in 1953. It was made of yellow clay with red clay for the rubies. Greg must have lost interest in the finishing stages so Mum purchased some purple velvet and completed the crown." She concludes this memory by succinctly expressing the different enthusiasms of the Curnoe brothers: "Through the years, Greg received several trophies as prizes for his work at the Hobby Fair, and Glen won prizes for his collections of coins."[11]

If one could ever construe any period of Greg Curnoe's life as 'lost', it would be his four long years at South Secondary School which he perceived as a dim but annoying nightmare. "I was totally out of my element at South," he told me in 1988. "I was a thoroughly mediocre student and person – no good at sports or my subjects and I just couldn't cut it socially, couldn't be bothered. My response to social tyranny was to lie low. Roy McDonald's was to act crazy. You couldn't say either one of us won acceptance in any genuine way."

Lynda concurs in her family memoir: "Beginning high school in 1950, at South Collegiate, a sprawling red brick building about four blocks east of our house, Greg still looked like a small, young boy, but by grade ten had started to grow. While almost happy at Wortley Road School, in high school he felt insignificant or as he told Mum, 'Like a young whipper-snapper.' He did not make many friends at South and there were few art courses for him to take."[12]

In a spring 1978 article for *artmagazine* on the enduring influence of Tom Thomson, Curnoe told Joan Murray about what minimal instruction he received at South: "When I was at South Collegiate in 1952-53, I was taking the art course, which was kind of a fill-in subject you took if you were weak in academic subjects. I took it because I was interested in it. The teacher had had some Tom Thomson repros, including *The Dam*. The other students didn't like it, but I remember liking it. This was my first exposure to any kind of modern art and I thought, 'This is good'."[13]

Luckily for Curnoe school wasn't everything. His extracurricular social life remained rich and various and as his commitment to making art broadened and deepened, his father helped him clear out and make over a space in the Langarth Street basement as his very first studio – a space which he christened by whipping up a hand-painted sign sporting flames and identifying the studio as 'Curnoe's Inferno'. As would ever be the case with Curnoe's studios, this space wasn't just the workshop where he concocted and brought forth his art; it was also his social headquarters.

Colleagues and friends always marvelled at Curnoe's willingness to let people hang out in his studios, never being reticent about letting people see what he was up to even during early or exploratory phases, never worrying about having concepts ripped off, and always seeming able to constructively work away in the midst of what could easily be mistaken for a full blown party.

In a 1999 interview with Judith Rodger, Nellie Curnoe remembered her son's studio in the basement of the family home: "'Curnoe's Inferno' somebody called it. They had all kind of sessions down there. It wasn't just an art studio. A lot of young men – not just young men, a lot of people – came. They gathered down there and had big discussions . . . There were people coming and going, running down my basement steps . . . I didn't know who they were . . . He made friends with everybody. They didn't have to be artists."[14]

In some reminiscences he provided for a 2014 show at the Michael Gibson Gallery, good friend and fellow artist Murray Favro describes the scene at Curnoe's King St. studio in 1964, capturing an atmosphere that was already in place in the space he carved out in his parents' basement:

"I saw all of his paintings at that time. He could paint with all of these people around. I was very impressed. Yes, I thought, this is what I want to do. It looked like fun. You just do what you want. Greg was enthusiastic about all things. He was a real collector of information and objects. At that time he was also making collages and pasting things together. He would talk to you and make the stuff. It never bothered him that people were around. Lots of people came up to visit him, and not just artists. There were students and university professors as well. He had a mixture of people. He read a lot and could talk about stuff that I had never heard about before.

"Greg had a huge collection of records and would always play music. Most of the records I was unfamiliar with. He had a real collection of interests and he was able to let the music and the books influence him, but not too much. Greg was able to handle it, with his work. Greg's studio was the real meeting place. That's where we would meet to talk. He would have parties there every Saturday, with 200 people, well, it seemed like 200 people, it was jammed. It was a very important hub for London at that time."[15]

In an extracurricular way, Curnoe was getting on with his education and artistic development as best he could. But instead of spinning his wheels for six hours a day at South, Curnoe should've been in the special art program at H.B. Beal. But his stated ambition to become a cartoonist was something that his parents and teachers were reluctant to lend encouragement and support to. Curnoe told me that the only times he ever heard about Beal (which despite its exceptional art school was most renowned locally as a technical and trades school situated in a rough part of town) were when his father would throw it out to him as a threat. "It was that tough school downtown full of thugs and creeps so they'd say, 'If you don't smarten up, then we're going to send you to Beal.' If only they had."

Having completed his junior and senior matriculation studies at South, Greg finally showed up at Beal in the fall of 1954. When he spoke to me about that educational shift more than 30 years later, I could still see the effects of that passage. The furrow left his brow as he visibly relaxed; everything about his physical attitude suggested that a prison door had just swung open.

"When I finally got to Beal, I couldn't believe it," he said. "That I could actually do what I wanted to do all day long – and this was school! I was taught by Herb Ariss and John O'Henly. They were nondirective teachers. In the mid 1950's, in London, these guys knew all about A.S. Neill and Summerhill. You had this autonomous department in a high school run by these people who were all wired up on the notion of free schools. Ariss would say, 'This is Bela Bartok and nobody understands him.' So I'd dig out all his records and see what was going on. Or, 'Here's a book that's too far out for everybody,' and I'd have to get a copy and read it. They'd talk about these things – Dadaism, cubism, surrealism – ask questions, point out doors that I never even knew existed . . . and I just ran with it. I guess I'd matured to the point where this approach was exactly what I needed."

From Beal, Curnoe went on to the Doon School of Art in Kitchener, worked doing commercial art at the Stewart Bender Screen Printing Company in London and then went to the Ontario College of Art in Toronto. He was only at the Doon School for one term in a class of amateur painters and school teachers. He didn't expect much and wasn't disappointed and even got some good out of it. While there he encountered the work of 19th century artist, Homer Watson, and appreciated it enough (perhaps seeing in Watson's work a precursor to his own 'regionalist' devotion) that he acquired one of Watson's old easels. His three years at OCA however, *the* Canadian art school, were so stupendously disappointing that they constituted a kind of anti-education – teaching him what not to do – and greatly assisted him in defining his own artistic philosophy and objectives.

"There was no comparison," he told me. "The lack of sophistication was appalling compared to what I'd known at Beal. These people hadn't even heard of Ezra Pound. They held up Picasso as some sort of god. I just thought it was a crock and I still think so. This notion that one person is the greatest in the world – I mean, that's silly – I rejected that completely. One of the first criticisms I got at OCA was that my work was too cartoony. It wasn't too cartoony. It *was* cartoony. I was a product of popular culture, the new folk culture, if you like. As an artist, I had to make use of that and that was what the OCA would've driven from my work if I'd let them."

Believing that ultimately, 'we educate ourselves,' Curnoe used his three years in Toronto (not 'four' as he tellingly mis-spoke in our interview; unconsciously extending this most disagreeable scholastic sentence) to bounce around from galleries to studios to public readings, talking to real artists and writers who made their livings from the original work of their wits and their hands. If OCA's fundamental message was, 'No, Mr. Curnoe, you can't do it like that,' then extracurricular consultations with artists of all kinds like A.Y. Jackson, Toni Onley, Graham Coughtry, Michael Sanouillet, Leonard Cohen and Raymond Souster told him otherwise, told him, 'You can do it anyway you want, anyway that you have to.' There is no question as to which of these messages was of greater value and inspiration for the young man.

In a 1983 *Globe & Mail* article by Judith Fitzgerald, Curnoe summed up the inadequacies of the OCA curriculum thus: "OCA was dull. It was also sterile. The instructors were formalists, pure and simple. I was reading Charles Olson and looking at Schwitters and listening to Little Richard and Louis Armstrong. OCA was into form and nothing more. They'd forgotten about content. I guess I was in a rebellious mood, but you can only talk about a certain shade of grey for so long."[16]

In a 1984 article on '60s art, *Three: The Sixties: All Together Now* printed in *Provincial Essays 2*, Barrie Hale included an exchange from an interview with then-OCA principal, Sydney Watson, in which Watson describes the treatment that rebellious upstarts like Curnoe could expect at his art college.

"Q: What about the romantic image of the rebel who revolts against the teaching of the atelier? Do you get many of that kind of rebel here?

"A: No – because the student can't rebel or he isn't going to graduate. I'd say that, per capita, our students are as conforming as any other students. I imagine you'd find more beatniks on the University of Toronto campus than you would here.

"Q: Is that good?

"A: It's good for us – it makes it a lot easier for the administration to run the college."[17]

In the spring of 1960, the poop hit the fan. "It was terrible," Curnoe told me. "I'd spent all this money and slogged away for four [sic] years, then I got into a big argument and I told my teachers how little I respected them. They went and failed me and my father had to come up and help me move my stuff back to London. I was really worried about how he'd take the news. My parents always got the usual guff from friends – 'Has Greg got a job yet or is he still painting?' – stuff like that. And so much of my art was geared to outrage everybody – parents included – that I couldn't really expect them to understand or approve but at least they usually had the patience to let it happen. When I told my father that I'd failed, that I wanted to set up a studio on my own, I remember he told me, 'Well, you've got to do what you think is right.' He understood. That was a revelation to me. A real milestone in our relationship."

15

TAKING A STAND IN LONDON

I T WAS IN THE immediate wake of that potentially crushing disappointment – being deemed a failed art student by the most highly regarded
college of art in the country – that Curnoe stepped into his own wobbly craft,
pushed his way into the open current and bloody well learned to paddle his
own canoe.

He submitted work to every group show going and mounted his own first
one man show within a year. Linking up with Jack Chambers when he returned
to London (and persuading Chambers by his example to stay here) Curnoe re-
connected at a deeper level with creative London stalwarts like Selwyn Dewdney and James Reaney and set about stirring up a whole community of fellow
painters, writers and poets and even some arts patrons who were ready, as he
was, to forsake the artistic dictates of Toronto, Montreal, New York and Paris
and see what was here in our own native soil that needed artistic exploration
and celebration.

It all came together so fast – with Curnoe at the hub of all of it – that you
can barely keep up with it. There was the legendarily awful Nihilist Spasm
Band for which he played drums and kazoo. Few people who ever heard them
could bear to return for a second gig. It was free-form noise rendered on mostly
home-made instruments; excruciating for anybody with any musical sensitivity.
But the band was so much fun to be around once they stopped playing, that
audiences learned to show up for their weekly gigs just as the lads were setting
down their instruments of torture. "Some husbands bowl once a week," Sheila
Curnoe told me once, releasing a long matrimonial sigh. "Greg has the band."

Though it was assumed that nobody else could've kept the Spasms up and
running for 30 years, the band has, in a manner of speaking, thrived in the almost 25 years since Curnoe's death. They released two albums during Curnoe's
lifetime and several more since and have had their back catalogue reissued by a
company called Alchemy that specializes in experimental or noise music. From
the mid 90's on they've toured Japan, Europe and the USA. "The Spasm Band
never performed in the United States while Greg was alive," his friend and *20
Cents* magazine editor Bob McKenzie told me. "That was totally out of the

question."

Curnoe was with the band for only one international gig in 1969 when Pierre Theberge of the National Gallery of Canada selected them for Canada's official delegation to the Paris Biennale. For the 2000 *no exhibition* at the London Regional Art & Historical Musem (a show that gathered together their distinctive homemade instruments, paintings, sculptures, posters and other band paraphernalia) Ben Portis wrote of that 1969 tour:

"The band gave two open air performances, at the Galerie de France and the Musee d'art modern de la Ville de Paris, reaching a few listeners and causing offense to most passers-by. The trip to Paris (including an added date at the Institute of Contemporary Art in London, England) was the first distant travel most of the NSB members had ever known. Curnoe collaged the whirlwind experience with tickets, receipts, and other incidental souvenirs in *Hands Across the Water* (1969). The band would not travel outside of Canada for another 27 years."[18]

Bob McKenzie first met Curnoe in June of 1960 at his studio on the third floor of 432 Richmond at the eastern foot of Carling Street, introduced by a woman who modelled for a class that was run by Selwyn Dewdney and Curnoe. "Deanna left and I was there with him. I don't remember what sort of conversation we had. There was a lot of his work hanging on the wall opposite where I was sitting. Then Brian Dibb came in sucking on a Popsicle. Greg said I was welcome to come there any time I liked so I did. I hung out at his studio at various times from then on. Greg and I figured out later that that was only about three weeks after he moved into his studio. He was five years older than me. It wasn't long after that that he rented a narrow little space farther north on Richmond – I can't tell you the exact address, I don't remember – but it was one of those really narrow storefronts. And he started an art gallery. I guess it was the first artist-run art gallery in London; in fact it might have been the first in the country. It didn't last very long. I remember going to one show there. I don't know how long it existed nor do I know how much play he would have gotten in the media – possibly none."

I mentioned to McKenzie the oft-heard lament at the time of Curnoe's death that not only have we lost Greg, we've lost all that stuff that happened around him.

"Greg always denied that he was the leader or instigator of anything," McKenzie said. "And to a certain extent that was true. He didn't deliberately organize things but stuff happened among the people who gathered in his studio. Everybody that was culturally alive in London would've visited Greg's studio at least once. Apart from his art the thing of greatest importance about Greg was that he received everybody and anybody in his studio. It was like the salons or coffee houses of the 18th century. It was where people could get together and exchange ideas and various enterprises had their beginnings from discussions that took place in Greg's studio – either that or the studio annex at the York Hotel."

In an historical footnote to our discussion, McKenzie mused on how the York Hotel became known as the official pub for Greg and his friends and is frequently cited as a sort of incubator for the London art scene of the '60s. "I can remember early on going with Greg to the London House at the corner of Talbot and Dundas, the Royal Alex, the Richmond Hotel and the Grigg and the York. But eventually the York became the only place."

In those first weeks and months back in London (sometimes sleeping at his parents' house but otherwise living at the studio) Curnoe also started up the first of a string of publishing ventures. I asked McKenzie who was a later editor of *20 Cents* magazine to sketch out some of that hazy history. "Greg had already started a magazine of his own called *Region*. I don't know how many were published. The only one I have is #8. It didn't have a regular publishing schedule. It came out now and then and he ran it off on a mimeograph machine at the Central Library. Because of the irregularity of the publication, he referred to it as a 'sporadical'. Some of the same people who contributed to *20 Cents* contributed to *Region*. [Bill] Exley [lead 'singer', if that is the term, of The Nihilist Spasm Band] probably has a complete set."

I got in touch with Exley who did indeed used to have a complete set of all nine editions published between 1961 and 1967 in print runs of five to 25 copies. Toward the end of his life Curnoe asked Exley for his copy of one of the earlier editions so that the publisher/editor would have a complete set. Exley now rues his generosity as he doesn't know what happened to Curnoe's set and his own now has this one crucial hole.

McKenzie resumes: "*20 Cents* grew out of a single-page publication which was invented by Robin Askew and Tony Pennicut while they were at Western. It was called *Homo Ludens* which I think translates to 'man at play'. *Homo Ludens* somehow got translated into *20 Cents* magazine, certainly with influence from Greg but also of course Art Pratten and Hugh McIntyre who along with Robin and Tony were the founders of the magazine."

The idea of 'region' and 'regionalism' was clearly bouncing around in Curnoe's mind during this critical period when he determined that he would find some way to play out his life as an artist in London. In 1973 he tried to define what he meant by 'regionalism' in an interview with Bruce Kidd in the August issue of *The Canadian Forum*. Unlike the American 'regionalist' tag which got affixed to artists like Grant Wood and Thomas Hart Benton, Curnoe's understanding of the term wasn't geographically determined by where an artist lived and worked but had more to do with independence from faddism and scene-making that could be realized anywhere. "Provincialism is what people do when they live, as they think, 'out in the sticks,' and they try to imitate what they think is hip in the big centres. Regionalism is simply what people do when they are an integrated people, when they are at ease with other people from other environments."[19]

20 Cents magazine always cost a quarter and – what sweet cultural revenge this was – a note on the cover said it cost more in the States (whether they actually sold any there at all is another question). Curnoe's column in *20 Cents* was called *Radio Journal*. Every month he would tune in a certain radio station – usually pop music but not always – and then speed-write his copy, free-associating all over the place for the next hour or so; talking about what songs were played, who was dropping by his studio for a visit, miscellaneous bits of London lore, anything at all that happened or occurred to him. It sounds pretty boring and might've been if anybody else had written it. Though he wasn't the editor, it was the Curnoe spirit that drove this wonderfully eclectic monthly magazine. One of my all-time favourite pieces by Pat Cole was an anthropological study of the graffiti she found scribbled on the playground equipment in Doidge Park behind St. Joe's Hospital.

For a 2011 exhibition at Museum London, *Cutout: Greg Curnoe Shaped Collages 1965-1968*, curator and artist, Robert Fones, wrote an essay describing the scene which had coalesced around Curnoe at this time: "This closely packed and very social community was an essential context for Curnoe's work. His Richmond Street and later his King Street studio were meeting places for discussion, argument and artistic exchange. The constant stream of people through Curnoe's studio brought new information and ideas, debate about current issues and an immediate audience for Curnoe's work. Some visitors left behind the paper ephemera used in Curnoe's collages.

"What is hard to imagine now, is how compact the London art scene of the 1960s was. Most of the artists' studios, art galleries, art centres and stores where artists could buy supplies were located within eight city blocks bounded by Queens Avenue on the north and King Street on the south, Ridout Street on the west and Wellington Street on the east. When I had a studio at 119A Dundas Street the studios of Ron Martin, Murray Favro, Greg Curnoe, Royden Rabinowitch, David Rabinowitch and Jack Chambers were all within a few blocks of mine. Alpha Centre, run by James Reaney was around the corner on Talbot Street. 20/20 Gallery was on King Street within the next block . . .

"Artists frequently visited each other's studios to talk about art and to keep in touch with what everyone was doing with their work. It was a very unique aspect of the London scene of the 1960s. This close-knit community remained intact until the city launched a process of so-called urban renewal beginning in 1971. From the roof of my fourth-floor studio I watched as the block bounded by Talbot, Ridout, Dundas and Queens was demolished and the old Georgian commercial buildings were replaced by a monolithic concrete courthouse.

The demolition then continued along Ridout Street south of Dundas. Curnoe prophetically asked in his 1969 Sao Paulo catalogue: 'Can one's sense of place survive the physical destruction of that place?'"[20]

Curnoe was incredibly fortunate that when he started to exhibit his work at any public exhibition he could wheedle his way into or put together himself, London's daily newspaper, *The London Free Press*, had a writer on staff, Lenore Crawford, who possessed a real eye for art and considerable critical acumen. (In contrast, the two reporters who succeeded her at the *Free Press* starting in 1974, Janice Andreae and Judy Malone, found Curnoe an exasperating figure.) Crawford's first mention of Curnoe in December of 1960 reviewing the 8th Annual Young Contemporaries show might not seem particularly auspicious: "The value of the media has to be tested – Mr. Curnoe's for example, might be valid for commercial art work but is inexcusable for anything wanted two months hence – but young artists should experiment."[21]

But almost one year later in reviewing his first one man exhibition at the Crouch Library, *An Exhibition of Things*, you can see that Crawford is starting to warm to the audacious fellow: "Some of the spoofs are scarcely worth the effort of moving them into the exhibit, for Curnoe, the producer, has not yet learned all about selection, which a good modern Dadaist should know. In the midst of the spoofs, though – those that have impact and those that don't – are things that are evidence of a competent craftsman and a sensitive artist."[22]

In December of 1961 Curnoe landed five works including *Drawer Full of Stuff* in an untitled neo-Dada exhibition at Toronto's Isaacs Gallery, winning him a glowing review in the March/April 1962 issue of *Canadian Art* by Michael Sanouillet. "Greg Curnoe displays an exciting genius and freshness of approach. From London, Ontario, a most improbable Dadaistic town, he brought a drawer filled with odds and ends such as we all conceal in the non-public corners of our Gracious Living Homes . . . It is to be hoped that this exhibition will be taken on tour throughout Canada. Started by talented young men, it indicates a healthy reaction against a lethal form of stuffy conservatism which has pervaded most of this country's artistic circles."

With this review in a national magazine, one can see the buzz of the 'wild child' or the 'rebel with a brush' attaching itself to Curnoe for the first time. Such notices undoubtedly brought his personality (if not his work) to wider recognition and, in their way, probably helped him to overthrow the Miss Grundy-ish tendencies of the old London art establishment – an establishment he would control as its unofficial but undisputed head in just a few years. But, in the short term at least, I don't think such notoriety did anything for the development of his art. The nadir of this sort of 'ooo, isn't he cool and who cares if he can actually paint?' media chatter was achieved the following February when Curnoe was credited as the main organizer of what gushing cultural historians are not ashamed to call, "the first 'happening' in Canada." This combination parade/protest/art exhibition drew some out-of-town artistic notables down to London such as Michael Snow and Joyce Wieland.

Michael Sanouillet (again) gave this eye-witness reflection on the event in 2000: "When the 1962 schedule of the London Public Library and Art Gallery [sic] was planned, one evening was tagged for 'demonstration of different techniques', and a group of London painters headed by Greg Curnoe was asked to present the program. Greg had planned a 'Tribute to the Group of Seven' (as a symbol of Canadian art) by laying a funeral wreath at the London Art Gallery in front of a Thomson winter scene. The event also included the construction of a huge wooden 'chance structure' inside the gallery's main hall: a truck dumped a load of scrap planks from a demolition site in front of the building's entrance. Each visitor was given a piece of wood and a few nails. Once inside, he would then nail his plank to the ones previously brought into the gallery by other participants. One of Greg's friends . . . sat inside the construction and was finally boarded in. Of course the gallery's staff (Clare Bice, chief curator?) was disgruntled and infuriated at the prospect of having to clear away all that mess, which was what Greg expected. Finally a parade, led along London's main thoroughfare, by Greg and his friends . . . all dressed up in dadaistic attire (ie: German 1914 Uhlan's uniform, complete with pointed helmet), each holding a six-foot pole supporting a huge plywood pane, painted white with a black border, like a movie screen. We were watched and followed suspiciously by the flabbergasted local police force who mistook us for a union protest march, but couldn't figure out why there were none of the usual aggressive statements on the posters."[23]

In a 1979 interview that Curnoe recorded with Michael Sanouillet, I get the distinct impression that nearly 20 years later the artist is a little embarrassed by the event and certainly wants to distance himself from the idea that he was part of anything as witlessly trendy as a 'happening'. "Happenings . . . were in the air," Curnoe explained, perhaps with a clearing of the throat, "but it turned out to be something quite different . . . What I had in mind for the happening or celebration or whatever it was, was the context, to change the context. To have someone in a big public art gallery do a washing. To have someone in a big public art gallery watch the hockey game, to play baseball and catch in that art gallery room. That was what that was about. That's very different from what happenings were about, I think."[24]

And then when I interviewed him about ten years later than that in a very wide-ranging series of conversations about his life and career, he didn't think to mention the 'happening' at all.

Greg Curnoe the Dada-ist does not hold the same sort of appeal for me as Curnoe the painter and the figurist. The above cited *Drawer Full of Stuff* is a prime and early example of a strain in his art that leaves me pretty cold. It is an actual four-sided drawer pulled from a battered old dresser or a desk; grooves along the side to facilitate easy sliding, a fixed brass handle on the front, and chucked inside are notes, bus transfers, receipts, pads, a tin of Gillette Foamy shaving lotion. I mean, my heart be still. I've got drawers like that in my own house that I can stare into any time I want and drink in the details of objects that will have considerably more significance for me than this self-conscious assemblage. Growing up I used to occasionally pull out the middle drawer of my father's desk and gaze upon its contents as a sort of evidential portrait of the man. But take it out of the context of our home and plant it in an art gallery à la Marcel Duchamp's 1917 urinal posing as a *Fountain*, and I expect I would be similarly unimpressed. Perhaps that's just me; your mileage may vary.

Here in an extract taken from his long essay that appeared in the catalogue for the 1982 retrospective at the National Gallery of Canada, the great Curnoe champion, Pierre Théberge, makes the case, such as it is, for *Drawer*:

"This accumulation of ordinary objects and common remains was not un-systematic, and there is a work by Curnoe that helps us understand his way of apprehending reality. The title of *Drawer Full of Stuff* (1961; cat. No 11) is a literal description. The drawer itself shows the disarray that follows several months' haphazard accumulation of all kinds of 'stuff' (odd objects, fabric, material substance). This 'stuff,' however, is bounded by a precise frame, the rectangle of the wooden drawer itself. Curnoe seems to say: 'Here is the world as it is, in disarray but understandable, capable of apprehension as a fragment within the limits that I impose – here, the limits of this box, this drawer.' Limits that were also imposed in the collages; there, the frame (before being framed itself) is the piece of cardboard or paper on which the work was done. Having fixed his frame, Curnoe turned to the descriptive stage: the inventory, the listing of the items in the box. One of those items is a handwritten list glued to a piece of wood; it is numbered 1 to 32 – each item in the drawer is listed, including the list itself. It is significant that this list is part of the jumble that it finally sets in order."[25]

And truth be told, just about all of the lettered works don't do much for me either though they too have their champions. I asked Ross Woodman why they worked for him:

"The nobility and majesty of them," he answered. "There's a kind of grandeur in the scale and in the kind of labour – putting his stamp on something: 'Here am I, here am I' – they're powerful but when you try to read them they're not so powerful. The inflation carries its own deflation and that's quite powerful."

I posed the same question to Nancy Poole and she said, "They work because they're very well painted. They're vivid. It's all there. I was never very interested in reading what was on the lines. I wasn't a bit interested in reading them. I just loved the way he used the letters as shapes – and they were wonderful shapes.

And he painted so well."

In May of 1962 a Curnoe piece, *Richmond and Carling*, was included in the 22nd Annual Western Ontario Exhibition. As this write-up from *The London Free Press* shows, the work's inclusion in the show was contentious; an early salvo in the power struggle that would soon see Curnoe emerge as not just the leader of the London art scene but its eminence grise:

"A painting mounted in an old window frame and bedecked with a cigarette package, a garishly painted megaphone, and an envelope from *The Farmer's Advocate* post-marked 1930 drew considerable attention . . . The painting by London artist Greg Curnoe is a grey disc on a yellow background. The envelope is pasted in the centre of the disc. 'I wouldn't have let it in,' said Clare Bice, curator of the Art Museum, as guests mulled past. But Tony Urquhart, ARCA, OSA, one of the jury of three, said he voted for it because it is 'aesthetically pleasing and very funny'."[26]

Later that same month, Curnoe sold his first painting to a Canadian gallery when the Norman Mackenzie Art Gallery in Regina, Saskatchewan snapped up, *Tall Girl When I am Sad* – a work Curnoe forthrightly described as being "about [a woman] as an object of desire." It would be almost two years until he made his next gallery sale.

In a September 1964 column in *The London Free Press*, Lenore Crawford wrote: "Twenty-eight year old Greg Curnoe strode into the office yesterday to announce he had just sold a painting to the Vancouver Art Gallery. It is the second painting purchased by a major Canadian gallery in four months. 'Things are beginning to perk,' was the way the tall, lean Greg expressed his satisfaction that after about five years of concentration on freelancing as an artist (with occasional stints as instructor), recognition is coming his way."[27]

In April the Montreal Museum of Fine Arts had purchased *Sunday Lacrosse at Talbot School*. This latest sale to the Vancouver gallery was *Myself Walking North in the Tweed Coat* [Plate 9]; by pretty universal consensus, one of the finest achievements of his earliest years which went on to become one of his most popular pre-bicycle prints. Curnoe mid-stride is featured in profile, his face quite featureless, the colours applied in bold, flat tones except the titular tweed jacket which mixes up different threads of dark colour. The draughtsmanship over all is pretty perfunctory but the thing is put across with such youthful elan that this becomes part of its charm. Text, in both of Canada's official languages, is worked into the image.

Curnoe's paternal aunt, Hilda Curnoe, loved Greg but had serious reservations about his calling as an artist. Lynda Curnoe reports, "When shown a print of Greg's 1963 picture, *Myself Walking North in the Tweed Coat*, all she said was, 'Where's his face?' The picture shows Greg, wearing the blue sweater Mum had given him, in mid-stride, his arms swinging, his colourful, herringbone-patterned coat flying open. Printed on the canvas are the words, 'Love doesn't last very long but thinking about it does.' Other words and phrases in French and English accompany Greg on his walk. The viewer sees only a blank profile of Greg but is immediately aware of his thoughts. Hilda could not understand Greg's occupation or the subtlety of this picture. But like my father, she became proud of him after he made a name for himself in London."[28]

A Professor Groome had written to Curnoe at about this time with questions about his artistic inspirations and practices and Curnoe's typewritten response, dated 17 November, 1964 is included in the Greg Curnoe Papers at the Art Gallery of Ontario. Portions of this fascinating letter were reprinted in the catalogue accompanying the exhibition, *Greg Curnoe '61-65*, at the Michael Gibson Gallery in 2014 and were also featured in the *Life & Stuff* catalogue where Groome is identified as an 'academic researcher'. First Curnoe talked about his influences and background:

"I do not consider myself to be a pop artist. I believe that Andy Warhol is the only one around, and he is mainly a watered down (chic) extension of some of [Marcel] Duchamp's ideas. As for my "granddaddies" – I am not that involved in the history of painting – most of the paintings I like have paralleled my own thinking at some point. I like Stanley Spencer's painting very much, living in a small city, painting the people and what happens. I like Henri Matisse; in fact these two are my favourite painters: his [Matisse's] colour, his simplicity. R.B. Kitaj – at last, I see another painter who's interested in the Anarchists and Socialists in a complete fashion. Jasper Johns' attitude towards objects has a lot of similarity with mine, that is, the juxtaposition and manipulation of surfaces and meanings . . . I like some of Robert Indiana's painting very much; in fact he has recently caused me to re-read Walt Whitman . . . When I first attended art school (1954) I got involved with Dada . . . that could be one of my major 'artistic' influences . . . Before that I would say that my biggest influences were games my cousin and I invented as kids, comic books, Spike Jones, also the fact that I was brought up on the edge of London and knew the surrounding country as a child, built shacks and undergrounds in the woods, and had gangs with badges and other paraphernalia."

Asked about his use of clear flat paint and the facelessness of his human figures, Curnoe talked about certain shortcuts and simplifying techniques that would not impress most art college teachers nor his good friend, Jack Chambers. Some folks are incredulous that these two artists could work together in the same room, even while painting the same subject (such as Victoria Hospital). Chambers clearly didn't have to worry about having his ideas or approaches poached by an artist who could talk like this:

"I like enamel because it feels nice and looks nice. I like white enamel chairs; the paint grows warm to the touch. I like shininess . . . It's easy simply to mix up a colour and paint in a shirt, much easier than using broken colour and indicating lights and shades. I wish to spend my time on other things, like what is interesting about the shirt, how many buttons it has, what is the shape of the smoke he blows out of his mouth, what does his membership card say on it, is that the way the line of her ass goes, or does it curve more at the top, what did she say that impressed me the last time I made love to her . . . When I wish to put a likeness of someone I know on a painting, I get them to sit in front of a lamp and then I trace their projected shadow on a piece of paper. What easier way is there to do it? People find them easy to recognize as well."

Commenting in a sort of aside on the wide disparity of painterly craftsmanship between the earlier Curnoe and Chambers that may have made it possible for them to work together without fear of conceptual influence, Ross Woodman couldn't help wondering how much regard they actually had for one another's work: "I often wondered, did Greg admire Jack as much as he sometimes appeared to admire him? And what was Jack doing when he hung his own copy of a Curnoe painting in his living room and painted the copy in one of his own paintings? [Woodman is here referring to *Hockey Stick Blades from West Lion's Park* (1965) which appears, framed and hanged on the living room wall in Chambers' perceptualist masterpiece, *Sunday Morning No. 2* (1970)] Greg couldn't do that kind of thing. Jack had a kind of sophistication. He could play with things in a way that Curnoe couldn't play with them."

And yet, Woodman pointed out, when it came to their characters, their emotional constitutions, Curnoe was the "much more playful" of the two; a gift of temperament that spared Curnoe much of the over-analytical angst that occasionally bogged down Chambers' productivity.

As for the ever-present text and printed comments that appeared on his canvases – the cartoony-ness that he never would shed – Curnoe quite guilelessly chalked that up for Professor Groome, once again, to easiness and directness: "What easier way is there to say you like something than to write 'I like orange'; what easier way to endorse someone than by writing their name on a painting?"

Asked what he regarded as his main drive as an artist, Curnoe again made it clear that he wasn't on a mission to master difficult techniques or probe great mysteries: "I like to do. I like to make objects that I can use. I like to make other people laugh. I like to be interested. I don't like to be bored. I don't like to solve problems; I like to contemplate what I am doing . . . Mainly my life is full and I like so much just to look, listen, read – to look at a cloudless summer sky. It doesn't threaten or seduce. It is just there, and I stand on the ground and look at it."[29]

There is a fecklessness on display in some of Curnoe's answers to Professor Groome that is a little jarring to those who knew him better in later years as a devoted family man. Never a scheming Don Juan collecting notches on his bed post and bragging about his amorous victories, one cringes a little to hear him showing off in this way to his professorial correspondent, loutishly asking: "Is that the way the line of her ass goes, or does it curve more at the top, what did she say that impressed me the last time I made love to her?" By the time he answered Professor Groome's questions, Curnoe was six months into the love match of his life with Sheila Thompson, a gorgeous, blonde English immigrant six years his junior whom he'd marry the following July.

16

"IT MUST'VE BEEN SOMETHING PRETTY FAST"

SHEILA CURNOE is reasonably certain that her first sighting of Greg took place in 1960, about four years before they were officially introduced by the wife of a member of the Nihilist Spasm Band, Barb Pratten. "He's kind of strange, Sheila," Pratten told her. "I think you'll like him."

"There is a very interesting story," Sheila told me, "and I still don't know if it was a dream on my part but I think it was real. Because I have a very good memory for these things and visually I have a very good memory and I don't think it was a dream. I went to Beal. I was in the art program; a complete misfit in every way. I didn't dress or sound like the other girls. I'm walking outside Beal and I look over to the funeral home across the street, Needham, and there's a metal fence along the front and Greg's sitting there with his bum on the metal railing and his legs straight out in front of him and his ankles crossed and his arms folded. That's how he would sit. And all the guys from my art class were hanging around him because he was a real artist who had just come back from OCA and he was setting up his studio. And he looked across at me and he said to one of the students, 'I'm going to marry that girl.' One of the guys came over and told me what he said and they were appalled that this guy would even think of marrying me who was a complete loser. And I said, 'I don't want to marry him.' To me he just looked kind of goofy because he had a blue sweater which his mother bought him and orange pants and work boots. Now, did I remember that when Barbara Pratten said to me at the dental office where we worked, that she wanted me to come and meet a friend called Greg 'Colonel', I thought she said? I don't think I remembered it then but I remembered it later. It's a very strange story."

How long had you been going together before you tied the knot?

"I met him in the spring of '64 and married in July of '65."

Did you have any idea what you were in for?

"No. I just thought that life would be interesting. When I met Greg all these people came up to the studio – Hugh McIntyre, all these different people, some were writers, some were poets, some were school teachers, whatever – and it was such a relief to actually be around people who talked about something interesting. Because I went out with a lot of guys and there were two things they all had in common. They had a car – a great big pink Ford or whatever – and they bought me French fries. And they got nothing from me at all. It was like, 'Thanks a lot. Bye.' I had no intention of mucking up my life in any way with that. I'd grown up in a Yorkshire village called Brampton and came over to Canada with my parents when I was fifteen. I hated Canada at first; everyone seemed so boringly normal. Greg and his friends were the first people I'd met who you could actually talk to, who were prepared or equipped to say intelligent and outlandish things. The atmosphere in his studio was very stimulating – all of the writers and poets and painters who hung around. This was what I thought life should be rather than what I was doing."

It was by all accounts a dramatic and volatile relationship from the get-go. In her essay in the *Life & Stuff* catalogue, Sarah Milroy writes, "Curnoe's sexual attraction to Sheila was ferocious, and the impact of their union on his creativity was profound. He found her feral and unpredictable, and he was intrigued by her in a way that was, for him, unprecedented."

Curnoe was clearly knocked off his feet and did his first drawing of Sheila that day and wrote down her phone number on a pillar in the middle of the room. Though he still wasn't doing much in the way of facial delineation, Sheila, frequently nude, immediately started turning up in some of Curnoe's most highly regarded early paintings like *Being Tickled, Feeding Percy* and *Spring on the Ridgeway* [Plate 10] – from 1964 and '65. Particularly with *Percy* and *Ridgeway*, the colours aren't so heavy and dark and the draughtsmanship is more delicate and fluid and playful.

The relationship also turns up in the text which, in the case of *Ridgeway*, runs around the perimeter of the image of a voluptuously nude Sheila, just risen from bed and looking out a window that is outfitted with real rayon curtains hanging on a rod. In *Ridgeway's* text, the names of various yoyo manoeuvres – "Around the World, Walk the Dog, Rock the Cradle" – are mixed in with Greg's lovesick broodings: "While I was in Toronto last week I kept thinking of you . . . My hands should be touching you . . . Why have we argued about this picture?"

In the case of *Feeding Percy*, Sheila told me the argument was about thighs. "I didn't like it because he flattened out my figure so it looks like I've got great big thighs. I mean, how dare he? And then around the edge of *Spring on the Ridgeway*, we're arguing some more. You'd have to say we started arguing quite early."

You weren't even married yet, were you?

"No."

And you're already arguing.

"I've never held back on my opinions and I've always been accused of talking too much. I really do love sharing thoughts but it gets me into trouble."

While it's a generally accepted truism that men don't like examining their feelings half so much as women, Greg seems to have taken that reticence a little further than the norm. Lynda Curnoe writes that this was a trait Greg inherited from Gordon. "Neither father nor son was aware of, nor would have ever admitted, that their life interests were almost identical. These included an intense love of their mothers, their families, London, sports and history . . . Greg and my father also shared an incapacity or unwillingness for self-examination, Dad, because he did not know how to, and Greg, because he refused to, insisting on following his instincts rather than analyzing them. For the viewer, Greg's paintings seem autobiographical, focussing directly on his life, family and beliefs. When commenting on his work, however, Greg would only discuss colour, the materials he used or technique."[30]

When I was conducting my interviews with Greg in the late 80s, I discovered that this thoroughly amiable man could get downright terse when asked about personal matters. "Was it love at first sight?" I rather inanely asked about his first meeting with Sheila.

"She was very attractive," he allowed; not exactly answering the question. "A friend brought her up to the studio. We were married about six months later." [Sixteen months later would be more like it.]

Not picking up on his discomfort, I doubled down on the stupid and asked again: "But was it love at first sight?"

"It must've been something pretty fast," he said in a way that made it clear even to me that it was time to move on to a different topic.

Sheila on the other hand more than 20 years after his death is still quite happy to diagnose the dynamics of their relationship. "In her book Lynda Curnoe says Greg became arrogant," Sheila told me. "And as much as everyone loved Greg and his gregarious personality, he could be quite arrogant. He could be very patronizing of me. I understand that if you're not a narcissist and arrogant, you're not going to make it as an artist. I was always caught in the middle. For Greg family was so important, supporting his family was important and children – all of that was really, really important to him. And then you have the other side that could be just miserable and stubborn – really awful. So I guess that's what kept me off balance and brought on our arguments."

Some of their arguments were about the roles they each expected the other to play. Sheila had no intention of giving up her work to stay home and bake pies – "I didn't make pies like his mom which really, really got him" – certainly not until there were children to care for and some sort of quasi-dependable income was rolling in.

"I continued to work after we got married because I thought, well, someone has to have money. I always had money. And if Greg got money, he spent it immediately. He would spend it on books and records and chocolate bars. So I continued to work and then I got pregnant and Owen was born on April 30th, 1966. I went back to the hospital to work so I could earn more money there, just for a short time, and then that was it."

By about Canada's centennial year, Greg was starting to earn a little more money and the couple were thinking of ways to buy a house. Indeed, his prospects were starting to look good and a momentum was building which Sheila thought might come to a screeching halt with the contentious Dorval Airport mural.

"I didn't like it. I thought, okay here you are, I'm home with two young children and you want a house. You want to prove to your dad that you can support your family by being an artist. Now, how many people can do that or actually did it? He was insistent that he would support us. And I thought, 'You go ahead, life is fun, just keep going and we'll see where this goes.' I just sat back and watched. I don't think Greg had a whole lot of respect for me."

The Dorval mural called *R34* was yanked from the wall because of its anti-American sentiments and put into storage one week after it was installed by an irate Department of Transport. Curnoe steadfastly refused to submit a revision of the work and still received his payment. With that and a timely sale of paintings to London collector Jake Moore, they were able to buy and overhaul an abandoned lithography shop on Weston Street where Sheila still lives today.

"We moved here in May of 1968," Sheila recalls, "and Galen was born on June 22nd 1968. The place was absolutely awful. It was ugly beyond belief. A big, square, flat-roofed building with nothing growing around it except weeds and maybe a couple of Manitoba Maples. It was baking in the sun. And I said to Greg, 'Well, if I'm going to live here, this has to be done and that has to be done and you've got to change this and replace that and get rid of those,' and he just did it. That was it. He did it. My mom's first response when she first saw it was, 'Oh, my poor Sheila'. He painted it all white, he got these carpets that were blue and all of a sudden everything was beautiful. He approached Jake Moore. If it hadn't been for Jake Moore, we wouldn't have had this place. It cost $14,600 and Jake took several paintings to help pay for the house. Greg loved wall papering and he was really good at it and it was a time when you could get the most wonderful patterns."

I reminded Sheila of my first visit to the place and how chuffed Greg was with the separation of workplace and home; the front part of the structure having been made over into their living quarters, and the big shop out back with its own separate outside entrance being turned into his studio. He walked me around there, saying, "I leave my house and I go to work." That separation of his private and professional life seemed very important to him and that struck me as odd in that so much of his art referenced his private life.

"Well, that was a bit funny," Sheila recalled. "He dressed up in striped train engineer's overalls and a hat and then he had this lunchbox and he wanted me to make his lunch and put it in there. And there he'd be standing and I had to make his lunch and he'd pick it up and he tended to walk in almost a robotic way and he'd turn and go out there and chunka, chunka, chunka, he'd go into the studio, right? I played along for a couple of days. I wasn't going to do it anymore. I ridiculed him and all that because this was ridiculous . . ."

Another one of your taunts?

"That's right. Okay. All right. And do you know what he would do in there? Sit down in that rocking chair that's still there and read comic books. You don't go to work to read comic books . . . if you want to play the working man's game. Isn't that funny?"

One area where Sheila tried to have some influence was regarding the resentment of the USA expressed in a number of Curnoe's works – such as the slogan, 'Close the 49th parallel' inscribed along the crossbar of some of his famous bicycle paintings or the 1972 ink drawing, *Map of North America*, in which the southern boundary of Canada runs right along the northern boundary of Mexico. Obviously no one was ever going to close the 49th parallel and from a strict cartographer's point of view if, in fact, the 49th parallel ever were somehow sealed off, then – oh irony of ironies – London, Ontario would then have been situated in the good old USA. Likewise, drawing a mischievous map wasn't going to change the reality of having the USA for a neighbour. But it was an effective way of saying, 'America, you're a little overbearing. You're a little hard to live next door to sometimes.'

Indeed a case could be made that Curnoe wasn't anti-American so much as he was looking out for himself and only wanted to shut out any domineering, external voices that might potentially throw an artist off his game. In a 2000 interview with Judith Rodger, Brenda Wallace recalled a little vignette that suggested Curnoe wasn't so much anti-American as totally xenophobic: "Greg rented my house during his stay in Banff . . . When I returned at the end of the summer, I found that Greg had rearranged my art collection – all the international works had been stored upstairs, face to the wall!"[31]

"I find the anti-Americanism a bit tiresome to tell the truth," Sheila told me in 2013. "What people don't understand is it was done with a lot of humour. That map he did was done with humour. I was sitting here, he came in and he was practically vibrating with joy that he'd thought up this thing. How clever that was, right? But it was supposed to be sort of funny. His goal wasn't to bash Americans. He was trying to elevate Canadian culture and let's not have the U.S. influencing our culture. He often would say, 'I'm playing the devil's advocate here'. And I would say, 'Well, then, why don't you just say that?' 'It's obvious,' he'd say.

"Robert Fulford right after 9/11 wrote a piece where he sort of accused

Greg of being part of the problem, saying it was this kind of attitude and this kind of thinking that contributes to what has happened here. I was appalled when I read it but then when I thought about it later, I thought, 'Well, he does have a point and Greg's kind of attitude really doesn't help'."

We'll never know whether Curnoe would've tempered his anti-American animus in the wake of 9/11. Sheila Curnoe isn't confident that he would have done so: "That would have been interesting, wouldn't it? To see if anything budged there. He could be so patronizing. I don't think so but we'll never know."

Nancy Poole feels quite certain that he wouldn't have budged an inch: "The anti-Americanism never bothered me at all. It was consistent with his nihilistic attitude. Greg was always going to be against. He was a super-nationalist which you need to have but not too many. And remember, those were really dreadful times. When you think what Johnson and Nixon and that dreadful Kissinger were doing in those days – America almost was a country out of control. We needed to have people like Greg. And of course he went to such extremes that he then nullified any value that he might have. [laughs] That was always the danger with Greg."

But at least he always did it with humour, I pointed out.

"Yes," Poole agreed. "And a twinkle in his eye and those are things I found quite endearing about him. He was the bad boy who always had a grin on his face."

Bob McKenzie pointed out that as a man of principle, "Greg wouldn't compromise for anybody. I suppose he could be described by some people who disagreed with him as being pig-headed. He was certainly open to ideas but whether he would actually change his mind in a significant way . . . ?"

McKenzie would also qualify Poole's comment about what actually animated his so-called nationalism: "To a large extent Greg's Canadian nationalism was anti-Americanism." McKenzie also recalled Curnoe's disparaging comment when he was praised as one of the best artists in the country. I wish I could remember who it was that said Greg Curnoe was one of the ten best artists in Canada. When he heard that Greg said, 'There aren't ten good artists in Canada.'"

Of those I interviewed, only Ross Woodman (who for all of his valuable insights was arguably the person who knew him least well) believed that Curnoe might have walked back some of his anti-American vitriol in the light of subsequent events. "Yes, I think he would," he said.

I shared my theory with Sheila that people who live with artists will inevitably be drawn into discussions about the artist's work. And your insights and opinions will be valued up to a point but they will not be given an ultimate stake in what does or doesn't get made; they will not be admitted into the innermost workings. They don't belong there and will do damage to the artist's instincts if they take up any sort of residence there.

"I think you're absolutely right. Okay, so that's what I was dealing with all this time."

All the evidence was that he was crazy about you.

"I know. But was it like, he couldn't understand, couldn't quite grasp, couldn't quite figure out what Sheila was about? And so he had to do the nudes because that's how men often look at women, you know, in the sexual way? You know, was that it? Was that him trying to figure out what Sheila was about?"

Let's talk about the nudes. They are loaded, aren't they?

"Yes."

They're heavy with conflict.

"They certainly are. I will be introduced to people – often businessmen – and they'll shake my hand and look in my face and say, 'I've seen you naked'. And I'll say, 'Well, so has everyone else. What's the big deal?' I was well aware of the history of art. Nudes go back thousands of years. It's just . . . there it is. So I didn't even think about it. It just seemed to be part of the whole thing. However, it was also an intrusion in my life. And it was boring. Posing was boring, boring, boring. I'd go, 'Are you finished?' I had to go back and cook supper or get groceries. I'd insist on certain music which would be Debussy or Erik Satie. And the room had to be warm. And he'd do lots of drawings and then he would want to do a painting. Greg was always watching and observing. He's an artist so that's what he does. And he struggled with this. He struggled enormously with object/subject."

Sheila recalled showing up for the opening of the *Life & Stuff* retrospective at the Art Gallery of Ontario. "I hired a great stretch limousine and I went down. There was champagne and everything. We arrived at the AGO and we walked up and apparently there were these huge banners flapping in the wind. They were enormous and they were pictures of me, nude, from the painting, *Genuine*, which says at the bottom, 'Subject/Object? Greg Curnoe asks this question.' He was dealing with that because feminists were challenging him. And Robert Fulford wrote, 'Even his own wife questioned it.' Well, that was just for irritation purposes. So I walk up the steps with my family and everything and there's this huge banner flapping in the wind and I didn't even notice it."

Sheila laughed mischievously when I shared with her another excerpt from Milroy's *Life & Stuff* essay discussing some of the personal challenges coming Curnoe's way in the late '70s: "His marriage to Sheila, always volatile, had taken a particularly perilous turn, with his paranoia fuelled by her taunts. Feminism was an idea he struggled with until his death, and his horror at *The Hite Report* is almost comical in retrospect."[32]

So what's that all about? I asked.

"We went to the Venice Biennalle, we were on the plane and I was reading *The Hite Report*. And I showed it to him and he was absolutely . . . he hated it."

Was it the idea of women objectively appraising the quality of their sexual experiences? Did he find that threatening somehow?

"No, I don't think it was that."

"What didn't he like about it?" I asked and she got me to read the sentences to her two more times, eliciting fresh gales of laughter every time I read out the words 'taunting' and 'paranoia'.

"I don't know," she said. "I can't remember."

And there, unanswered, we left it.

Every couple has to find (and continually re-find) their own best way to relate and taken all in all, the Curnoes' marriage was a happy and decidedly productive union. Nevertheless there was a mutually fuzzy sort of standoff that seems to have at least intermittently troubled their relations. Clearly Sheila loved and admired Greg but, irked by his self-sufficiency and emotional imperviousness (Ross Woodman had once said he couldn't conceive of the self-contained Greg ever suffering with anything so jejune as a broken heart), Sheila couldn't resist taking the piss out of him and occasionally knocking him off balance. Greg manifestly adored Sheila ("The weekend before the accident on his last visit to Langarth Street he had said, 'Mum, I really love Sheila'," Lynda Curnoe reports in her memoir) but I believe he was regularly perplexed at just how tetchy Sheila could be when he failed to respond to her more intuitive cues and overtures.

17

THE WILD CHILD BECOMES A FATHER FIGURE

IN THE FALL OF 1966 Pierre Théberge, the newly hired assistant curator of Canadian Art at The National Gallery, was pulled off his assignment working on the catalogue of early Quebec religious sculpture in the Gallery's permanent collection by his boss, Kean Rene Ostiguy, and told to travel down to London, Ontario to visit an utterly unknown young artist who had written to the Gallery asking them to consider buying one of his works. If he deemed it warranted, Théberge was instructed to reserve a small work for purchase by the Gallery. At first writing in French, Théberge recounted that first visit to Curnoe shortly after the artist's death in 1992. In 1997 this essay was translated into English and published in the Spring/Summer issue of *Canadian Literature*:

"I had no idea who Greg Curnoe was or even exactly where to find London on the map. I had never heard it spoken of as a centre of creativity and knew only that it was the birthplace of Paul Peel (1860-91), one of the most famous Canadian painters of his time. In fact, the only previous contact of any depth I had with contemporary Canadian art was through the Musee d' art contemprain in Montreal and that city's commercial galleries . . . I had only been to one artist's studio, Guido Molinari's in Montreal, which I visited twice while at university, on student assignment . . .

"I walked to 202 King Street and climbed the stairs to his studio. Inside, I was immediately bewildered by the total disorder. Magazines, collages, assemblages, drawings and all sorts of papers littered the tables . . . In the course of our conversations, I soon realized that Curnoe was highly cultivated. He had the entire range of modern art history at his fingertips . . . As I was well acquainted with a number of his artistic and intellectual points of reference, our first contact was stimulating. Curnoe also expressed curiosity about Quebec politics."

Though he was clearly impressed by the man, initially at least (while looking at smaller works which were all he was instructed to consider for purchase), Théberge wasn't that impressed with the artist. This is a point which Théberge makes more clearly in a reminiscence he supplied for the 2014 exhibition of Curnoe's early '60s work at the Michael Gibson Gallery: "Greg must have sensed my lack of real interest in what I was seeing so he offered to show me a much larger painting he had just finished."

Now we return to his 1992 essay: "Curnoe invited me to come with him into a second room to get a large painting he had just finished. Together we carried it out into the studio proper and set it up so we could view it more conveniently. I reacted with immediate enthusiasm to the colourful exuberance of the painting, *The Camouflaged Piano or French Roundels*, and its simple straightforward eloquence. I reserved the large painting for the National Gallery on the spot . . . Soon after the painting entered the National Gallery collection . . . Curnoe's painting and Guido Molinari's *Black Angle*, from 1956 . . . were among the first works I suggested for purchase. I still savour the pleasure I felt when my suggestions were approved by Mr. Ostiguy, Jean Sutherland Boggs, and a majority of the committee."[33]

With this purchase by the big national gallery of *The Camouflaged Piano* – the biggest and the boldest of his one-dimensional cartoony works which incorporated a wooden hotel sign that was splattered with decorative pigeon droppings and had working electric lights (that are switched on whenever the work is displayed) that he scavenged from the Richmond Hotel – a tectonic shift had occurred beneath the ground of the just-about-to-burst London art scene.

This was the moment when Curnoe started to unofficially become the go-to guy, the grand mediator for anything having to do with London art. As if to confirm this psychic shift, almost immediately following the sale of *The Camouflaged Piano*, The London Public Library and Art Museum – finally figuring out which way the wind was blowing – bought *Feeding Percy*. In an interview with Lenore Crawford, Curnoe was a little caustic about the tardiness of their support:

"It's very nice the London gallery is taking one of my paintings. It would have been nicer though, if it hadn't waited until the National Gallery bought one and thought it was 'safe' to get one. It would have been a real help three years ago. I really needed it then. It was the Regina gallery – and Regina isn't any bigger than London – that was willing to take a chance on me, not the gallery in my own home town."[34]

As an illustration of how rapidly Curnoe's star was rising in the national firmament, consider how prominent a part Curnoe was to play in the next year's Centennial exhibition put on by the big national gallery which not 12 months before didn't even know who he was. Here is curator, professor and art historian Dennis Reid's memory of the great centennial cake ceremony which was Reid's introduction to Curnoe:

"The National Gallery celebrated the Canadian Centennial with two large exhibitions. The first, *Three Hundred Years of Canadian Art*, a 378-work survey of art in Canada in the European tradition, was organized by Robert Hubbard and Jean-Rene Ostiguy, chief curator and curator of Canadian art respectively. Curnoe's *Camouflaged Piano* . . . dominated the last room of the exhibition. I began working at the Gallery just days before the opening, which was marked by a gala party in the cavernous workrooms in the Gallery's basement. Curnoe had won a limited competition to design a Canadian birthday cake and was there for the official cutting, resplendent in new yellow suit, chartreuse shirt, and sky blue tie. The huge cake, flat and rectangular like a painting, was iced in "Curnoe" colours as well – blue lettering on orange. The text paraphrased a popular song of the day, *Wild Thing* by the Troggs: "300 YRS OF CANA / DIAN ART, I THINK / I LOVE YOU! / BUT I WANT TO KNOW FOR SURE! / 300 YRS OF CANA / DIAN ART, HOLD ME / TIGHT! I NEED YOU!" I first met him on that occasion and remember being not quite sure what to make of his curious mix of hip sophistication and down-to-earth charm."[35]

Also in that Centennial year Pierre Théberge approached Curnoe with the idea of a national touring show of works by Greg and that other up and coming titan of London art, Jack Chambers. An opportunity like this would establish both artists at the national, even international level. It is impossible to exaggerate the generosity and courage of what Curnoe did next. He said yes, in principle, but couldn't we open the show up beyond just me and Jack? Let's call it *The Heart of London* and include the work of about a dozen other artists who are also working in London.

And so it came to be and a whole raft of other artists like John Boyle, Murray Favro, Ron Martin, Beverly Lambert Kelly, David and Royden Rabinovitch, Walter Redinger, Tony Urquhart and Ed Zelenak received national exposure which gave all of their careers a boost. The show also vindicated what Curnoe always knew; encourage people to cultivate their own arts scene and they will. The regionalist explosion was upon us. Arts journals and newsmagazines from Canada, the States and Europe were all running stories about the remarkable goings on in London, Ontario.

Along with personifying the idea that artists should work from where they are, Greg's enduring status as a benevolent father figure for London artists was forged when he opened up *The Heart of London* show in this way. Yes, Jack Chambers wins somewhat similar Brownie points for starting up Canadian Artists Representation but the origin for that was self-interest. 'I'm getting ripped off. How can I make them pay for using my images?' In correcting that situation for his own profit, Chambers coincidentally improved the lives of all Canadian artists.

But Curnoe had nothing to personally gain by opening up that touring exhibition to include a dozen other artists. Indeed he stood to lose some of the spotlight and some of the money. Curnoe exerted what power and influence he had by sheer strength of character and generosity; not by dint of any professional or political position. Only Nancy Poole, Jack Chambers' agent and director of the London Regional Art Gallery in the late '80s and early '90s, is inclined to qualify the legend of Greg Curnoe's heroic largeness of heart:

"You see, you describe the Greg that Greg wants you to describe. I don't think Greg was nearly as nice as Greg's fans think he was. Pierre Théberge gave Greg the power that Greg had. It was Pierre Théberge who made the Canada Council not go to Clare Bice anymore to see who the young artists were. You're dealing with the father figure in power when you're dealing with Greg. I have to put it in these terms. Pierre Théberge would be in touch with Greg – 'I'm going to be in London, who should I see?' Well, the young artists pretty fast figured out who they had to make God. It's true. This is the reality of the father figure. He had the power. Jack? No, he didn't want the power and he didn't need it and he was coming out of a different personality. But the adoration that the young artists had for Greg gave him power and Greg used that power. I really did not have any animosity towards Greg. Quite the contrary. But let me say this – I had no illusions about Greg."

Nancy Poole told me that she could not recall any time when relations between her and Curnoe were unfraught. "There was an emotional thing in his dealings with me which I don't completely understand. I always felt that Greg thought I had no business in his world. I didn't belong. I think it was he who introduced words like 'dilettante'. He was not generous about me at all."

There undoubtedly were points of contention that arose between Curnoe and Poole. The first big one was probably her work as Jack Chambers' agent when, at Chambers' request once he'd received his fatal diagnosis, Chambers' asking prices shot sky high overnight. Poole points out that all the artists jacked up their prices too (though not nearly so precipitously as Chambers) but Curnoe did express his fear at the time that this sudden escalation would, as he said, 'skew the market'.

"He was outraged," Poole told me. "Which was so funny because they all raised their prices immediately and I was supposedly the culprit. He literally stomped down the front steps at 554 Waterloo Street [Poole's London-based gallery]. He was so angry. Jack thought it was very funny and said, 'He's taking out on you what he's feeling about me'."

If Curnoe was vastly more prolific than Jack Chambers, I think it has to be admitted that there is less universal consensus about which are the truly great works. If Curnoe is predominantly identified with any one of his works it would be the 'bicycles' which he first produced in 1973 and continued until the year of his death. "He turned them out like sausages," Bob McKenzie told me. I had been explaining my quandary to McKenzie; that with the incredibly prolific Kurelek and the more abstemious Chambers, you could point to six or a dozen works over the course of their lifetimes and say, 'There's a lot to be said for everything they made but these here, by anyone's consensus, are masterpieces.'

"It's easy to do that with Jack," I said to McKenzie. "But not so much with Greg. Would you concur?"

"It's hard to think of Greg's work one at a time," McKenzie replied. "When you think of the whole body of work, it all seems to relate together."

McKenzie then went on to share this observation about the two artists' different approaches to their work: "I used to shoot pool with Jack and Greg. Jack was really good. I was really good because John Boyle and I spent a whole year shooting pool after we saw *The Hustler* and we got really good at it. So Jack and I were playing seriously. Greg seemed to be only interested in the way the different coloured balls looked on the table. And I think that's a good illustration of the difference between them. Jack was really serious about things. Greg took things seriously, of course, but he was never serious, he was never solemn about anything."

I floated McKenzie's idea past Ross Woodman.

"I would agree with that completely," Woodman said. "And that is why I like Greg so much now. I'm able to do that. I have the whole to experience. And I've been through all of these stages at a great distance. Now I can go through much more closely. And I agree with what you're saying about Chambers; there are six or seven masterpieces here – the film *The Hart of London* is one – and of course, *401 Towards London*. And the *Victoria Hospital* is a beautiful painting and to put that beside Greg Curnoe's *Victoria Hospital* is to reduce Greg Curnoe's painting to ludicrousness. I couldn't have Greg Curnoe's painting in my own collection. I wouldn't enjoy it at all. I still wouldn't enjoy it – especially with all those sound effects built into it. But when I see it with the rest of his work, I feel differently about it. I wouldn't want a house full of Curnoes. It still wouldn't be me. Greg was a great stylist. He had flair. And I admire a man who could dress the way he painted as if he were dressing himself up for his paintings. He was so identified. It's not that you have to see all of Greg's paintings. You have to see all of Greg. And I can do that now."

Any visit to Curnoe's studio included a moment of jarring recognition. To the north, across the river and ravine that cut just under the back studio wall, was Victoria Hospital. Curnoe was born there, both his parents, both siblings and all three of his children. He'd painted the building at least twice, once from the two windows in the studio's north wall. Jack Chambers painted it once, already stricken with leukemia and taking his sighting from Curnoe's studio roof. Chambers died at Victoria Hospital in 1978 and Curnoe, never overtly emotional or sentimental, nonetheless commemorated the site where his friend had stood by removing that portion of the roof and replacing it with a window, a portal opening onto the sky that flooded his studio in light. I wish I could remember the exact terms Curnoe used when he told me about that renovation during a studio tour. Struck by the perfunctory and un-allusive nature of his words, I probed him a bit, hoping that I might get him to venture into quasi-mystical territory for the sake of his departed friend and colleague, but politely yet firmly he let me know that he would not be going there.

Though she was the most forthright and outspoken of his critics, Nancy Poole was hardly the only high profile player in the art world to get on Curnoe's wrong side. Some critics really were out to get him. I regret imposing myself (or, at least, my first novel) into this narrative, but Ross Woodman's review of *The Goof* published in *The London Free Press* on Valentine's Day of 1976 under the headline *Herman Goodden: Huck Finn from the Forest City*, is a stark example of the kind of animus that Woodman used to have for Curnoe. And if it was only Woodman who had ever reacted this way, I might not include this, but – owing perhaps to the self-identification which was so central to getting or not getting what Curnoe was up to – throughout his entire career Curnoe could be a strongly polarizing figure.

Let me just add for the sake of context that I was a 23 year old puppy when this review appeared and totally ignorant of the game Woodman was playing here. Indeed, I was delighted by whatever coverage I could get even if my reviewer did mis-identify minor characters and devote more than half of his review to going after Curnoe with a cudgel. I will spare you the bits that pertain to just the novel but should explain that its autobiographical transparency (the narrator is even named Herman) invited the sort of conflating Woodman does here of fictional and real life. To feel at home back in the Forest City from a disorienting trip to the West Coast, *The Goof's* recently dumped narrator has built and moved into a tree fort; in real life I was working as a dishwasher and living in a dive across the road from an East London strip club.

Woodman wrote: "A vastly similar sort of thing, though set in Hamilton rather than London, can be seen in *The Great Canadian Sonnet* by Dave Mc-Fadden with Greg Curnoe doing the illustrations. It's also self-conscious in an art-is-just-honest-plain-living way. Much has been written and even more has been said about the so-called London school of art. Official recognition was bestowed in 1967 when the National Gallery spent in excess of $100,000 organizing a travelling exhibition of the work of London artists. Though there was no real leader of the pack, the kind of regionalism evident in the work of Greg Curnoe and Jack Chambers largely defined what the exhibition was about. A far more recent exhibition of London artists at the London Art Gallery (I mean the second floor of the London Public Art Gallery and Art Museum) reveals that the regional spirit has largely been lost and that what has replaced it is not worth talking about.

"*The Goof* assumes some larger importance in the light of this very recent, very sad show. Here is a novel that celebrates a region (London) in a manner that Curnoe's diaries and drawings (as well as [James] Reaney's *Dance of Death at London, Ontario*, with Chambers' drawings) have long rendered familiar to about a hundred people. And it does it without any indebtedness to this distinguished company.

"Herman likes Chambers but has never met him. He's met Curnoe but I doubt that he has ever visited him in his studio or listened more than once to the Nihilist Spasm Band. And that is probably all to the good. Regionalism is as natural to Herman Goodden as it is to Greg Curnoe. Yet there is a difference. Curnoe belongs and he knows he belongs. He doesn't have to live in a tree fort, and a broken heart (psychic adolescent wounding) is the very last thing one could associate with him. Herman is more like Huck and . . . he may just have to head out for the territories again (right now he's in exile across the street from Striperama).

"Curnoe doesn't have to go anywhere, and if he does, as often as not it's CAR or the Canada Council or the National Gallery that send him, and so they should. When Curnoe travels he's an ambassador of sorts, one of the best. His drawings for *The Great Canadian Sonnet* are sent on tour by the National Gallery, complete with a glossy catalogue and lots of quotations. Of course, it wasn't always that way. And it's certainly not that way yet for Herman Goodden, who until very recently washed dishes for a living in a restaurant where Curnoe fairly regularly eats.

"What I am saying is this: *The Goof* gives me a great deal more hope and a good deal more pleasure than the recent gallery exhibition of London painters. Now that Curnoe is establishment (small "e") and on his way at last to Venice [as the artist selected by the National Gallery in Ottawa to represent Canada at the 37th Biennale di Venezia], it's nice to know that Herman Goodden is around, bringing up the rear without kissing it."

Local poet Jamie Hamilton was rightly outraged by Woodman's critical dereliction and score-settling and zapped off a letter to the editor: "As a regular reader and sometimes writer of book reviews in the *Free Press*, I can neither accept nor subdue my reaction to Ross Woodman's review of *The Goof* by Herman Goodden in your Feb. 14 editions. No book, especially Goodden's, and not even the insipid bedroom wailing of Xaviera Hollander should be used by a "reviewer," and I use the word with abandon, as an excuse to direct personal criticism, praise, or jealousy toward something as distant from *The Goof* as Greg Curnoe's status in the art community. There are other forums for personal statements like Woodman's; there must be, somewhere. Unfortunately little in his review relates to *The Goof* as a work of art, in itself. It demonstrates his struggle to reach the middle, a painting under one arm, Goodden's book under the other, comfortable crutches for otherwise lame comments."

I don't know if Hamilton's letter registered on Woodman's consciousness at the time. I showed it to Woodman a good many years after his book review ran and he heartily agreed with the poet, saying that what he had done was an inexcusable violation of a reviewer's prime duty. He admitted this, God bless him, quite happily; all the while laughing with a sort of incredulity at the magnitude of his gall. And so, at Christmas of 2013, I decided to revisit the subject and asked Woodman why he had resisted Curnoe's charms for so long.

"When I came to London, I was not interested in Greg Curnoe because I was exceptionally interested in Jack Chambers. And I was aware that my attitude reflected the London attitude. If you were for Chambers, you tended to be against Curnoe because they were so unalike. And I only became interested in the late Curnoe and in his drawings and then in his bicycles and bicycle wheels – I found them quite exceptional. But I had never thought of Curnoe as in any way the equal of Chambers. I thought Chambers represented a higher level of art and not only that but that Chambers reflected London and that Curnoe's was an art that came not from London but from New York – though Curnoe would be the first to deny such a thing. And I held that attitude for a long time. There was a certain kind of snobbery in it. I found that I couldn't really talk to him that much. I would ask him questions but he wasn't really interested in anything I had to say. He considered me one of those academic types and he had no use for them. He had no use for me in that respect. I think we got along as well as we did because appearing to not have much use for each other, we could carry on. I didn't have much use for Greg as a person but I admired him enormously.

"I don't know how to put this . . . Greg Curnoe's paintings never looked as bad as they did the first time I saw them. Whenever I saw them again and again and again, they got better and better and better. That was the most disturbing thing. And the more familiar I became with his work by frequent viewings of it – and mostly casual viewings of it – the more engaged I became with it because I became engaged with its social and political history which was Greg's own history. In that respect, I respected his personality and in respecting his personality, I respected the paintings and the drawings – particularly the drawings. Greg, unlike Jack, continued to improve as an artist. Gradually, as I became more aware of what was going on in art outside of London, the more I saw that he was being influenced by Dada, by surrealism, and by American art – Warhol, pop, all of those things. But he was being influenced in his own way. He wasn't idealizing them. He was in there doing it. Gradually I saw that he was as good as they were."

I shared with Woodman my impression that when Curnoe had the most buzz, the draughtsmanship wasn't that great and when he started to feel he was being ignored, his work was progressing hugely.

"You're describing my own experience," Woodman said. "When he went on with his own work, drawing on his own work, it got better and better. I saw it more clearly as I think he saw his own work more clearly. So he could do with a watercolour what so few people could do. Greg was very sensuous without being sensual. That was always amazing to me. I would have thought that his paintings – particularly of Sheila – would be very sexual but they weren't. They were not sensual; they were sensuous. They were quite beautiful. When he painted Sheila he was so interested in the beauty of the brushstroke in a way that Jack never was. It was never vulgar. It was never brash. That was amazing to me. He became more and more a serious painter in a way that I hadn't seen earlier. When I saw the recent exhibition of Jack's silver paintings and films at Museum London, that showed me Jack picking up on Greg's work and doing something with it. And that really gave me pause. I began to see Jack more in terms of Greg and got over my early idealization of Jack and the more I got over that, the more I liked Greg."

I mentioned to Woodman that when my shrink was writing his book on Carl Jung and his synchronicity theory, he sought experiences and impressions from a lot of people, including Greg who was known to have a fascination with coincidences. In her memoir, Lynda Curnoe says of her brother, "Greg loved finding connections between disparate themes and connections between events. They provide a sense of completion." So Curnoe was interested in principle but he thought the idea behind a Synchronicity Society or whatever it was called was pretentious. "Just call it the Coincidence Club," he told my shrink "and I'll come out."

Woodman howled in appreciation of Curnoe's comment and told me, "Thirty years ago I didn't appreciate it. I was a young academic intellectual getting started and Chambers seemed a nice person to get started on and Curnoe didn't. Curnoe wasn't serious enough for me. He wouldn't let me use the word 'synchronicity' and get away with it. I realize now what I was denying myself in doing that."

For the big Curnoe Retrospective at The National Gallery of Canada in 1982, Pierre Théberge wrote an extensive essay for that show's catalogue in which he charted the evolution of other critics' opinions about Curnoe. Of particular interest is his take on Gary Michael Dault, whose development was diametrically opposed to Woodman's.

At one time a sturdy champion of Curnoe who fought back against other commentators who were lazily inclined to regard him as just another pop artist, Théberge wrote that Dault "decided to bow out of the Curnoe picture in 1978, taking a few parting shots as he left: 'Curnoe has made a huge reputation for himself in the Canadian art world over the past decade by an almost obsessive whacking away at certain high-profile, easy-to-read ideas': these ideas being regionalism; 'simplistic' nationalism; autobiography ('boring – insufferably, languishingly, narcissistically boring'); and, equally dull to Dault, the 'theatrical, almost aggressive parading of his hobbies as the content of his work . . . As Jose Barrio-Garay rightly pointed out . . . 'the response to Curnoe's persona has often been unduly mixed in with the criticism of his art'."[36]

The independent Region Gallery which had been opened by Curnoe and other London artists eventually morphed into the 20/20 Gallery and then the Forest City Gallery which still operates today. And it was at the Forest City Gallery where I was put in charge of literary programming through most of the '80s that I got to know Curnoe fairly well. He wasn't the president or anything official like that but he was the Gallery's guiding spirit and someone everyone looked up to and deferred to. Often at our regular executive meetings I was a little awestruck by how much Curnoe knew about all the other artists in town and what they were up to and his sincere interest in how they were faring. He also repeatedly asked what we were doing to make sure that new, emerging artists were being encouraged to come out and try to get shows at the Gallery. I thought it was a beautiful summation when David McFadden was quoted in *Greg Curnoe, A Hero's Journey,* by Douglas Fetherling, saying, "Greg was my best friend. But then he was many people's best friend. That's how much energy he had."[37]

One of the shortest entries in *Moustache,* George Bowering's compendium of personal memories about Curnoe reads: "I remember that Greg Curnoe always knew guys with names like Ernie."

He also knew old communist geezers called Matt. At the Gallery I would arrange and host about eight readings a year, bringing in a mix of local and national and internationally known writers. By the end of my regime, I was roping in some pretty big names like Timothy Findley, W.P. Kinsella and good old Richard B. Wright. I lived in constant fretfulness about what I would do if one of these writers failed to show up but except for the very first reading of the very first series, that never was an issue.

The morning of that first reading – announcements having appeared in local papers, fetching homemade posters having been plastered onto poles throughout downtown – I heard from painter, Ron Martin (I no longer recall what sort of literary project he was working on at that time) who said he had a family emergency on his hands and he would have to cancel. Utterly new at this post, I didn't yet have the confidence to say to Mr. Martin: "What do you bloody well mean? Is there an axe lodged in the middle of your wife's forehead as we speak? Because if it's anything less than that, pal, I personally will put one in the middle of yours." My brain seizing up in panic I think I managed to mutter, "Well, thanks for letting me know," and then the defector hung up on me.

Of course I called Curnoe in a panic and he dropped whatever he was doing and within about three hours came over to my house to let me know he'd been able to persuade an elderly labour organizer and Marxist working-class intellectual, Matt Wherry, to give a spur-of-the-moment talk about the proper sequencing of Shakespeare's sonnets. "It won't be exactly as advertised," Curnoe admitted, "but Matt's a good egg and he knows his stuff and I think he could use the money." It was undoubtedly the strangest reading I would ever host but utterly charming in its way (Wherry had run off his own Gestetnered copies of the sonnets in his preferred order with supplementary notes and sold these at cost to a handful of attendees) and reinforced my impression that Curnoe's circle of acquaintance was wonderfully wide and deep.

Curnoe never did make his peace with the establishment gallery which was relocated in its own freestanding building at the forks of the Thames in 1980 and today is called Museum London. It was Curnoe's contention that a big splashy building would devour money that should be going into acquisitions and programming. But as one of his main benefactors, Jake Moore, played no small part in funding and overseeing the main gallery's expansion and reloca-tion (as well as handing over the great bulk of his Curnoe-heavy collection to the gallery) Curnoe wasn't very vocal at first in his disapproval.

Nancy Poole was appointed the first interim executive director of the place, then in October of 1981, curator Brenda Wallace began what was supposed to be a five year contract as the gallery's first permanent executive director. As it turned out, she was forced to bail out in three. Poole had also wanted the position but as she was already interim director, she assumed folks would know of her interest and failed to secure a formal nomination for the post. Curnoe backed Brenda Wallace and his choice prevailed . . . for a while.

Poole changed horses completely after Wallace was instated and set about researching and writing her indispensable *The Art of London*. Poole recalls, "When I was writing the book I said, 'Now I have taped everybody, Greg, and I want to have an interview with you.' Well, he wasn't much on that. In the end I went to his studio and he gave me a kind of interview but it was not – the tapes are all at the university; you can hear it if you want to – there's nothing there. I don't think his animosity towards me was based in logic. It was an emotional reaction to me and what he thought I was."

Then in August of 1985, Poole was appointed the new executive director of the London Regional Art Gallery which was $400,000 in debt, about to have its mortgage foreclosed, was being sued for wrongful dismissal by Brenda Wallace, and was being warned by an engineer's report that the five year old structure might be in danger of collapsing.

So, I asked her, what didn't Greg Curnoe get about how art galleries run?

"Well, he had a difficult time with economics. He never understood that we actually had a very large acquisition budget and we acquired a lot of art. We didn't acquire any more of Greg's because we already had an enormous amount of Greg's work through the Moore Collection. The Gallery had been buying Greg's work all along. He did however come to the lunches that I used to give before our openings. I felt that openings should not be in the evening but should be on Saturday afternoon at two o'clock and everybody was invited. Before we had the opening – say we were having an opening of Doug Mitchell's work – we would have people who were interested in Doug's work, people who had lent their paintings for the exhibition and other artists would be invited. Herb and Margo Ariss always came, Bernice Vincent would be there and I always asked Greg. We would have a very inexpensive buffet. You've no idea how inexpensive. It was very basic – sandwiches and cold veggies and cookies. Greg and Sheila frequently would appear because this was an opportunity for the artists to meet collectors and collectors to meet artists. I felt that was important and it also allowed me to have the staff there – the people who would install the show and the curators. There would be between 30 and 40 people for lunch and he found this difficult but he came. When I say he found it difficult, I mean there I was but he was there. Greg was not going to miss out on that opportunity. It always pleased me when I would see that sweater coming through the door.

"The only time I wished he had just not been there was when he was determined that Brenda Wallace would be the director. He didn't know enough to understand that curators for the most part do not have the skills necessary to be a director. Just as directors for the most part do not have the skills to be curators. Brenda was a marvellous curator. I remember when I had my own gallery and we would welcome Brenda because she came with such knowledge and so much energy. But she knew nothing about budgeting. She knew nothing about the political end of keeping an institution with a budget of $2 million going. She just didn't understand any of that. She was there for three years and it was tragic because she didn't understand. Never was there a better example of a round peg in a square hole. She was so good at what she did. Money was the issue and she didn't understand that at all. She came out of government. She came out of the Canada Council. She came out of a world where you know you don't have to worry about money because it comes from the government. Well, I came out of the private sector and I knew where money came from."

Poole was director of the LRAG at the time of Curnoe's death and the following spring the gallery mounted The Heart of London Revisited, paying homage to that touring show from a quarter century before that had put the London art scene on the map. For a feature article that ran at that time I asked Poole if it was accurate to describe her professional relationship with Greg as 'prickly'?

"Absolutely," she answered. "I had tremendous respect for him. And there's no question that he was the conscience of this gallery. In my head I always used to ask, 'How will this play with Greg?' And I didn't always go along with what I thought he'd like. Quite the contrary. But I like to think there was a creative and dynamic tension that helped each of us define our positions. I think he knew the respect I had for him. I hope he did."

Though Greg came to watercolours comparatively late in his career – he started to make the shift around 1971 – he won some of his best reviews for his work in that unfashionable medium. No pale miniatures these. The colours burn with the intensity of hot oils and the size of major pieces could measure in at eight by five feet – preposterous dimensions for watercolours. [Plate 11]

"That is his genius, isn't it?" Sheila Curnoe told me. "He wanted to be a cartoonist and then he starts to experiment with watercolour. And the early watercolours didn't work but you could see he was experimenting. I watched it all happen. The colours, some of them weren't very good at first and then it just started to get better and better and better."

In *The Concise History of Canadian Painting*, Dennis Reid presented a running survey of 300 years' worth of Canadian art in just under 400 pages. Where someone like A.J. Casson had to get by with four scattered references (and William Kurelek, in the first edition, wasn't mentioned at all) Greg received 11 pages worth of intensive and enthusiastic scrutiny. In appraising the watercolours, Reid pulled out all the stops, claiming that Curnoe was confidently pushing watercolour "to a previously unheard-of scale and to new heights of inspired emotion and visual force."[38]

Until the mid '70s London artists enjoyed an indulgence, a special interest on the part of national critics who looked fondly on Curnoe et al as brave constituents of 'the little community that could'. As is the way with such things at the snooty pedigreed cat show of modern art, that mood passed and the claws eventually came out. John Bentley Mays writing in *The Globe and Mail* about the 1980 Jack Chambers retrospective at the London Regional Art Gallery referred to London as 'the Sleepy Hollow of the north' and suggested that Chambers had always been a second rate talent whose light would've shone less brightly in any city but dim old London.

Irritating, mildly depressing perhaps, but Curnoe found such critical missiles to be about as threatening or meaningful as phlegmatically discharged furballs. Curnoe's nourishment and inspiration was always drawn from his region, his family and his personal experience and there wasn't a blessed thing he could do about that except carry on – mixing his paints and training his eye to set it all down in images, colours and words.

Most folks consider the phrase – 'a career in visual art' – to be an oxymoron. It's a notoriously difficult thing to pull off even if you remain a bachelor. But for a family man with three kids in a medium-sized Ontario city . . . it took some doing. In the financial flush of the mid 80's, Curnoe could see $30,000 for a single work. But as he told me in '88: "We drive a beat up 1978 Oldsmobile. Usually it's a feast and famine kind of situation. I'm earning more of my income from sales all the time so I'm not as dependent on grants as I was. We've held back a lot of paintings from different stages in my career so there's a real good collection on hand which is kind of like our insurance. Also, we own the house."

Sheila concurred with this appraisal at that time and even pointed out some perks: "We've lived well. We've travelled to England, Paris, all over Europe. We were just in Cuba where Greg had some work in a show. Somehow or other, the money always comes through."

Any recession or downturn tends to hit the arts community first (art heading most people's lists of 'inessentials') and the early 90's were especially hard that way. Just before he died, Curnoe's main preoccupation was researching the history of his Weston Street neighbourhood. According to Frank Davey, executor of Curnoe's literary remains, "Greg had compiled 800 single spaced pages of material researching the history of his house and street "past crown deed back to First Nations occupation and contextualized the information in terms of the street, recounting the changes going back to 5000 B.C."

This work ultimately would have fuelled the next phase in Curnoe's development as an artist – had he lived that long. But the research phase was largely un-remunerative and putting that together with the recession and a time when two of his kids were attending out-of-town universities . . . things were getting really tight. Curnoe was contemplating some pretty desperate expedients to generate some cash; he was looking to paint a bunch of flowers which were always easy sales but unrewarding in other ways and he was also taking on more teaching and lecturing gigs at UWO and Fanshawe College. The Dean of Western's Journalism School, Peter Desbarats, sadly recalled in that *Canadian Art* memorial piece, a visit to Curnoe's studio by journalism students who videotaped an interview: "He was supposed to get a $150 honorarium. I later heard that he called the university administration two or three times for the cheque."[39]

The *Deeds Abstracts* exhibition which debuted at the Forest City Gallery in March of 1992 and the related *Self Portraits* show which opened at Toronto's Wynick/Tuck Gallery exactly one week after his death, contained the first fruits of Curnoe's archeological researches into his home turf. An essay he wrote for the catalogue shows Curnoe happily toiling in his favourite vineyard; digging into London history and records and mixing that in with his own investigations and observations to make vital connections with where and how we live today. In one richly representative paragraph he wrote:

"South Central London, where we live was developed as a residential and light industrial area where proprietors could live close to their shops. Our building was built in 1891 by Thomas Knowles senior (1841-1926), an immigrant from England (who had lived on Weston Street since 1873) as a lithography shop for his sons Thomas (1866-1933) and Joseph Knowles (1868-1954). London artist Albert Templar [who gave art lessons to Curnoe's mother, Nellie, in the 1950s] apprenticed here in 1917. He ground litho stones as part of his apprenticeship. (He boarded on Maryboro Place, now McClary Avenue). My son Galen and I have dug up Knowles Company litho stones from the back of our building. My most recent prints were three editions of lithographs, drawn directly on litho stones. The lithographer / owners who worked here were well connected socially to the extent of belonging to the exclusive Forest City Bicycle Club around that time with the then famous author Arthur Stringer and the Saunders family of the Saunders Drug Company. The club rode ordinaries and safety bicycles. The Knowles brothers rode their bicycles from 38 Weston Street to their club rides. I leave from the same place for club rides with the London Centennial Wheelers."[40]

Roses are red, violets are blue . . .

On that awful morning of Saturday, November 14, 1992 (as the Santa Claus Parade was wrapping up in downtown London) a pickup truck, in a horrible fluke accident on Highway 2 near Delaware, went ploughing through 12 members of The Centennial Wheelers. The driver said his eyes had been distracted from the road for just a second by the vision of a barn that was perfectly reflected in a field of standing water. Six of the cyclists ended up in hospital with everything from minor scrapes to a fractured skull. One of them was killed.

Curnoe loved bikes. He was simply besotted with them; in love with both their utility and their high artistic form which most of us hadn't twigged to until Curnoe brought it to our attention. He certainly painted enough of them. And he made them his own personal emblem – their taut, skeletal, pastel-shaded frames reaching out to every corner of the canvas; positively Zen in the way that their emptiness defined them. The ever present Curnoe message stamped along the crossbar: 'Close the 49th parallel'. Lists of lovingly compiled bicycle statistics pencilled in just to the left of the raised leather seat: "Frame specification constructed in chrome (Reynolds?) tubing with C.C.M. forged, chromed fork crown . . ." The tight, clockwork axis of the pedals, stirrups and chain, the power radiating outward to the wheels – the mystical colour wheels – ribbed with mandala type spokes, each spoke rendered with the kind of hard precision that you're not supposed to be able to capture with watercolour. [Plate 12]

In the wake of his death the sight of all those bikes in paintings and prints and photographs of Curnoe – the sight of those bikes stabbed us. 'God, that's how he died.' But we soon realized that we'd never be able to banish those two-wheeled emblems from the Curnoe equation because they comprised such radiant testimony – 'God, that's how he lived.'

If there is less universal consensus today regarding which paintings are Curnoe's masterpieces than there is with Jack Chambers, there is no question which artist is the most highly regarded and the most frequently referenced by artists working here today. I expect this is because the work he produced comes with so much less baggage. Certainly with his earlier work, although he unquestionably had an eye and an audacious kind of flair, you didn't have to marvel at what an incredibly accomplished artist Greg Curnoe was. This changed later to a considerable degree but for me at least, Curnoe's work always comes rushing out to meet me with an arresting sort of boldness; like a flag or an emblem or that gamboling mutt who's just broken free of his leash and wants to see what sort of trouble he can rustle up. I don't have to go to it and when I do, it doesn't draw me in and hold me like the best of Chambers or Kurelek. As he freely admitted, his work remained – however exquisitely rendered – cartoony and lighthearted; as Curnoe himself retained a young and mischievous aspect until the very end.

For all his rebelliousness and his stubbornness, his occasional moodiness and his scraps with authority and the old order of arts bureaucracy and management, things fairly quickly fell into place for Curnoe and for the most part continued to go his way. While he can't have been happy to be turned down for an "A" Canada Council grant five months before his death, his career was mostly played out in a golden era of arts council funding. This was not a man who ever seemed to be broken by his experiences and then had to painstakingly put himself back together again. As Ross Woodman said in that long ago book review when he wasn't supposed to be talking about Greg Curnoe at all, "A broken heart is the very last thing one could associate with him." Nor as things turned out did Curnoe ever get the chance (even if he ever would have developed the inclination) to contemplate mortality's long and inexorable descent upon his life.

Until the accident, Curnoe had seemed uniquely blessed. He had pretty well raised three gorgeous and whip-smart children with a wife he still adored and seemed set to move into a new phase in his life as a widely respected elder. I remember thinking a number of times after Jack Chambers' death 14 years before (and also recalling Paul Peel's premature death in 1892 – exactly 100 years before Greg's) that the curse had somehow been broken and that finally a leading London artist was going to get to live out a full and generous allotment of days.

I remember the last time we met. Nothing all that remarkable happened but as is the way with these things, once the news came of his death, you cast back your mind and every miscellaneous detail you can scavenge from the past becomes vivid and precious. It was Labour Day weekend of 1992 and Greg and Sheila threw an end-of-summer open house on the night before two of their kids would be heading off to university. Out in his studio Greg was talking with Bill Exley about some of the finishing touches being applied to the second

Nihilist Spasm Band album, *What About Me?*, that would be released later that year. Greg was toying with Exley, asking him to allow them to issue a version of one of the songs with considerably more vulgar lyrics but, mindful of the reputation he needed to uphold as a teacher of English in Elmira, Exley wouldn't budge. Then Greg insisted that Exley listen to a tape he'd recently acquired of the speed metal band, Motorhead. Greg didn't think much of it as music but was hugely impressed by how fast Lemmy and the boys played and wanted Exley to sample just one song. "Isn't that something?" he asked an obviously underwhelmed Exley at the song's conclusion.

Usually there was such a crush of guests at Curnoe parties that your hosts could not be expected to either welcome you officially or see you off when you left. But that night (perhaps he was headed from his studio into the house anyway) Greg escorted us as far as the gate at the south side of their lot and showed us the latch he'd recently repaired to keep in Sheila's Dalmatians. For once we got to say our proper goodbyes; none of us suspecting that it would be the last one ever.

In our big 1988 interview, I wrapped things up by asking Curnoe to summarize what sort of mark he thought he'd been able to make as an artist. I was fascinated by the way his answer morphed from an appraisal of his own situation, to that of other artists, then the country as a whole and finally London:

"I know some works of mine have managed to get into some kind of national consciousness. The bicycles, the big painting of *Victoria Hospital*, the *Camouflaged Piano* – and I know that's typical of the artists of my generation. Younger artists haven't been able to achieve that because nobody's looking, nobody's giving them a hearing. It sometimes seems that everything I stood against has come back. I really thought we had it on the run for a while. The whole notion of independence for this country is going. It couldn't be worse. The possibility of working in your own community is going. We're back to that same situation where critics in the main centres seem to believe that art has to fight its way through to them in order to be deemed worthwhile. And here at home we'll bend over backwards to put up a convention centre for out-of-town businessmen but we make our committee for a performing arts centre crawl through mud just to get a hearing at City Hall. No, no, don't get me started. The climate will change. I know it will. I've seen it change before. And when it changes, I'll be here."

As I write 24 years after his death we still don't have that performing arts centre and its presumed major tenant, Orchestra London, has gone bankrupt and officially disbanded. But sooner or later when that climate does change for the better – and it will because it has to – it will be due in no small measure to Greg Curnoe's life and career; the attitudes he changed, the perceptions he opened us up to. And having said that, it naturally follows that Curnoe was right on the second count too. He will be here. Not in any sense that he would have had any patience with. But this man who always identified himself first and foremost as a "London artist" will continue to influence this community he did so much to discover, disrupt and define for 56 rambunctious years.

PLATE 9 Greg Curnoe: Myself Walking North in the Tweed Coat, oil on plywood, 183 x 122 cm,
November,1963. Vancouver Art Gallery, purchased with the financial support of the Canada
Council for the Arts Acquisition Assistance Program, VAG64.23

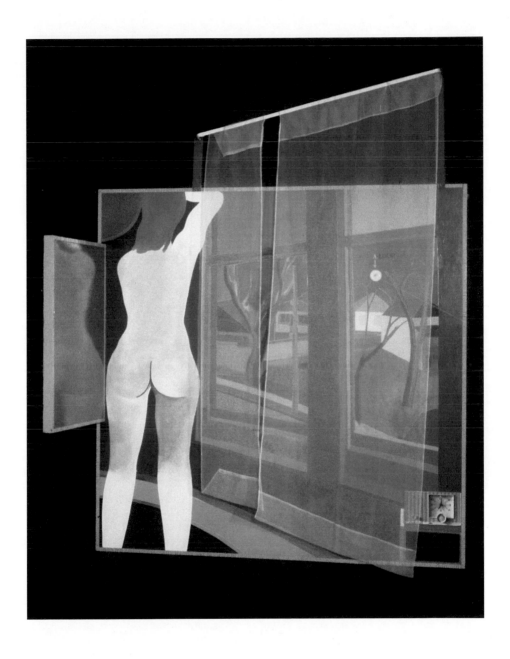

PLATE 10 Greg Curnoe: Spring on the Ridgeway, oil, rayon/nylon, metal, wood, paper and string on plywood and masonite, 187 x 187 cm, 1964. Art Gallery of Ontario, purchase, 1965, 65/24

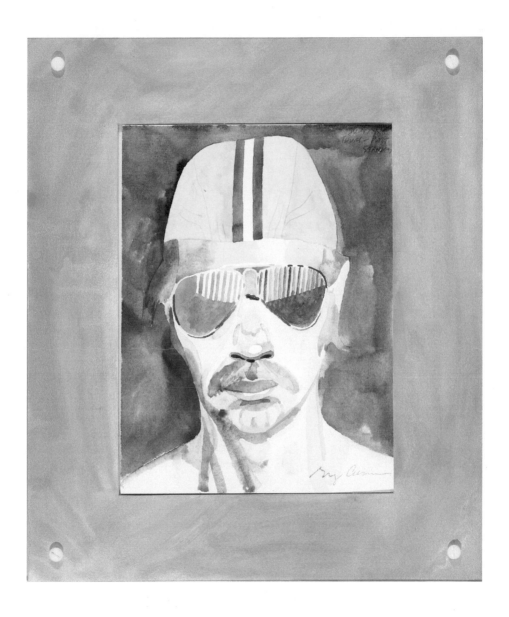

PLATE 11 Greg Curnoe: Self Portrait July 10, 1980, watercolour and graphite on wove paper, 30.4 x 22.4 cm, 1980. Art Gallery of Ontario, gift of Sheila Curnoe, London ON, 1997, 97/124

PLATE 12 Greg Curnoe: Gitane 5-Speed, watercolour, gouache and graphite on wove paper, 109 x 182 cm, 1973.
Art Gallery of Ontario, gift of Sheila Curnoe, London ON, 1997, 97/107

GREG CURNOE

Works cited in this essay:

CHP	Reid, Dennis (editor). *A Concise History of Canadian Painting*, 2ⁿᵈ edition. Toronto: Oxford University Press, 1988
CO	Curnoe, Greg; Fones, Robert; Portis, Ben; Ryan, Carol-Ann M. *Cutout: Greg Curnoe: Shaped Collages, 1965-1968* (exhibition collection). London, Ontario: Museum London, 2011.
CS	Fetherling, Douglas. "The Curnoe Story." Toronto: *Canadian Art*, (Summer, 1993).
DA	Curnoe, Greg; Davey, Frank (essay). *Deeds Abstracts* (exhibition catalogue). Wynick/Tuck Gallery, Toronto, 1992.
GC	Curnoe, Sheila; Favro, Murray; Gibson, Michael; Théberge, Pierre, Vincent, Charles (essays). *Greg Curnoe – '61-65* (exhibition catalogue). London, Ontario: Michael Gibson Gallery, 2014.
L & S	Reid, Dennis and Teitelbaum, Matthew (editors); Sarah Milroy and Dennis Reid (essays). *Greg Curnoe: Life & Stuff* (exhibition catalogue). Toronto: Art Gallery of Ontario and Vancouver: Douglas and McIntyre, 2001.
MBG	Curnoe, Lynda. *My Brother Greg: A Memoir*. London, Ontario: Ergo Productions, 2001.
MGC	Bowering, George: *The Moustache: Memories of Greg Curnoe*, Toronto: Coach House Press, 1993.
NE	Nihilist Spasm Band; Portis, Ben (essay); Curnoe Greg; Boyle, John; Clement, John; Exley, Bill; Favro, Murray; McIntyre, Hugh; Pratten, Art. *no exhibition, the art and spectacle of the nihilist spasm band* (exhibition catalogue). London, Ontario: London Regional Art & Historical Museums, 2000.
NGC	Theberge, Pierre. *Greg Curnoe: Retrospective*. Ottawa: National Gallery of Canada, 1982.

Citations from newspaper articles and unpublished papers are listed in full below.

CHAPTER 13: IT CAN HAPPEN HERE
1. *CS*
2. *The Telegram*. Elizabeth Dingman: "The Art World Beats a Path to London, Ont." 28 November, 1970
3. *MGC*, p. 34

CHAPTER 14: GORDON AND NELLIE'S FIRSTBORN
4. *CS*
5. *MGC*, p.49
6. *MBG*, p. 33

7. *MBG*, p. 42
8. *MBG*, p. 31
9. *MBG*, p. 24
10. *NGC*, p. 117
11. *MBG*, p. 48
12. *MBG*, p. 100
13. *L & S*, p.140
14. *L & S*, p. 141
15. *GC*
16. *L & S*, p. 143
17. *L & S*, p. 143

CHAPTER 15: TAKING A STAND IN LONDON
18. *NE*
19. *L & S*, p. 144
20. *CO*, pp. 36-37
21. *L & S*, p. 144
22. *L & S*, p. 144
23. *L & S*, pp. 145-47
24. *L & S*, p. 147
25. *NSC*, p. 5
26. *L & S*, p. 147
27. *L & S*, p. 150
28. *MBG*, p. 69
29. Greg Curnoe's letter to Professor Groome, 17 November, 1964. Greg Curnoe Papers, Correspondence File, 1964. E.P. Taylor Research Library & Archives, Art Gallery of Ontario, Toronto

CHAPTER 16: "IT MUST'VE BEEN SOMETHING PRETTY FAST"
30. *MBG*, p. 68
31. *L & S*, p. 183
32. *L & S*, p.87

CHAPTER 17: THE WILD CHILD BECOMES A FATHER FIGURE
33. *L & S*, p. 154
34. *L & S*, p. 155
35. *L & S*, p. 111
36. *NGC*, p. 47
37. *CS*
38. *CHP*, p. 326
39. *CS*
40. *DA*, p. 14

WILLIAM KURELEK

Canadian, 1927 – 1977

William Kurelek © The Estate of William Kurelek. Courtesy of the Wynick/Tuck Gallery, Toronto

PLATE 1 In The Autumn of Life, oil on tempered hardboard, 59.1 x 120.3 cm, 1964. Art Gallery of Ontario, gift from the McLean Foundation, 1964, 64/9

PLATE 2 Pre-Maze, watercolour and graphite on paper, 25.3 x 37.7 cm, c.1953. Art Gallery of Ontario, gift from the collection of Bruno M. and Ruby Cormier, 1983, 83/300

PLATE 3 The Passion of Christ (And So They Reached A Place Called Golgotha), gouache on paper, 52.2 x 48.1 cm, 1960-1963. Niagara Falls Art Gallery

PLATE 4 Self Portrait, watercolour, gouache and ink on paper, 47.5 x 38 cm, 1957. The Thomson Collection © Art Gallery of Ontario,103679

JACK CHAMBERS

Canadian, 1931 – 1978

Jack Chambers © The Estate of Jack Chambers. Courtesy of John and Diego Chambers

PLATE 5 Portrait of Marion and Ross Woodman, oil on wood, 80.5 x 91.5 cm, 1961. Art Gallery of Ontario, Toronto. From the collection of Ross and Marion Woodman. 98835

PLATE 6 401 Towards London No.1, oil on mahogany, 183 x 244 cm, 1968 – 1969. Art Gallery of Ontario, gift of Norcen Energy Resources Ltd., 1986, 86/47

PLATE 7 Sunday Morning No. 2, oil on wood, 121.9 x 121.9 cm, 1968 – 70. Courtesy Loch Gallery, Toronto

PLATE 8 Lake Huron No. 4, oil on wood, 121.9 x 121.9 cm, 1972 – 76. Courtesy Loch Gallery, Toronto

GREG CURNOE

Canadian, 1936 – 1992

Greg Curnoe © The Estate of Greg Curnoe / SODRAC (2016). Courtesy of Sheila Curnoe

PLATE 9 Myself Walking North in the Tweed Coat, oil on plywood, 183 x 122 cm, November,1963. Vancouver Art Gallery, purchased with the financial support of the Canada Council for the Arts Acquisition Assistance Program, VAG64.23 (PHOTO: Trevors Mills, VAG)

PLATE 10 Spring on the Ridgeway, oil, rayon/nylon, metal, wood, paper and string on plywood and masonite, 187 x 187 cm, 1964. Art Gallery of Ontario, purchase, 1965, 65/24

PLATE 11 Self Portrait July 10, 1980, watercolour and graphite on wove paper, 30.4 x 22.4 cm, 1980. Art Gallery of Ontario, gift of Sheila Curnoe, London ON, 1997, 97/124

PLATE 12 Gitane 5-Speed, watercolour, gouache and graphite on wove paper, 109 x 182 cm, 1973. Art Gallery of Ontario, gift of Sheila Curnoe, London ON, 1997, 97/107